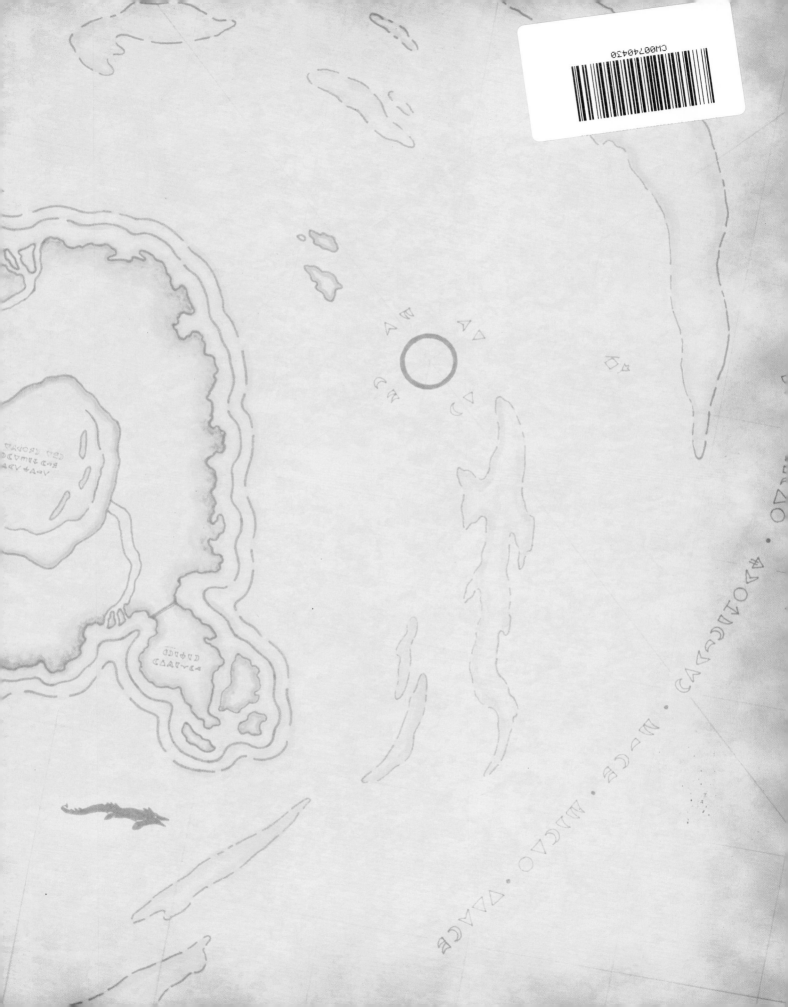

KONG

KING OF SKULL ISLAND

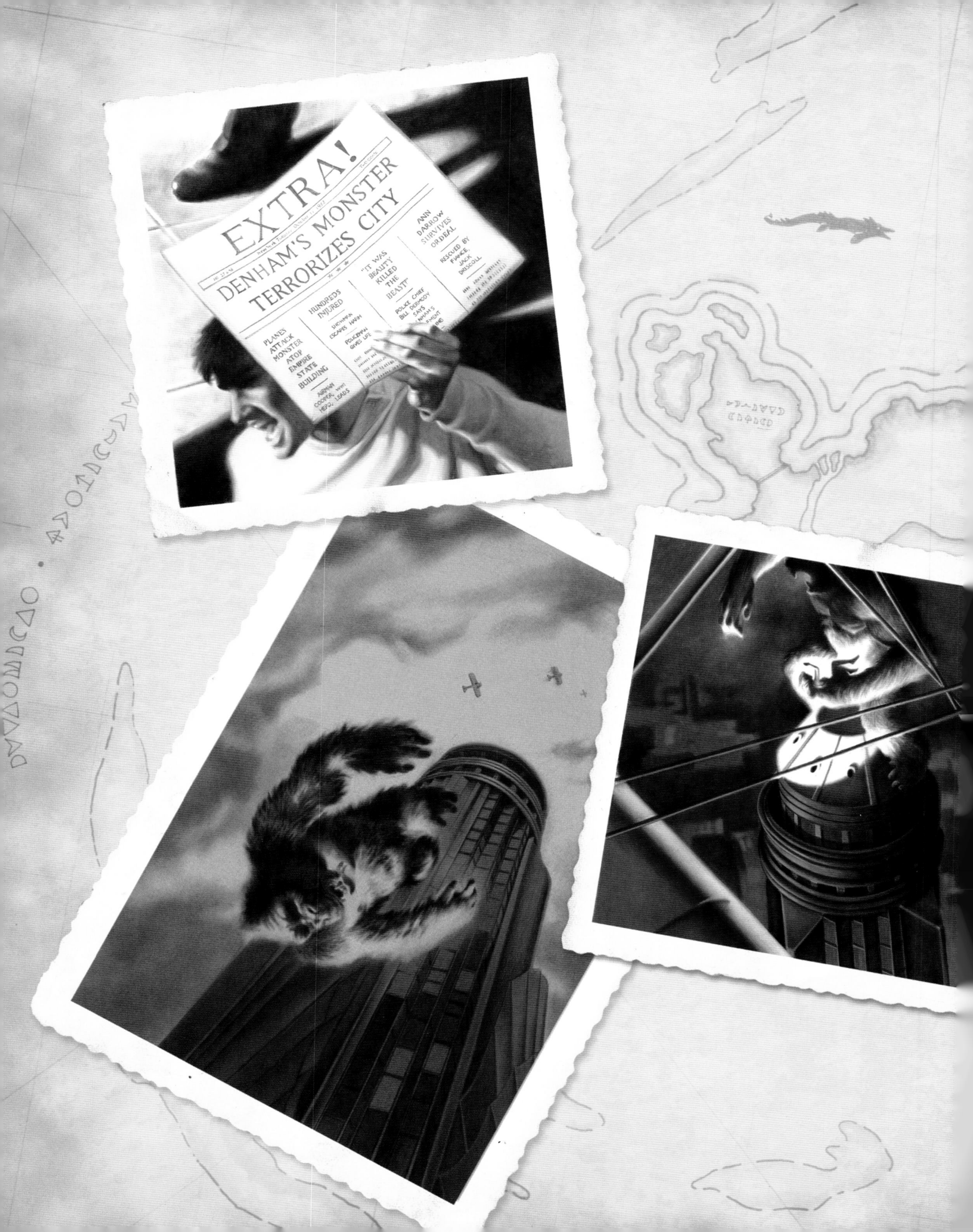
EXTRA!
DENHAM'S MONSTER TERRORIZES CITY
PLANES ATTACK MONSTER ATOP EMPIRE STATE BUILDING
AIRMAN COOPER, WWI HERO, LEADS
HUNDREDS INJURED
SHOWMAN ESCAPES HARM
POLICEMAN GIVES LIFE
"IT WAS BEAUTY KILLED THE BEAST"
POLICE CHIEF BILL DERMODY SAYS
ANN DARROW SURVIVES ORDEAL
RESCUED BY FIANCE, JACK DRISCOLL

KONG
KING OF SKULL ISLAND

Created and Illustrated by
JOE DEVITO

Written by
BRAD STRICKLAND
with JOHN MICHLIG

Inspired by and based on the novel *King Kong*
conceived by
EDGAR WALLACE and **MERIAN C. COOPER**
novelization by
DELOS W. LOVELACE

DH PRESS™

To my wife, Mary Ellen, and our daughters, Melissa and Emily, for their unshakable love and support; to my brother Vito, who first introduced me to King Kong and was my artistic guide throughout childhood; to my brother Vincent, who opened the door and made this book possible; to my late Aunt Ann; and in loving memory of my parents, William and Yolanda DeVito.

I would like to thank the following people

Colonel Richard M. Cooper, the entire Merian C. Cooper family, and the late Charles B. FitzSimons for their kindness and acceptance; my publisher, Mike Richardson, my editor, Chris Warner, and everyone at DH Press for their enthusiasm, expertise, and guidance; Barry Klugerman, who has been an extraordinary artistic and literary mentor over the twelve years of this project; Jennifer Goetz and Sharon Vale Chapman, for their valuable contributions toward pulling storylines together; attorneys Alan Franklin and Randy Merritt, for help and advice far beyond business; Richard Curtis for introducing me to Brad; Joe Viego, for his invaluable help and support; Arnie Fenner, for his steadying advice and unwavering confidence; Michael Friedlander, a kindred spirit; Arnold Kunert, for connecting me with two of my childhood idols, Ray Harryhausen and Ray Bradbury; and Cilius Lam and John Routh of Birchfield Design Group.

There are many others who provided inspiration and support. In the professional world: The late Ralph Amatrudi, Jill Bauman, Rick Berry, Georg Brewer, Vincent DiFate, Dr.'s Jane and Howard Frank, Charlie Kochman, Bill Logan, Michael Mims, Will Murray, Frank M. Robinson, Dr. Jack Seydow, Rob Simpson, Mark Cotta Vaz, James Warhola, Bob Walters, and Pat Wilshire. On the home front: Joe Stallone, Ed Russo, Ron Schiller, Bug, Dean Balosie, Elmer Schiller, Billy Kowalczuk, Anthony Manganelli, Pete Rippa, Joe Bigley, Kevin McLaughlin, and Dan Hogan. I want to sincerely thank all those whose constant prayers saw me through; and last but first, Mother Mary and St. Jude — the novena worked!

—*Joe DeVito*

Publisher **MIKE RICHARDSON** • Editor **CHRIS WARNER**
Publication Design **DEBRA BAILEY** • Art Director **LIA RIBACCHI**

Special thanks to the **MERIAN C. COOPER ESTATE**

KONG: KING OF SKULL ISLAND

Published by
DH PRESS
A division of Dark Horse Comics, Inc.
10956 S.E. Main Street, Milwaukie, OR 97222

dhpressbooks.com • darkhorse.com • jdevito.com

First edition: December 2004 • ISBN: 1-59582-006-X

1 3 5 7 9 10 8 6 4 2

Printed in China

INTRODUCTION

When I first read the book and saw the 1933 film *King Kong*, I had no idea it would father so many concepts and interpretations over the years. To me it was mainly a wonderful, rip-roaring magical adventure into the never-never land of fantasy. Its fascination was not only in the unique technical effects of the film, at the time, but the basic story, which was structured in a most unusual way. The book and the film took the audience by the hand from the mundane world of the Depression into the most outrageous fantasy ever to be put onto the "silver screen" and made us believe that such an adventure was possible.

Merian C. Cooper's concept was developed into a cohesive whole by including ideas from the never-completed Willis O'Brien project, *Creation*, and *The Lost World*. O'Brien's contributions to the story have many times been overlooked. But it was Merian Cooper's love of and flight into the fantastic that pulled the complete project together as a masterpiece of unusual adventure and fantastic entertainment.

Unfortunately, in today's world the many outlets for presenting entertainment have reduced the unusual visual presentation to the mundane by overexposure of the computer-generated image. In a thirty-second commercial on television, we are now inundated with the most amazing sights. Before CGI, spectacular visual images were rare and unique, but alas, no more.

Joe DeVito's original story and artistic conceptions have gone deeper into the history and background of the adventure's hero, Carl Denham. It was a concept I am sure was never anticipated by Mr. Cooper. DeVito's story and his imaginative illustrations have added a new dimension to the idea of spectacular visual imagery.

—Ray Harryhausen
March 5, 2004

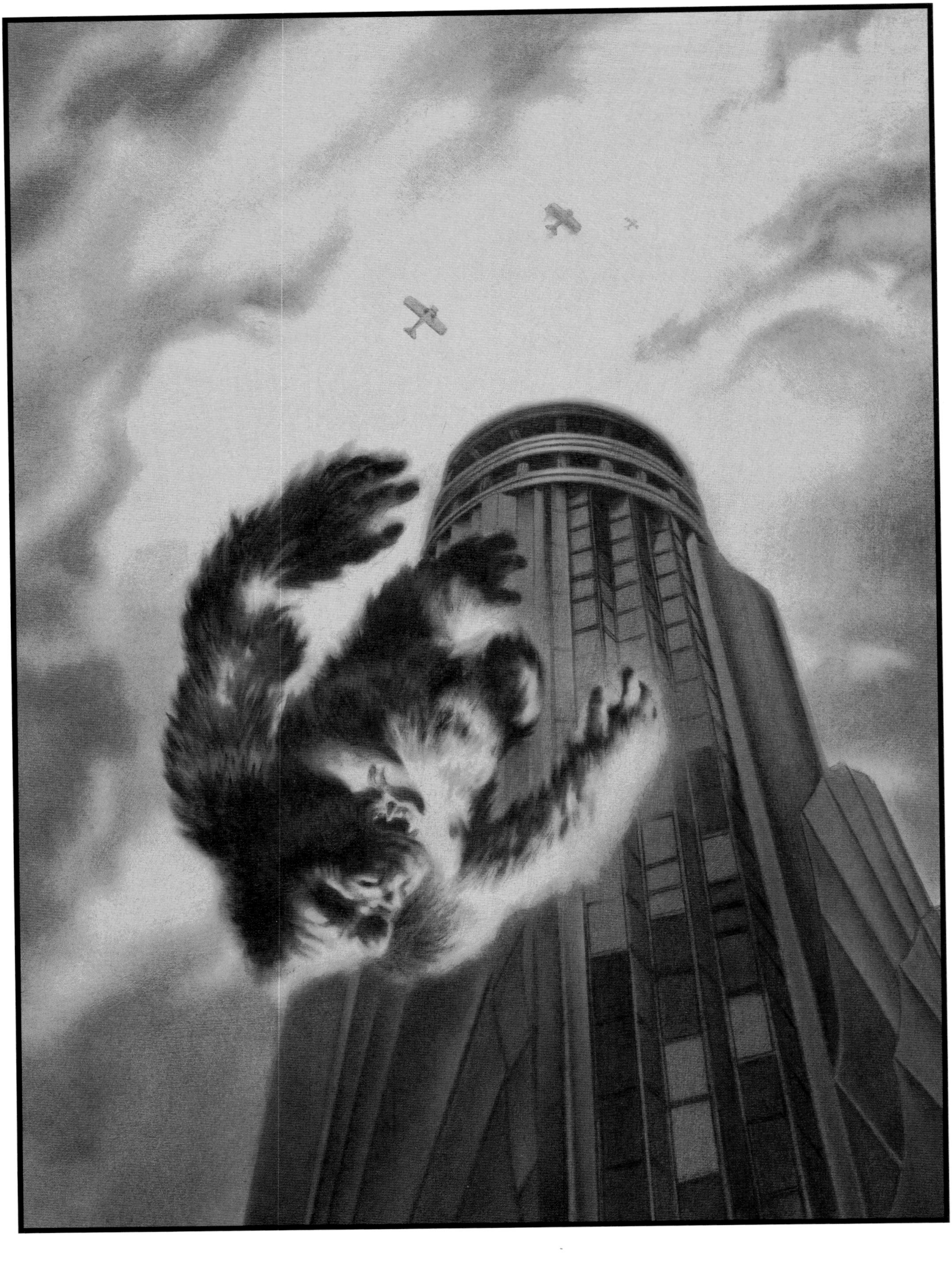

PROLOGUE

SOMEWHERE IN THE WESTERN PACIFIC
November 18, 1933

Carl Denham could smell land. The hazy tropical night still lay too dark for him even to glimpse it, but the breeze from the east brought the well-remembered scents: the odor of riotous vegetation, the ammoniac reek of predators, a whiff of wood smoke. Somewhere not far ahead lay Denham's destination. He leaned on the ship's rail, staring into the darkness, every nerve, every sense, alive and aware.

A soft footstep behind him. Without turning, he said, "Good morning, Captain Englehorn."

"Mr. Denham." Beside him the captain stopped. He struck a match and lit his pipe, his craggy face golden in the momentary glow. "You've been standing here a long time."

"I didn't sleep well. But you're here, too."

The captain chuckled. "Yes, but it's my job. I've ordered dead slow. No use tearing her heart out on the reefs. Not with dawn coming."

The tobacco in Englehorn's pipe glowed cherry-red, and the aromatic smoke masked the land odors. "Plenty of time," Denham said. "As long as the ice holds out."

"Yes. Well, there it is."

Straining his eyes, Denham could barely see a faint gray horizon line. That would be breakers, pounding the rocky shore of the island. Above them rose a humped, rounded shape, a darker patch against the sky. "I remember it."

The captain took a meditative pull at his pipe. "I swore never to come back."

Denham sighed. He had made that same vow to himself. "You're a good friend."

"You're paying me well enough," replied the captain.

"Still, I never thanked you. Not the way I should have."

The dawn was coming. The east was bloody with it. The captain, a silhouette in Denham's peripheral vision, turned his head. "That sounds as if you're not planning on making the return voyage."

Denham did not answer. He reflected that the captain's remark might not be a bad idea. After all, what lay behind? Lawsuits, accusations. His family, of course, but his wife and the boy were well provided for. And he hadn't exactly been a model husband and father, had he? Always chasing around the globe for images on film. Chasing shadows. Until he had caught the greatest one of all, the Eighth Wonder of the World.

He shifted his weight and rubbed his eyes. What would the islanders think of this mad return? He was bringing back their king—a fallen king. Like himself. He smiled grimly.

Sunrise, and the breathtaking flood of tropical daybreak. Denham shielded his eyes as the golden light gleamed on the rounded dome of the island, and the curiously eroded volcanic monolith that loomed over the blackish-green jungle seemed to stare back at him with empty eye sockets. The island was closer than he had thought. He could even glimpse the line of the great wall.

"We're a little too far south to suit me," said the captain. "I'll put that right." He left Denham alone at the bow.

Denham strained to hear. Surf—he could hear the steady pounding of breakers on the rocky flanks of the island. Was there another drumbeat behind that one? He couldn't tell. He rubbed his palm over his face, feeling the rasp of his unshaven cheeks. Time to wash up, break out the razor. Maybe today he'd have some appetite for breakfast. He pushed up from the rail and turned, heading back along the starboard side of the ship. Ahead of him he saw one of the sailors, the young Clancy, securing a line. "Morning," Denham said.

Clancy looked up, his homely, pug-nosed face breaking into a smile—and then he screamed, looking not at Denham but at something beyond him.

Denham spun, instinctively ducking. A winged horror filled the sky, a flying dragon, descending, forty-foot wingspan stretched out, translucent against the rising sun, arteries and veins roadmapping the leathery flesh, gleaming black eyes, talons outstretched, claws rusted red from the blood of old kills—

All this registered in an instant, together with the thought *If I only had a camera—*

The beast seized Denham's up-flung left arm, claws searing into his flesh. The wings beat once, twice. Desperately Denham hooked his right arm through the rail. He heard Clancy's shouts, saw the fierce beak above him, the crested orange head swiveling to bring the pterosaur's gleaming black plum of an eye to bear. Denham groaned against the strain, feeling the trickle of blood over his skin. It was an impossible contest. The creature couldn't lift him, but it was too stupid to know that. If it dragged him away from the rail, though, it would slash and tear at him with its wicked teeth. If he managed to hold on, at the least he would lose his arm—

He lost his grip on the rail, felt himself dragged aft, past the overhang. The monster's wings flapped twice as it tried to rip his arm off.

An explosion from the water, a flash of green and silver, and Denham fell tumbling, seeing the world whirl past. He had one glimpse of a body as long as a freight engine, frightful jaws clamped on the still-struggling pterosaur. Sea beast. Prehistoric. He saw it as if in a photo flash, frozen in time.

He plunged into blood-warm water, sank deep, kicked, rose, lungs aching, eyes burning, arm trailing red streamers. *No,* his mind shrieked, *not now, not when I've come so far —*

Somewhere above him, something broke the surface of the water in a burst of silver bubbles.

But Carl Denham was in the murky depths already, and sinking fast.

CHAPTER ONE

NEW YORK CITY
March 16, 1957

Tyrannosaurus rex. King of the Tyrant Lizards. It dwarfed him, made him feel like a child facing a tiger. A child? No, smaller—a squirrel, a rabbit. Dr. Vincent Denham stared up at the dinosaur, shaking his head, dissatisfied. He could visualize the various muscles and orchestrate their movement over the living bones. He knew the size of the brain, the exact length of the teeth, and saw the mad gleam of its eyes in their stereoscopic, ridged sockets. Could anyone else? He doubted it. Except to those gifted with a paleontologist's knowledge or a Charles R. Knight's artistry, the exhibit was just an articulated skeleton, maybe a fantasy from a kid's book.

A tall man, despite the way the skeleton made him feel, Denham sighed and checked his watch for the third time that hour. And it was still only 3:11. The appointment wasn't until 3:30. If—

A chatter of voices distracted him. A family group, father, mother, two sons, a daughter, sauntering toward the tyrannosaur exhibit, the father pontificating in a self-important way: "These animals lived a million years ago, kids. They all died out in caveman times."

Denham clamped his jaw shut. A million years? Try seventy million years, you ignoramus. And don't tell the kids that cavemen and dinosaurs co-existed. That was a delusion or a lie. People need to read more books and watch less movies.

Except, taunted a voice in his head, *for the island your old man discovered*.

Denham strode away from the dinosaur hall, heading for the elevator and for his office. A few staff members nodded to him as he passed, but no one spoke. Denham carried his own silence with him, wrapped himself in it like a cloak. He opened his office door and smiled as he saw a gray-suited man turning from the wall of photographs on the wall to the right of his desk. Same muscular build, though heavier; same earnest features, though the hair was grayer, the jaw a little fuller. "Hi, kid," Jack Driscoll said with a grin. He jerked a thumb at a framed diploma. "Or I guess I should say 'Doctor Denham.'"

"Kid's okay," Vincent told him, shaking hands. "Good to see you again, Mr. Driscoll."

The other man winced. "Not 'Mr. Driscoll.' Jack, please. How long has it been?"

Denham gestured toward a chair, and he sank into his own chair behind the desk. "Too long. Mom's funeral."

Driscoll sat down, crossing his legs, and nodded. He didn't say anything.

Watching him, Denham thought, *He knew exactly how long it's been. He wanted to see if I'm still grieving. Still angry.* Aloud, he said, "How's Ann?"

"Fine, fine," Driscoll said. "Waiting for our first grandchild to be born." He chuckled. "You're not much good at small talk, Vince. Want to tell me why you asked me to come see you?"

Denham nodded without smiling. "It's about Dad," he said. "And about King Kong."

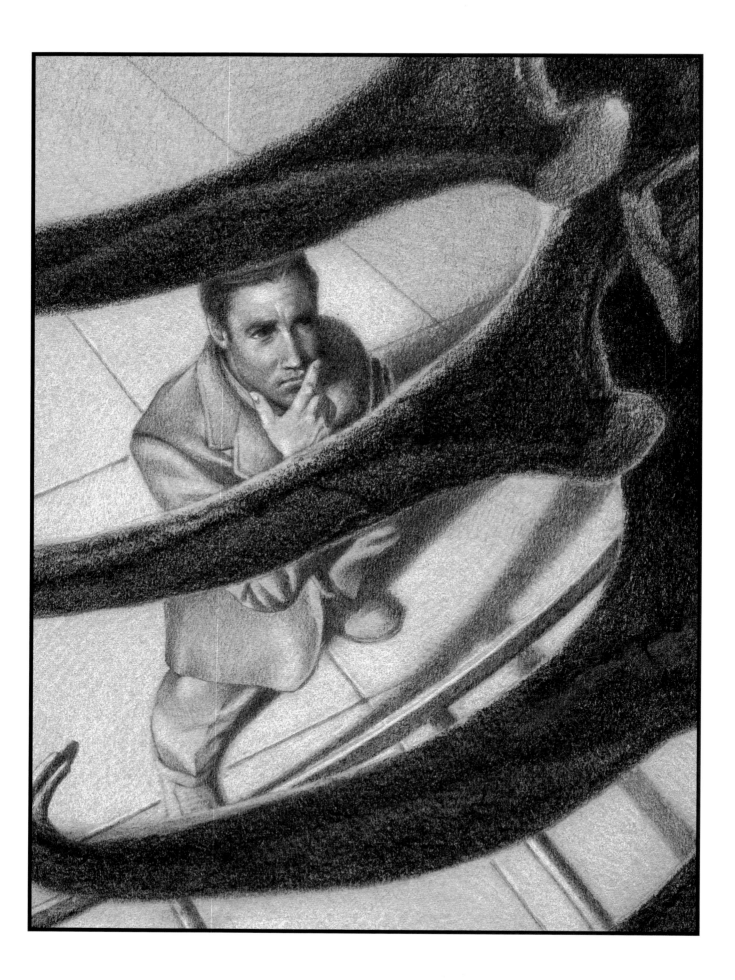

Driscoll regarded him impassively. "I thought you didn't believe Kong even existed."

Denham opened the top right drawer of his desk. He took out a stack of photos and papers. The pictures, all eight-by-ten black and whites, he tossed to Driscoll. "A scientist has to have evidence, Jack," he said. "We need it the way living creatures need food, water, air. This is what I've always had." He watched as Driscoll thumbed through the photos. "As you see, the pictures of King Kong aren't very good. A black mass, in most of them. The one with Dad and Ann could have been faked. The one of Kong dead on the street just shows a heap of something against a background of buildings."

"I was there that night," Driscoll said with a grim smile. He placed the pictures back on the desk. "Let's say his photos don't do him justice."

Denham didn't respond to that. Instead, he picked up a slim scrapbook. "Then there are the news stories. 'Denham's Monster Terrorizes City.' Six or seven days' worth—Kong wasn't even a nine-day wonder."

"It was the middle of the Depression, kid," Driscoll said. "There were other things to worry about. Is that why you won't accept Kong's existence?"

Denham shook his head. "Not entirely. Part of it is scientific. The descriptions of Kong don't match any known primate. The newspapers called him a gorilla, but no gorilla of that size could exist. He'd have to be an unknown species, and where do you hide a species that size?"

"He wasn't easy to find," Driscoll pointed out. "What else?"

"Personal things, I guess. You know, three or four years after the war, when I was still in college, a reporter interviewed me about my dad. What did I think of King Kong? Did I feel my father was responsible?" He laughed without much mirth. "What was I supposed to say? I wasn't even ten in 1933, and Mom and I never saw Kong. Dad kept us away from the city. But you know the question that really bothered me? It was 'What happened to the body?'" Denham leaned forward over the desk. "Jack, what did happen to the body?"

"You got me," Driscoll said evenly. "It was there, and then a crew came and hauled it away, and no one knows for sure where it went."

With a sigh, Denham replied, "Exactly. That's why the debunkers had a field day later on. Was it really a freak of nature? Was it some bizarre hoax that Dad pulled off?" He leaned back in his chair. "You know the way I think, Jack. I'm a paleontologist. I've got to see the bones. That's what I want."

"No," Driscoll said quietly. "You want to sleep at night." When Denham started to object, he held up his hand. "Hear me out, kid. I know what you went through. Not even a month after Kong rampaged through the city, your old man disappeared. Your mom was left to fight the legal battles, make the explanations, hear the accusations."

"It killed her," Denham said.

Driscoll nodded. "I know it did. So now you want—what? To prove the whole thing never happened? Because you can't do that, kid."

Denham did not answer at once. He could hear the slow ticking of the Regulator clock in the hall outside. At last he said, "I want to discover the truth."

"All right. How?"

Reaching into the open drawer, Denham pulled out a manila envelope. "Last week I was rearranging the pictures on the wall there, putting up new shots of our last Montana dig. I bumped a photo, and it fell off the wall. The glass broke." He pulled the picture out of the envelope. "This is the last picture taken of the family before Dad vanished." He looked at it, his mother, his father, and himself as a tow-headed eight year old standing in the sun before a white house. Carl Denham stared into the camera, a cocky grin on his face, as if in challenge. His mother had her eyes turned toward her husband, and she was not smiling. Vincent himself looked almost lost, in front of the other two but somehow not fully part of the family group, his face solemn, looking older than his true age. Denham handed the photo to Driscoll.

"Looks just like he did the first time I met him," Driscoll said. "What about it?"

Denham took a folded piece of heavy paper from the envelope. "This was hidden in the frame behind it," he said.

Driscoll took it from him and unfolded it. He whistled. "Is this the real McCoy?" he asked.

With a shrug, Denham said, "You mean is it a fake, like the one in the lawsuit? I don't know. What do you think?"

Driscoll shook his head. "Looks right to me." He stood, completely unfolded the map on the desk top, and studied the bearings scribbled in the margins. "This is a redrawn version of the original map, but it's by your dad's hand, all right." He pointed at the chart. "This strange writing wasn't on the original. And these rivers—or whatever they are—weren't on it either. This is a close copy, though. The coordinates are on target. But someone's fooled with it."

"Who could have done that? And why?"

Driscoll glanced up from the map. "I don't know."

Denham stood beside him, hesitating for a moment. Finally he took a deep breath and said, "I need your help."

"To do what?"

Vincent thumped the map. "To find this place," he said. "To see what's really there." He looked Driscoll in the eye. "Jack, I'm going to Skull Island."

CHAPTER TWO

ABOARD THE *DARROW*
June 28, 1957

Jack Driscoll leaned back in his chair and drained the last of his coffee. "She's an old Liberty ship," he said. "I bought her back in '46." He shrugged. "I'd come through the war all right, had some money saved, and figured there was no point in crewing for someone else all my life. Started in the Mediterranean. By the time we began taking jobs in the Pacific, I had a fleet of six. Anyway, the *Darrow* was the first."

"She's a good ship," Vincent said, wishing that she had a somewhat better cook and a less pervasive stink of diesel. Still, breakfast was tolerable, and he poured more coffee for Driscoll, then for himself. "I didn't know you were still sailing. Personally, I mean."

Driscoll grinned. "Vince, this is the first trip I've taken in four, no, five years. Mostly I navigate paper across my desk now. I've done all right for myself, I guess. And for Ann."

"I'm glad she wasn't upset by your taking off with me like this," he said.

Driscoll looked at him over the rim of his cup. He put the coffee down and said, "She liked your old man, Vince. She still feels he saved her life by getting her off the breadlines—in spite of the fact that he almost got her killed. Besides," Jack said with a smile, "I reminded her that if it weren't for your dad, she never would have met me. How could she argue with that?"

They were in the captain's wardroom, where they had eaten every morning and night for weeks. Vincent had wondered what kind of sailor he would be. Now he knew: except for a touch of seasickness during a heavy blow, the answer had been a pretty good one. Still, he woke every morning to—not nausea, exactly. Butterflies. The feeling that something big was coming, heading right for him.

"How close are we?" he asked Driscoll.

Driscoll shrugged. "Not far now. We're lucky—when I sailed with Englehorn, sonar hadn't been invented." With a sweeping gesture, Driscoll added, "This isn't what they call blue-water sailing, Vince. This whole area is shallow, bottom at no more than twenty fathoms anywhere, reefs coming to within a fathom or so of the surface. Volcanic. Unpredictable currents, shifting sands. Already we've learned that the old chart isn't a hundred percent accurate anymore. We have to take our time."

Vincent nodded. "What happened to Englehorn?" he asked. "I tried to trace him, but—"

"He vanished about the same time your old man did," Driscoll said. "Him and his ship." He gave Vincent a long, appraising look. "There was some talk that your dad went back to Skull Island. Went back and never returned."

The squawk box overhead crackled to life: "Mr. Driscoll to the bridge."

"Come along," Driscoll said, reaching for his hat. "It's probably land."

It was land, land on the very edge of visibility. The water shaded from deep greenish-blue to a pale emerald, and in the center of the emerald patch was a gray-brown smudge, a shining patch of cloud above it. "Good work," Driscoll said, staring through high-powered binoculars. "Are we in the channel?"

First mate Hansen, standing on the far side of Driscoll with folded arms and a dissatisfied frown, nodded. "Not much of a channel, if you ask me. The depths you gave me are way off."

Driscoll winked at Vincent and handed him the binoculars. "To be expected," he said. "Assuming no one's been there for nearly a quarter of a century, and the chart's at least that old. What do you think, Vince?"

Vincent was trembling with excitement. He struggled to hold the binoculars on target. Through them he saw towering peaks, an etched white line of surf. No detail. Not close enough for detail. "How soon?" he asked, not heeding Driscoll's question.

"Hard to say," Hansen replied. "With these dog-leg turns, maybe three hours. If the channel hasn't shoaled up completely."

Three slow hours, with the island growing every minute of them. Vincent and Driscoll stayed on the bridge, staring ahead. Vincent kept thinking, *Big. Much bigger than I'd thought.* But then it would have to be, if it harbored any respectable range of life.

Once or twice the ship came to a dead stop while Hansen swore, reversed engines, reversed them again, and jockeyed her through an almost impossible turn. Still, they progressed. Vincent kept staring at the cliffs through the binoculars, recognizing them as eroded volcanic plugs. From the dark green tangle of jungle, wafts of steam suggested that the island was still volcanically active—hot springs, at the least. Lost in distant mists were hints of mountains. But the peculiar geological formation that gave the island's central mountain its name showed clearly: eye sockets, empty nasal cavity. The skull of an earth giant.

"There's the lagoon," Driscoll said at last. "We'll anchor there."

Vincent lowered the binoculars. So far, he had been disappointed. He had caught no glimpse of life. "Where's the village?" he asked.

Driscoll gestured to the left. "On that peninsula. Can't see it from here, though. You can see part of the wall. There, coming over the rise and going right down to the water."

Even with the naked eye, Vincent spotted the straight feature, its base deeply shadowed by the late morning sun. Through the binoculars, it became a sight to make him gasp, a towering structure fifty or sixty feet high. Its architecture was oddly . . . *reptilian* was the word that came to mind, sinuous like a snake, gigantic in proportion like a dinosaur. "Who could have built something like that?" he asked.

"Your guess is as good as mine," Driscoll said. "Your old man thought it was Egyptian, but—"

The deck lurched, and Vincent fell against a bulkhead, grabbing wildly for support. Driscoll lost his footing and fetched up against the forward bulkhead. The captain was already barking orders. The ship's engines groaned, screeched, the *Darrow* gave another heave—

"We're over," Hansen said, helping Driscoll to his feet. "You all right?"

"Pride's a little bruised." Driscoll looked at Vincent. "You?"

"I'm okay," Vincent said. "What happened?"

"We grounded," Hansen said, lifting a telephone handset. He spoke into it, then shook his head grimly. "We've sprung a plate or two, but the pumps are handling the leaks. We may have bent the drive shaft or damaged the prop. Can't tell without diving."

"There's a few days of work," Driscoll said.

"I'm dropping anchor," Hansen told him. "We have to check the damage. I'll tell you one thing, though: we're not getting out of this lagoon until the spring tide."

"In that case," Driscoll said with a grin, "we've got a couple of weeks to do the work." He clapped the captain on the shoulder. "Always look on the bright side, Max."

"When can we go ashore?" Vincent asked.

Driscoll laughed. "Why did I know you were going to ask that?" He stared across the water for a moment, as if lost in thought. "Well, you won't be much use aboard, and you're itching to get onto the island. Tell you what: I'll have some men row you ashore. Rafaelo speaks more Pacific island lingos than there are islands. If anyone can communicate with those strange birds ashore, he can, so he'll go along as interpreter. And just in case they can't understand Rafaelo, I'll have rifles and sidearms issued to the crew. You'd better go armed, too."

"I never—"

"You will now," Driscoll said. "Listen, Vincent: These are primitive people. Human sacrifice is as low as it gets. You're going into real danger now—this ain't a museum. I'll stay aboard to supervise the inspection, then later I'll join you ashore. Okay, kid?"

Vincent nodded.

It took less than an hour to assemble the shore party, though Vincent felt as if days were passing. He changed to khakis, stowed some equipment in a backpack, clapped on a pith helmet, and strapped on a holster. The unfamiliar weight of a Colt automatic dragged at him. It was not as if he were going to use it, he told himself. Not as if he could even hit anything.

He went back on deck to find the weather had turned around. A gray cloud hung over the island, its underside ominous, as purple as a bruise. A jagged streak of lightning strobe-lit the eerie peak in the west, the rocky facade that grinned over the island with a skeleton's sardonic expression. Vincent stared at it, thinking, *Dad saw this twenty-five years ago. The gateway to the beast-god Kong's lair. Skull Island.*

"Ready, Vince?" Driscoll asked, bringing Vincent out of his reverie.

"I guess so. I—" Vincent broke off, noticing Driscoll's expression. "What's wrong? How badly is the ship damaged?"

Driscoll shrugged. "I've seen worse. It's going to take a lot of work, though. And probably it would be wisest to get out of here in two weeks, when the tide is highest. Get to port, make some real repairs."

"You can leave me," Vincent said. "We'd planned for six weeks."

"Comes to that, I'll stay with you," Driscoll said. "Look, kid, get to shore and then find cover, fast. If the islanders show up, and they probably will, let Rafaelo do the talking. My best men will go with you. Stay on this side of the wall and you should be okay." Driscoll slapped him on the back. "Take care, now."

The dinghy was waiting, two oarsmen holding her close to the side of the *Darrow*. Vincent had never climbed down the side of a ship before, but the sailors rigged a sling and lowered him like a side of beef. Hands seized his legs, dragged him into the boat,

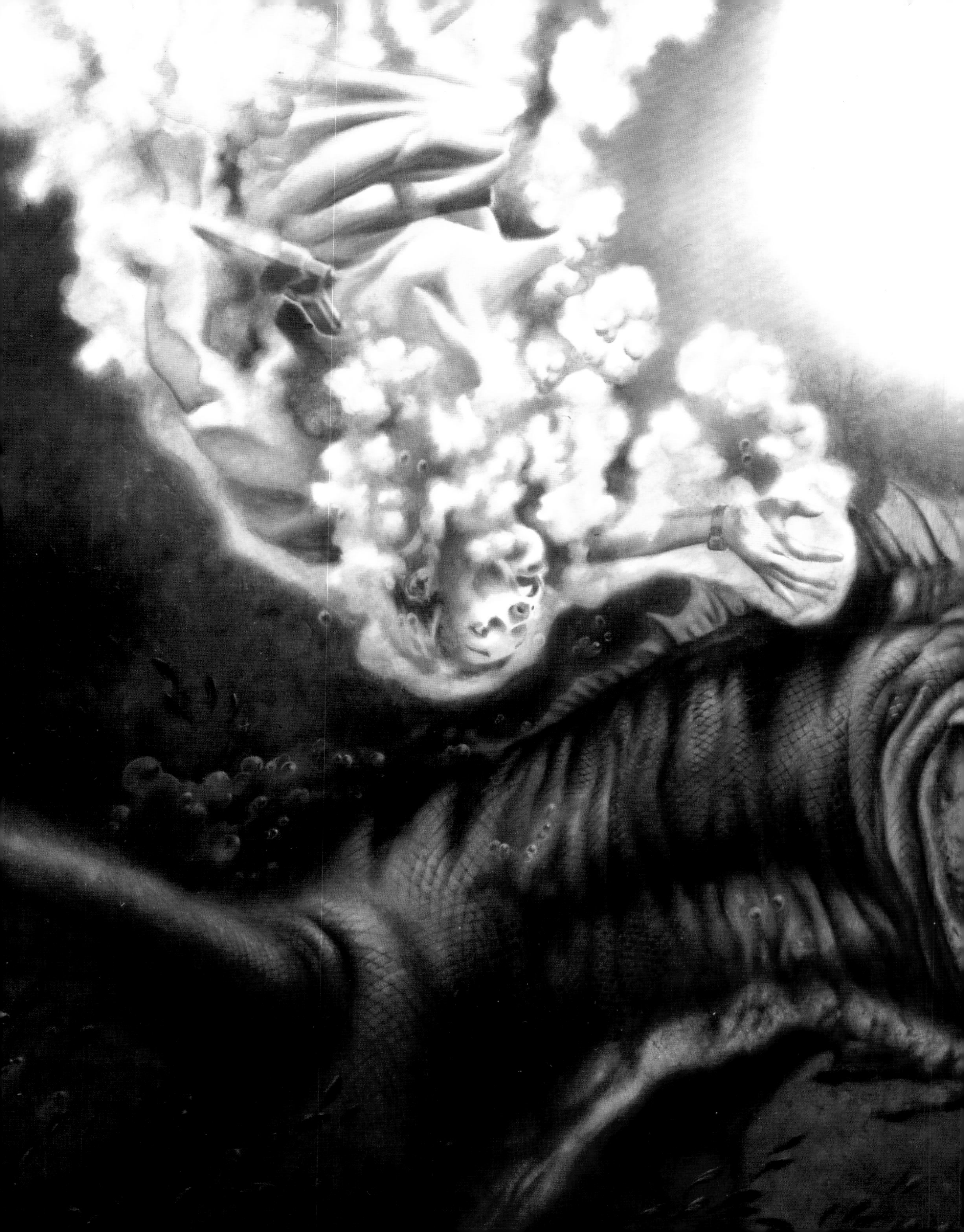

and settled him near the stern. The man named Rafaelo dropped easily into the bow and grinned back at him. "Get wet soon, no?"

Thunder rumbled ominously as if in agreement. The men pushed off and bent to their oars. Off to the right, the squall swept over the jungle toward them. Fascinated, Vincent watched it coming, a dark wall of rain silvered with lightning blasts, as inevitable as sunset or death.

"Hold on!" shouted Rafaelo, clapping a hand on his hat. The dark wall of rain came hissing and boiling across the green surface of the lagoon, hit them with pelting, drenching force. Vincent shrank from the cold, stinging lashes of rain, gasped for breath, heard the hammer of the storm on his helmet and on the boat. And then—

The world turned upside-down. Vincent felt himself falling, heard the terrified yells of the men. He plunged into the warm water and into silence. Frantically, he snatched at his bootlaces, dragged his feet free, unbuckled the holster and let the drowning weight of the Colt pull it away from his body. With his lungs clenching for air, he kicked and flailed desperately, eyes wild.

Before righting himself, something immense glided past him, an arm's reach away. Whale? No, impossible, not here in the lagoon—

Vincent's head broke the surface, and he gasped in a long, shuddering lungful of air. The overturned boat spun nearby, the two sailors clinging to it, trying to right it. Rafaelo was nowhere in sight. The pounding rain whipped the lagoon's surface to something like foam, smothering and blinding. Vincent trod water, gathering strength for the swim to the boat.

A commotion near him, a huge shimmering, scaly back breaking the surface, dragon jaws gaping.

Vincent shouted as the monster seized the nearest sailor, lifted him screaming, shook him as a terrier shakes a rat. He heard, or imagined he heard, the crunch of those ferocious jaws. Then, with a strange liquid grace, the creature turned sideways to dive, and only a red cloud in the water showed what had happened to the man. It was no whale. It moved like a crocodile, but its build was different—

Mosasaur? No, not quite right. New species maybe. New? Living species! Vincent swam toward the boat, stunned, numb, but his brain working, instinctively seeking to classify, to understand.

The man still clinging to the boat yelled and flailed his arm. Gull-sized birds—no, not birds, feathered but not beaked, their heads split into toothed weapons—dived at him. One scooped a golfball-sized chunk of flesh from his arm and soared away. The man shrieked again, clawed at the boat, and sank. No.

Something had dragged him under.

Something that swam below.

It, or another huge creature, broke the surface, breached, hung suspended for what felt like an eternity, then fell atop the overturned boat, splintering it. Vincent whirled in a welter of froth, tumbling over and over. He went limp, letting himself float to the surface. He turned on his back and panted for air. Through the rain-darkened air sailed an immense winged creature, swooping low, coming at him with extended claws—

Something closed on his leg like a vise.

Exhausted, lungs clogged with water, Vincent struggled as something pulled him under, into darkness. He heard his own pulse pounding in his ears, felt his lungs burning. This was what it was like to be eaten alive, to be prey, not hunter. This was . . .

CHAPTER THREE

SKULL ISLAND
June 28, 1957

Hansen said, "I wish you wouldn't do this."

"I'm not gonna ask anyone else to do it." Jack Driscoll had been hunkered down, studying the traces in the fine, tawny-gray sand of the narrow beach. Someone had been dragged inland by two barefooted people. The pith helmet that rested upside-down said the person being dragged was probably Vincent Denham. The streaks of blood on the beach said he was hurt. Driscoll rose and tightened his gunbelt. "You've got your orders, Hansen. Get back to the *Darrow*."

"Aye, sir," Hansen said. "Good luck."

Hansen climbed back into the dinghy. The sailors immediately pushed off and began to row. They had seen what had happened in the lagoon, Driscoll knew, and they were in a hurry to get back to the ship.

Driscoll turned from the retreating dinghy and toward the island. "I hate this place," he muttered to himself, and tapped his pocket, making sure the map of the island and his compass were there. His rifle leaned against a drooping palm tree, and he reached for it. If only the men had been willing to row him into the lagoon—but they were scared, and he couldn't blame them. Well, he could walk to the wall, but not along this beach. A hundred yards away it petered out, replaced by an overhanging cliff of dark volcanic rock. It would have to be overland.

He had made it through that jungle once before. Sure, back when he was twenty-odd years younger and twenty pounds lighter. But he had learned that a group of men looked like appetizing morsels to the wild animals that roamed here, while one lone man could find ways of sneaking through. "So sneak," he told himself. A last glance showed him that the dinghy was tied fast to the ship again, the men safe on deck. He waved and pushed into the brush.

Within minutes sweat was pouring into his eyes. Insects chirred and zinged all around him. Fine, let them. They shut up when something big was around. Suited Jack Driscoll to have some warning. From time to time he heard distant shrieks and growls, fewer it seemed to him than he recalled. Well, if some of the dinos had died off, he had no objection.

At last Driscoll broke out of the tangled undergrowth and into the open floor of the jungle. A heavy overhead canopy cast everything into a green gloom but kept the smaller growth on the jungle floor stunted. And it was cooler, too. Driscoll had a compass, but he didn't need to refer to it. One thing that hadn't left him was his unerring sense of direction. He knew that the wall had to be ahead and to his left. Far off and to his right was the broad river, and beyond the steep-sided canyon. And beyond that the mountain, once the lair of Kong.

Well, he wouldn't be going that way. Shouldn't even be going this way, but Hansen had seen through his binoculars Vincent ashore, moving feebly and looking semi-conscious. And then, judging from the footprints, someone had taken him away.

If the kid was still alive—

Something big crashed through the forest somewhere behind him. Driscoll saw a deadfall, three or four gigantic trunks that had collapsed and left a triangular opening, just about man-sized.

The crackling of branches came again, nearer. Without hesitation, Driscoll crept into the opening, wedged himself, waited with his rifle at the ready. An indistinct creature was moving among the trees, something as big as an elephant. Driscoll pressed himself back. The branches behind him yielded, feeling springy. The place smelled of mold. Beads of sweat crawled down his face like ants.

The creature lumbered into sight, munching on a leafy branch it had torn from a low tree. Driscoll breathed easier. It looked like a cross between a triceratops and a rhinoceros, he thought. Definitely like the former, with its thick barrel body and short, powerful tail. It also had the massive, parrot-like beak. But like the rhino, it had a single huge horn and no shield-like frill. At any rate, it was a plant eater, not—

The branches crackled, and he felt himself slipping. His instinct was to grab for a handhold, but he was clutching the rifle. Driscoll tried to lunge forward.

Too late. A branch snapped, and he felt himself falling. He had no time to brace, and maybe that saved him from breaking his leg as he came down hard after a fall of eight or ten feet. Leaves and twigs showered around him. He got to his feet. He seemed to be in a cave of some kind, though he could see almost nothing. A faint shaft of light came down through where he had fallen.

But there was no way to climb up to it.

"Oh, great," Driscoll said aloud. "This is just great." About par, he added mentally, for what always happened on Skull Island.

"Jack! Help me, Jack!"

Vincent knew that voice—Ann Darrow's voice! He struggled to the surface of consciousness and jolted awake into darkness—a dank, closed-in darkness, smelling of earth and dust. He had memories of nightmares. But the voice, the voice was surely not from inside his mind—

A sound in the dark, an insane, cackling laugh. "For the luvva Mike!" His father's voice? His father?

"Who's there?" An echo died in the dark, but no answer came. Not unless he counted a grunting, feral growl.

Instinctively he froze. He knew now exactly how prey felt, and he had no wish to attract attention to himself. He felt clammy, sweating and chilled. Something lay over him, soft, a coverlet of some kind. Beneath it, his muscles ached, and he felt the fire of other wounds along his side, on his leg. His left arm felt numb. With his right, he explored his naked chest, stopping when his palm found a jagged but closed rip in the flesh over his ribs. Someone had stitched up the tear.

Vincent shivered. Had he been delirious? Somehow memories of his father floated to the surface, the big man laughing, dressed for yet another expedition. "For the luvva Mike," his dad had often said to him—when? Maybe when Vincent had been four. "For the luvva Mike, kid, you have to stay here and take care of your mom. When you get a little height on you, you can come with me."

The day had never come, but now, flat on his back in the darkness, Vincent felt an unfamiliar kinship with Carl Denham. Vincent's travels had been to sunny places, dinosaur digs. He had felt far more at home in the cool, shadowy recesses of a museum than on the road. Now he had followed his father halfway around the world—but to what?

Vincent strained his senses. What at first he had thought to be his heartbeat had a different quality, ominous and musical: a primitive drumbeat, muffled and far away. Cautiously, he raised himself on his right elbow.

Something rustled in the darkness, and he felt a cobweb-touch across his face. Reflexively, Vincent dropped back, batting at the air. He connected with something feathery, heard a shrill screech from the thing and heard at the same time from behind a woman's cry: "Oji!"

The thing fluttered away, scrabbled at something. Vincent heard a shattering crash, as if a jar had fallen and broken.

"For the luvva Mike." Not his father, but the woman's voice again. "Here."

Panting, Vincent sat up as a phosphorescent glow, orange at first, then greenish, pushed back the darkness. He strained to turn, needles of pain jabbing at him. "Father? Dad? Is that—"

"No. Be still." A hand pressed him back, and in the smoky, shimmering light, Vincent saw it belonged to an old woman, withered, a white-haired crone. Exhausted, he fell back as in a dream. She stooped over him, her hooded eyes black in the strange light. Even in the haze of pain, his trained mind noticed the garment she wore: leather, but certainly not cowhide. It was scaly, mottled in the uncertain glow in a way that reminded him of lizard skin. Reptilian, certainly. "Would you like a better light?"

Vincent reflexively nodded, fighting to quell his fear. Her English was unaccented, but slow, each word carefully pronounced. She reached to the floor and produced a torch. This she touched to something outside of Vincent's field of vision, and the torch flared to slow life, burning with an unearthly greenish-white flame.

When she settled the torch into a holder, Vincent recognized it as a curved section of rib—dinosaur rib. And in the light he saw that the woman wore a necklace of teeth and claws, curved and gleaming. A flesh-eater's teeth. A predator's claws. "What—?" Vincent mumbled, trying to put together his thoughts.

"Here." The woman pulled back the coverlet, touched his chest gently, probed the wound he had felt. Vincent groaned, yellow pain exploding behind his eyeballs. "Hurts, does it? Healing, though." She was so close that Vincent could smell an unusual scent on her breath, somehow green and growing. Not mint, but something with that tang.

"What is your name? *Fortheluvvamike?*" The woman's seamed face broke into a smile. "Crazy name like that would be good for a man who swims in those waters."

"My name is Vincent Denham," Vincent said. "Who are you? I heard my father's voice—where am I, how did I get here?" His chest ached, and the effort of speaking made his head spin. He felt a flutter of panic at his weakness, at the strange surroundings.

Despite the calm assurance of her voice, the old woman's eyes seemed to stare malignantly at him through the glowing light, and her smile was distorted to a sneer. "We saved you in time. Look at your wounds, Vincent Denham."

She helped him sit up. He looked down at his bare chest and abdomen. A red welt, nearly black in the green light, jagged down his left side from two inches below his nipple to just beside his navel. It looked lumpy. But he had been wrong about its being stitched. Vincent focused and then gagged.

Insect heads, maybe twenty of them, clasped his flesh together. They might have belonged to ants, if ants grew three inches long. Their mandibles had clamped into his flesh, and the insects had been decapitated. Only then did the full horror of his predicament flood his mind, and he lost all control. Screaming, Vincent reached with his good hand to tear the things away.

The woman's hand closed on his wrist in an iron grip. "No. You stay still!"

The crack of her voice and the strength of her grasp shocked him back to reality. Trembling, weak, Vincent fell back. "The—the heads—"

"Hold your wound closed so I can treat it," the woman said, concern on her ancient face. "They are harmless, and they keep you from bleeding to death."

"Where is my father? I heard his voice! What have you done with him—or was I dreaming? Who are you?" Vincent asked, shuddering. "A witch doctor?"

"You can call me Storyteller. That is close enough. As for your father, he is not here. But that is a story yet to be told. Lie still now." In a louder tone, she called, "Kara!"

Vincent stared as a form emerged from the darkness, a strikingly attractive woman, no more than twenty. Her face had a timeless beauty, a symmetry and perfection of feature.

But her expression was mingled pride and anger. She did not even look at Vincent.

The Storyteller said something to her in a rapid, low voice. The young woman walked past Vincent's bed off to his left. He heard the clatter of some kind of earthenware vessel, and then he felt the cold touch of a viscous liquid. While the young woman stood beside her, holding the container, the Storyteller was painting his wound with some mixture. "More light, Kara," she said.

Kara set down the vessel and turned away. Vincent heard her moving, and a new torch flared. The Storyteller had settled onto a stool beside the bed, her brooding eyes never leaving Vincent. Weakly, he looked around. He seemed to be lying in a vault of vast proportions. A cave, he supposed, or a tunnel. When he raised himself, he stared down an endless expanse of darkness, the light just touching some gigantic carvings to the left and to the right.

"Tyrannosaur," muttered Vincent, studying the carving to the left.

"My people carved that from stone," the Storyteller said. "An age ago."

"Not right, though. Proportions are off." The statue looked at least half life-sized, Vincent thought.

A nagging thought crossed Vincent's mind. The tyrannosaur wasn't right, wasn't the way he knew it should look—something about the head, the hunch of the shoulders, the stance were all wrong. But what if it were not a tyrannosaur at all? What if it were a different species, maybe even—understanding dawned, even in Vincent's dazed mind: sixty-five million extra years of evolution could have made the difference. Not the Tyrant King, but a descendant of the great killer dinosaurs.

Vincent tore his gaze away from the predator and saw that its companion was an ichthyosaur, carved and poised as if it were swimming in an antediluvian sea. The statues were beautifully executed, with perfectly detailed limbs, claws, teeth, scales, eyes. Vincent knew archaeology, and he could tell that these carvings were not stylized, not typical of primitive art. The artisans were brilliant in both art and in scientific knowledge. The idols looked almost alive.

"How old?" he croaked, pointing to the statues.

"Old beyond memory," Kara said from somewhere behind him. Her voice was cold, scornful.

Vincent heard the fluttering sound again and winced as something flew over his head, landing with a clumsy thump on the foot of the bed. It gave a creaking call and ruffled its feathers. In the strange torchlight, it looked green, with highlights of yellow, scarlet, and orange. It began to preen one wing, its long tail moving for balance as the creature held onto its perch beside Vincent's right foot.

"Archaeopteryx," Vincent said, mesmerized by the crow-sized dragon-bird.

"Oji," corrected the old woman, rising from her stool to stand beside Vincent. She clapped her hands, and with a piping call the creature flapped into awkward flight, scrambling onto the Storyteller's shoulder. Its long neck curved and it delivered a quick peck to her cheek.

"Oji," Vincent said. The primitive bird swiveled its head to look at him, its eyes bright as jewels. It grinned at him with carnivorous teeth.

Vincent had to rip his attention away from the living fossil. "Listen," he said. "How did you learn English?"

"You rest now," the old woman said. "Time for questions later."

"I came to find my father," Vincent said in a rush. "He—do you remember King Kong?"

From behind him came the sharp intake of Kara's breath.

"Kong," the old woman said without expression. "You must rest. Sleep. Kara! We will leave him." She turned and walked away, into darkness, followed by the young woman. But Kara turned her head back over her shoulder and glared at him, a withering look that was as sharp as a dagger.

Vincent settled back, too weak to protest. Feverishly, he remembered the tales Driscoll had told him on the outward voyage. How Kong had rampaged through the village on the island, how later in Manhattan he had run amok, spreading death and destruction.

And then he was dreaming. He was standing in New York City's American Museum of Natural History, in a new wing, the Carl Denham Wing. The architecture was a strange mixture of the familiar and the bizarre.

The central display was the mounted skeletons of a tyrannosaur and a gigantic ape locked in combat, the dinosaur on its back, ready to deliver an eviscerating kick to the enemy that towered over it. Flashbulbs popped, and in Vincent's dream he imagined his father's voice saying, ". . . the Eighth Wonder of the World!"

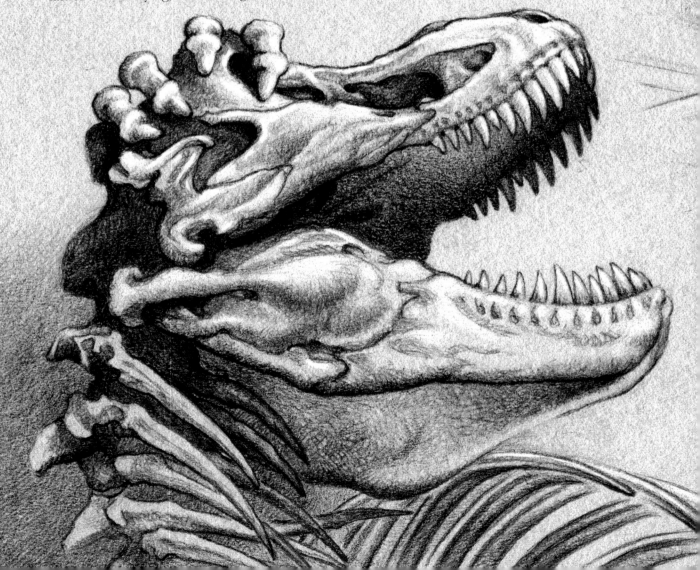

And the dream changed. Vincent was back in the museum, but the crowds had departed. He stood alone before the exhibit—but only the tyrannosaur was a skeleton. Kong was a living, breathing behemoth, his eyes burning into Vincent's. Vincent felt ice in his bones. Kong roared deafeningly and took a step forward. His shadow fell over Vincent, a shadow that seemed to have weight and suffocating substance. The beast's massive hand reached towards him. Vincent couldn't run, couldn't move, couldn't even breathe—

Gasping in terror, Vincent yelled himself awake. He felt a touch on his forehead and realized that Kara sat near him, wiping his brow. "You dream of the Kong," she said. "You said his name twice. And you called for your father."

"My father," Vincent said, hearing the coldness in her voice.

"Carl Denham," Kara said in a voice dripping with venom. "And now I know what I must do with you, Vincent Denham."

"What?" Vincent asked. "What is that?"

The young woman bent close, her eyes glittering like stars, but as deep and black as the grave. "Nothing," she said slowly and ominously, "that your father has not already done to my people."

CHAPTER FOUR

UNDERGROUND
June 29, 1957

Jack Driscoll rose and stretched. His fire had burned down to ashes, but the thin light streaming through the break overhead told him it must be morning. He rummaged around in the semidarkness, finding the torches he had prepared before settling in for a fitful sleep. He thrust all but one into his belt and lit the last one. It was a stout branch, its head wound around with dried creeper. In its wavering light, he unfolded the map of the island. His finger traced a line that snaked toward the wall.

Had to be the tunnel he was in, he decided. Had to be. He had often wondered how the islanders had been able to survive cooped up on the peninsula. Here was the answer: secret passages that let them get out into the jungle and back in one piece. And that would give him a chance to find Vincent. Driscoll grinned.

He took a look at his compass and turned to the right direction. Savages couldn't have built this tunnel, he thought. Lava tube, he supposed. Just his luck the ceiling had collapsed right under the deadfall, just his luck to topple through. But it seemed to be plenty big enough for him to stride through it. He should still make far better time here than struggling through the jungle.

If nothing hungry denned here, he thought with a twisted smile. If there was an opening at the far end. If he wasn't trapped here for good and all.

But there were no signs of animals, which was strange. As if the creatures avoided the place for some reason. Or maybe they hadn't ever discovered it.

Anyway, according to his compass readings and the map, he was headed toward the wall. With some luck, the tunnel might even take him beyond the wall. He might come out somewhere on the village peninsula. Only one way to—

Something crunched under his boot. Driscoll took a step back and lit a new torch.

In its flickering light he saw something long and white.

He had stepped on someone's foot.

But whoever it was felt no pain. He or she had become a skeleton ages ago.

SKULL ISLAND
Date Unknown

Delirium: Vincent was prey again. Monsters loomed all around him, eyes, teeth, claws. A sharp snake-house reek, cold in the nostrils. Hisses, roars, shrieks that could never be torn from mammalian throats.

And beyond the monsters, behind them, larger than they were, as large as the night itself, blackness. A darkness that lived and moved and was worshiped as a god.

27

Kong.
Kong.
Kong.

How long the fever madness lasted, Vincent could not tell. He was aware of intervals, of the old woman, the Storyteller, lifting his head, holding an earthenware vessel to his lips, of a taste astringent and bitter, cold and yet spiced with a heat that burned its way to his gut. Sometimes the beautiful Kara was there, treating him gently but with obvious hatred in her glare. Then, like a man clawing at the side of a cliff as gravity pulls him down, he always slid back into sleep, into nightmares.

Until he pulled himself into the light. He raised himself in bed, his head reeling. A few of the bone torches burned with their lazy, oily, almost liquid flames. The skin on his chest felt tight, drawn like a drumhead over the frame of his ribs. The scar had turned pale, was no longer purple and puckered, and the ant heads were gone.

The Storyteller sat not far away, her back against one rough wall, her head forward. She seemed asleep. The Oji, the impossible archaeopteryx, perched nearby, its long claws closed over the handle of a basket. Eyes bright as black pearls regarded him. The scaled beak opened, a black tongue vibrated. The creature made a faint cawing sound, ending in his father's voice: "For the luvva Mike!"

Vincent wanted to rise, but he lacked the strength. His arm trembled even supporting his weight in bed. He let himself fall back with a sigh. He lay exploring his feelings. The dead spots, the numb places, were gone. He had an interesting variety of pain now, ranging from the deep muscle ache of unaccustomed exertion to abrasions, cuts, scratches, bruises. And his mouth tasted foul, as if the Oji had been roosting in it.

"You are awake." A hand cool on his forehead. Kara looked down on him, and again the elegance of her face, the loveliness of it, caught his attention. "The fever has passed. You will not be strong for a long time."

The old Storyteller stirred and her cracked voice said, "He was never strong enough to swim in the lagoon, to face the water beasts."

A flutter, and the archaeopteryx landed on the side of his bed, near the crook of his right elbow. Vincent stared at it, seeing its feathers clearly for the first time, seeing the reptilian snout, the face of a predatory dinosaur. It tilted its head, studying him. "Where I come from, we'd call that a living fossil," he said. "How can it imitate my father's voice like that? When did it hear him speak?"

"Here I call him Oji," responded the Storyteller. She ignored his questions. "Vincent Denham, your fever cried out. It called 'Kong! Kong!' What do you know of Kong?"

Vincent shook his head. "Almost nothing." And that was true; he knew so little of his father's find, the Eighth Wonder of the World, the beast that hulked through his dreams and haunted his memories. "Only what I have heard."

The woman leaned close, her fingers exploring the scar on Vincent's side. "He was unlike any other creature. Like nothing that ever walked, hunted, or fought. He had, almost, a soul." She put an arm behind his shoulders. "Stand up. Walk now. We will help you. Only a short way."

"But what about my fath—"

"Not now. Come, Vincent Denham. You will hear what you wish to know in time. Come with us now."

Her voice was hard to resist, almost hypnotic. Vincent struggled up on rubber legs. His head spun, and he heard, or imagined he heard, that insistent, mournful drumbeat from somewhere not close, yet not very far away. Kara, with a supple strength, put his arm around her neck and bore most of his weight. He felt her body, warm against his. "Where are we going?" he asked.

The Storyteller gestured with one of the torches. "This way. Not far."

Vincent put one foot in front of the other, then again, and again. Kara's deceptively thin frame felt muscular and strong beside him. The torch chased wavering shadows ahead of them. He wondered where he was—the place had the feel of a natural cavern, vaulting up to unguessed heights, lost in darkness, but the rough walls were shored with balks of timber, lined with carved idols. To Vincent's dizzy sight, the dinosaurs seemed almost museum-quality recreations, and yet—"They're not quite right," he muttered. "Not for the species I know."

"Maybe you do not know them all," said the Storyteller.

"He knows nothing!" Kara's voice was like a cracking whip.

"He will learn," the Storyteller said quietly. She stopped in her tracks and lifted the torch high. "There," she said. "Ahead."

Vincent's heart thudded. There before him reared a gargantuan form, bent forward, fists raised, mouth agape, fierce eyes fixed on him with a vengeance that made his blood run cold. The flicker of the torch made the creature almost breathe—

No. It, too, was an idol. Yet the eyes, the eyes practically glowed with an intelligence that was almost human.

"You see," the Storyteller said. "Kong."

Vincent staggered. Kara supported him and then led him back to his bed, a wooden-framed cot, he could see now, with a thin mattress, made of thin, tough leather stitched over a stuffing of something soft, resting on the stretched, heavy skin of some great reptile. Kara helped him lie down, then the Storyteller held the bowl to his lips again. He drank, first tentatively, then greedily. The liquid must have been the juice of some tropical fruit, spiced and warming. He was hungry, ravenous.

As if reading his desires, the Storyteller said, "No solid food for a little time yet. More of this if you wish it, and all the water you want. You can hold the vessel?"

Vincent took the bowl in both hands. He forced himself to take small sips, not to gulp. "It's good," he said.

"You have had nothing but medicines and water for several days," she told him. "I know why you have come."

Vincent drained the bowl, let it rest on his stomach. The archaeopteryx fluttered to his knee, pinch-walked up his thigh, then pecked at the bowl. "I came to find my father," he murmured.

"The murderer!" snarled Kara.

The Storyteller raised a thin hand, shushing the younger woman. "I will help," she said.

"How?" Vincent asked, warily eyeing Kara.

The old woman pulled her wooden stool close to the side of the bed and sat on it. "By doing what I do," she said simply. "I am the Storyteller. I will tell you a story." She tilted her head back. "It is day," she said. "Look up."

Vincent did. In the darkness overhead he saw what he at first thought was the moon. It was round, at least, and shone with a silvery light. "A window?" he asked.

"A window now," the Storyteller said. "It is covered with hide, scraped, stretched thin, and oiled. But once it was more than a window. Once it was a portal to another time. A time when the fate of my people hung in dangerous balance."

"When?" Vincent asked.

"I cannot tell the count of years," the Storyteller said. "But I can tell you this: My story is different from anything you know or have heard. And yet, Vincent Denham, it grows, like a jungle vine, and it twines around other stories. Yours not least of them. Listen to me. Listen to my story."

And Vincent lay back and listened. . .

CHAPTER FIVE

UNDERGROUND
June 29, 1957

Jack Driscoll had wandered into a catacomb. Six skeletons lay on the floor of the tunnel. He crouched, studying them, not liking what he saw.

"The devils," he grunted aloud. The nearest skeleton wore rotten shreds of clothing, and not the wraps and skins of the islanders, either. Canvas clothing. European clothing. At first Driscoll wondered if these were the bodies of some of his shipmates from the first expedition, but he had found a pistol that dispelled that notion. It was an Eley's, a weapon manufactured in England, according to the engraving, in 1873. Carl Denham had not equipped his men with antiques.

But the skeletons were European, at least. And the tough shaft of a spear still transfixed one rib cage, showing how the man had died.

The islanders. The devils.

Grimly, Driscoll stood up and lifted his torch high. The tunnel, floored with dark sand, led off into the distance. Something faintly gleamed ahead. And patches of some kind of fungus or lichen on the walls nearly glowed in iridescence when he moved the torch. With his rifle slung on his back, his torch in his left hand and his drawn pistol in his right—a Colt automatic, not an antique—Driscoll left the chamber of death and headed deeper underground, either toward the Wall or the unknown.

SKULL ISLAND
The Past

Gray rain lashed the village. The wind tore at thatched roofs, and lightning stabbed from roils of cloud. Young Ishara knelt beside the opening of her hut and gazed at the world, her eyes bright as the lightning.

"This is what Bar-Atu prophesied," said her betrothed, Kublai, from behind her.

"Just a storm," she replied. "That's all."

Kublai growled. "Not to Bar-Atu. He'll call it a sign, an omen, and he'll make the people believe that, too. You know the Shaitan. That's what they do."

Ishara closed her hand over the artifact that had been given to her long ago by the Storyteller of the village. It was a simple statuette, graceful in its lines, worn by time. There was no telling how old it really was. It came from the time when such things were plentiful, from a time before the Shaitan priests swayed the minds of the people from understanding of the beasts beyond the Wall to stark fear. To worship.

"Your father doesn't have long to live," Kublai said, kneeling beside Ishara and staring out into the storm. "When he passes, Bar-Atu will proclaim the kingship at an end.

He'll make himself ruler." He gave Ishara a sidelong glance. "Then he'll want to kill you. Bar-Atu can't leave the old king's only child alive."

"But you're of the Atu," replied Ishara. "Bar-Atu can't object to one of his own people. When we marry, you'll be king."

Kublai turned his troubled eyes back to the rain. "Bar-Atu knows I don't agree with him. I'm as dangerous to him as you are."

Ishara did not answer. She was thinking of her childhood. It seemed so long ago, and yet she could count only fifteen suns, her betrothed only two more than that. If she had been an ordinary young woman, she would have been married by now, would have a child. But she was Tagu and of the ruling house of that people. The rules were different for her.

Lightning found the top of a wind-whipped tree, snapped it into flame, and the earth shook with the explosion. With the thunder deafening her ears, Ishara stared into the darkness. The fitful, hissing flames showed her the Wall.

Beside her Kublai rose, took his shield and spear, and strode into the rain. She saw him standing tall and strong, like a prince indeed. She put down the statuette and stepped into the rain, joining him. "The Wall," he said bitterly, pointing with his spear. "Long ago our people built it to protect themselves. Not to become slaves to it."

Ishara pushed her thick hair back from her eyes. No matter where she stood on the peninsula, the Wall was always to be seen, hiding the world beyond. She had grown up with it, had become so accustomed to it that she never thought of it.

Or had not, until Bar-Atu had made a god of Gaw.

The wind rose even more, sending spears of rain stabbing against their flesh. Ishara stood against it, staring at the dark outline of the Wall, at its serrated spine. Was Gaw out there now? After a storm like this, Bar-Atu would cry out for sacrificial victims, would claim that the beast-god Gaw was angry and had sent the lightning and the wind. To ward off more storms, he would say, the villagers would need to feed the blood-cravings of their god with human sacrifice.

"It's wrong," Ishara said in a voice hardly louder than a whisper. The voice of the Storyteller filled her mind, stories of the days when the islanders controlled the creatures of the island without fearing them. Without worshiping them.

Without feeding them—

The world turned white. Ishara stumbled back, collapsed to her knees, her ears ringing.

Kublai staggered before her, pointing with his spear, yelling something. "What?" she asked, after-images dancing before her eyes.

"The Wall!" Kublai shouted. "Look! The Wall!"

Ishara struggled back to her feet. The tree had gone out, its flames put out by the torrents of rain, but part of the Wall smoldered with a red light—

No. Not part of the Wall.

Part of the Gate.

Ishara saw at once what had happened: the last bolt of lighting had struck the Gate, had blasted a smoldering hole near the base of one of the two massive doors. And now the wind came howling through the Gate like the groan of some wounded giant.

"Get the people into the longhouses!" shouted Kublai. "Warriors, to me!"

Ishara dived back into the hut, emerged a moment later with a spear and shield. She dashed through the village, shouting a warning. She heard voices raised in alarm, saw the villagers struggling through the wind and rain toward the strongholds. The younger men joined her, and in a group they ran to Kublai, who stood at the foot of the Wall. Lightning showed his furious face as he shouted, "Ishara! You get to safety!"

"I have a spear!" she shouted. "You need every weapon!"

She could see now that the lightning bolt had broken more than one of the massive timbers of the doorway. A gap much wider than her body, and more than a head higher, jaggedly ran all the way to the sodden earth. "Close in!" yelled Kublai to the young men. "A shield wall! I've seen slashers!"

Ishara caught her breath. Slashers! Man-sized killers that hunted in packs. And if one of the deathrunners, the stronger, eerily cunning herders of the slasher packs, had found the gap in the Wall, a whole group would descend on them. Kublai was pointing and shouting directions for a work party to repair the gap. She stepped through the rain, up to the opening. Her breath came tight and hard. She had never looked through the Gate before.

Warriors were bringing torches that sizzled and spattered in the rain. Their light did not go far, but in the darkness beyond the Wall, Ishara saw two green sparks and then dozens.

Eyes.

"Slashers!" she yelled. "Slashers!"

She felt rather than heard the charge as the creatures piled into the Gate. In momentary flashes, she saw the beasts launch themselves screeching, felt their claws assault the wood. An evil head, half-bird, half-reptile, burst through the gap, teeth ripping at the opening. With a shouted battle cry, Kublai charged past Ishara, stabbing with his spear. He found his target, and the wounded slasher jerked back through the opening, screaming.

Ishara heard the other slashers fall on the bloody creature, heard their snarls and the ripping of flesh as they tore it to pieces, heard the crunch of teeth on bones. She turned toward Kublai. "Can we—" she started.

A scream, a human scream, spun her around. A slasher had thrust its head through the opening, had closed its jaws on a warrior's leg. Knifelike teeth effortlessly sliced through skin and hooked on bone. Ishara saw him dragged out, his frantic hands clutching at the earth, clinging for a moment to the Gate, then jerked through. This time the feasting was over in a second, and the beasts hit the gate with such force that the ground shook.

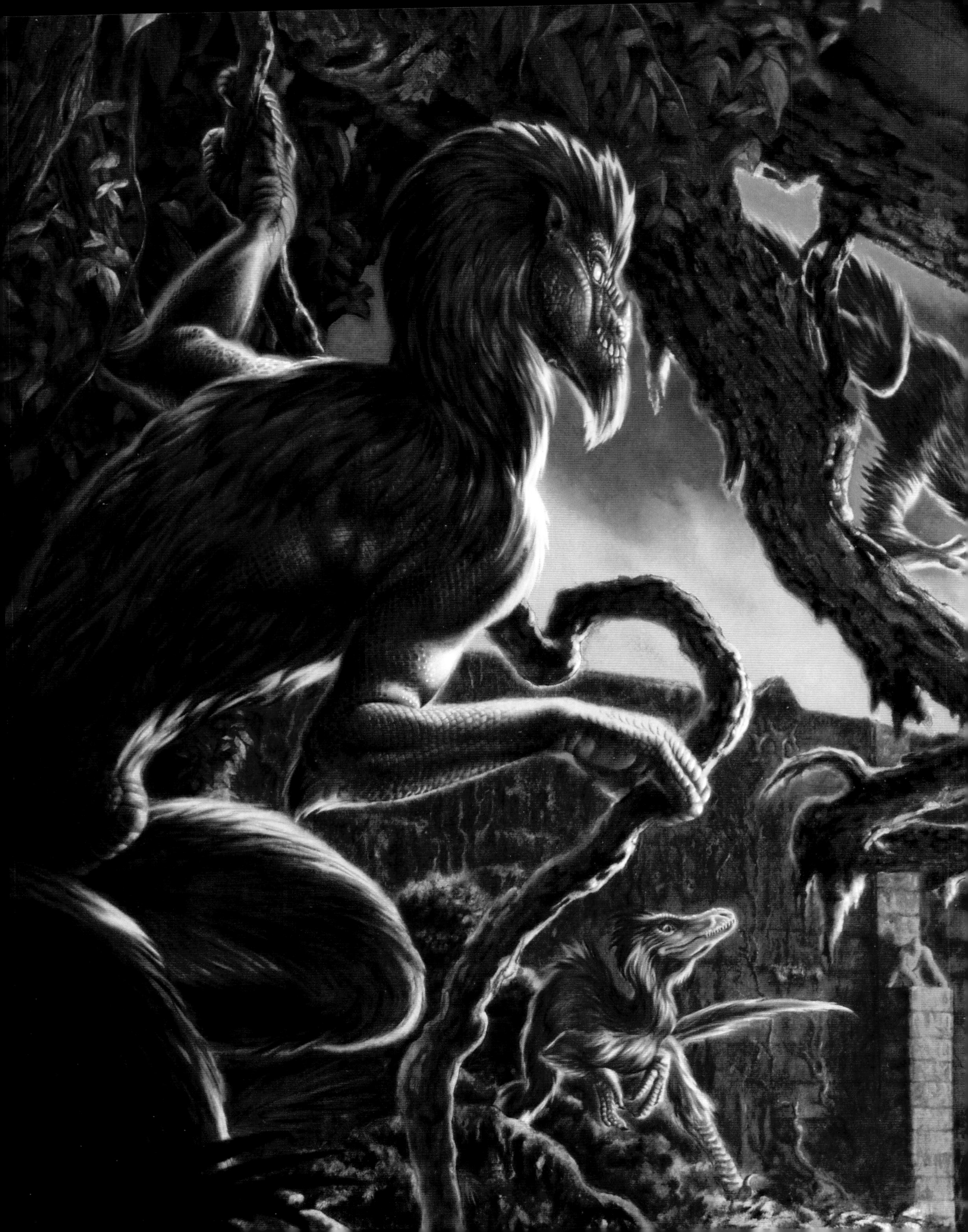

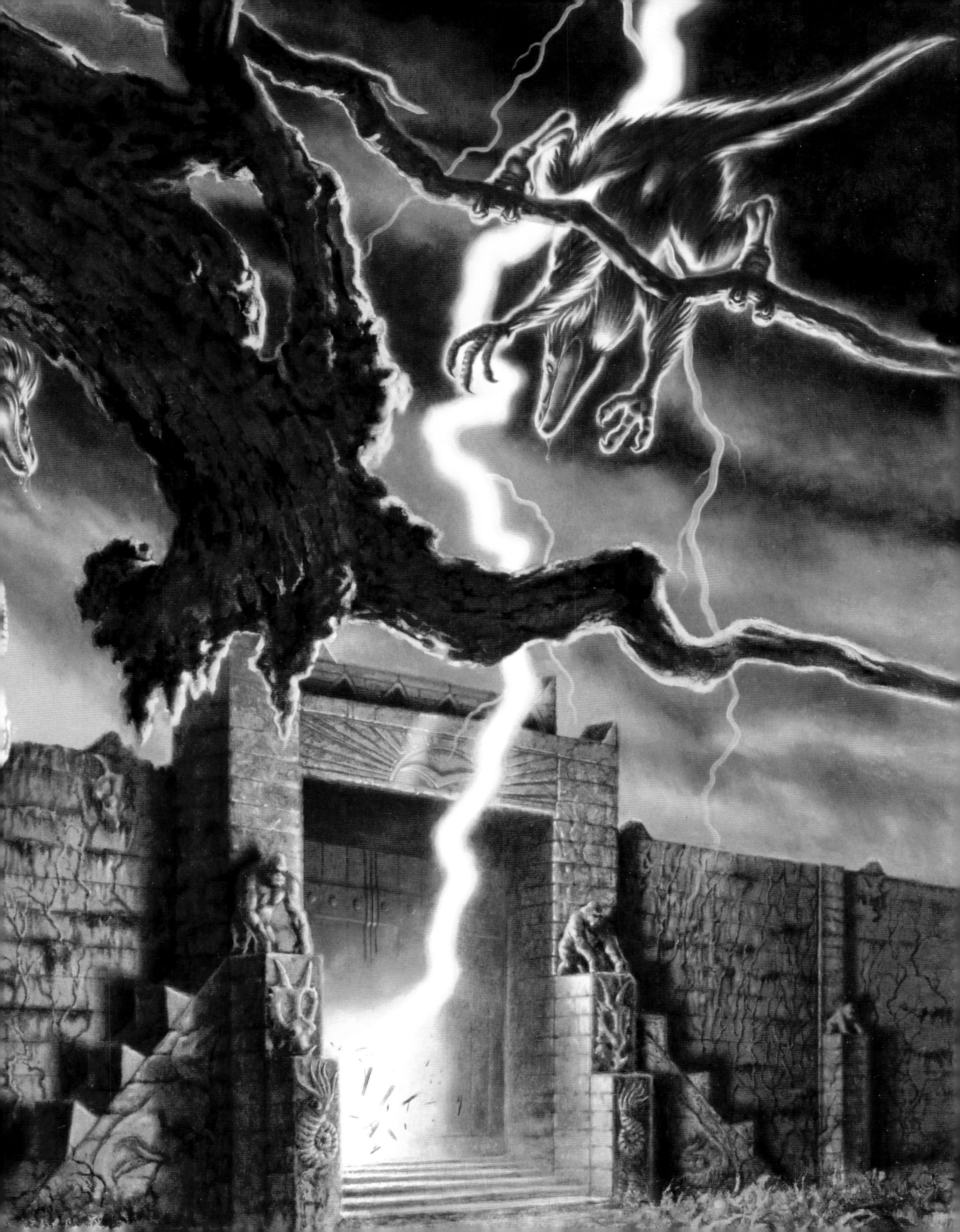

"Hold them!" screamed Kublai.

Three of the creatures had pushed in. Ishara saw a group of men running toward the breach in the wall with a patch, a lashed-together grating of timbers. Warriors at the hole were holding the rest of the slasher pack out by thrusting torches at them. The beasts feared fire, but fire was an uncertain defense in the wind and the rain.

Kublai led a furious charge against one of the creatures, cornered it against the wall, thrust one of a dozen spears at it. Its death-screech pierced the chaos as its rasping body fell, rose, and collapsed again. Another of the beasts had ripped open a warrior, but now it lay dead, too. The third had dashed toward the village, and Ishara heard sounds of the pursuit as a party of warriors harassed it. From beyond the gate came the shrieking voice of a deathrunner! With evil intelligence it was urging the slashers to assault the opening, to press through—

"Close the gap!" Kublai yelled as the work party moved their lattice into position. "If they—"

Splinters flew. Ishara cried out in alarm. A creature, larger than the others, had wedged its feather-covered body into the gap. It could not push through, but it kicked furiously, its talons slashing the air. It caught a defender, not with its clawed foot, but with something it held in its hand, and sent him tumbling, blood erupting from his body like a fountain. The wood groaned and the monster roared as its sinewy, human-like arms groped for better leverage. Horrified, Ishara hesitated a split second—had the creature actually used a weapon? She screamed and charged with all her strength, aiming her spear to catch the thing in the throat—

The beast saw her, kicked, splintered the shaft of her spear. She fell forward, just as she heard the wood give way. Three clawed fingers of a powerful, scaled hand strained to grasp her arm. The deathrunner's eyes glinted in murderous rage as they locked their knowing gaze onto Ishara's.

Kublai yanked her backward, jerked her to her feet. The monster screeched in fury as its plumed head wildly strained from side to side in an effort to get to them. "Up!" he yelled. "Here! Up! The Storyteller!"

Ishara grabbed the rope he handed her—part of a ladder, she realized, that led to the prayer hut atop the Wall, the hut where the Storyteller meditated.

"Come on!" she screamed, pulling herself up the ladder hand over hand. She knew beyond certainty that the monster was a deathrunner, the pack leader, that it would burst through. With it and a dozen of the slashers loose in the village, there would be no safety—

The dinosaur roared again from somewhere far beneath her. Ishara looked down. "Kublai!"

She heard a scream, a human scream. Wind tore at her.

"Kublai!"

A hand closed on her arm, and Ishara tried to jerk away. Too late; it hauled her up, away from the blood, away from the red death below.

CHAPTER SIX

BEFORE THE STORYTELLER'S HUT
After the storm

"**I**t is over." The ancient woman turned from the edge of the Wall and leaned on a gnarled staff, its knotted head taller than she was. She beckoned with a hand twisted by time into a talon. "Come, child. You can look."

Ishara had never looked down on the village from such a height. Though she had climbed trees often enough, she had never been atop the Wall. She felt dizzy, as though the world were reeling, though her senses told her the Wall was as solid and firm beneath her as the earth itself.

Although she had grown up with it, she had never realized how thick the Wall really was. Here, above the great gate, it was as broad as a moderate hut at the top. In fact, it was even broader, for the old woman's prayer hut was in fact built into the top of the Wall, with space enough on the village side to pass by. Ishara swallowed hard and forced herself to stand beside the old woman, looking down.

Bar-Atu's hut, apart from the others, was guarded by two of his followers. She saw the fierce priest enter and the two guards step closer together. "He is going to have *visions*," the Storyteller said acidly. "Bar-Atu has learned enough to know that some of the island plants can make him dream even while he is still awake. He calls his dreams visions and claims they come from his god."

Ishara did not reply, but stood looking at the village. It seemed so different from this point of view. Far below them the work party was repairing the gate. Scattered before it were bodies of dinosaurs and of men. Butchers were already at work on the dinosaurs, stripping meat from the carcasses, meat that Bar-Atu would distribute at the Feast of Victory that he was sure to declare. To her relief, Ishara saw Kublai directing the repairs. He glanced her way, lifted his shield in brief salute, and then turned back to his task.

"He knows you're safe," the Storyteller said.

Ishara hugged herself. "Thank you. I'm just glad to see him alive." She backed a few steps from the Wall's edge and studied the seamed, ancient face of the Storyteller. The old woman's eyes sparkled from deep nests of wrinkles. Ishara felt herself smiling back at the old woman. "I thought you came here to meditate and pray. I never knew you lived here."

"Where did you think I lived?"

Ishara said, "I always wondered. You're in the village on feast days, never any other time. I never knew where you went."

For a moment, the Storyteller gazed into Ishara's face. Then she turned away, leaning on her staff as she walked toward her hut. "Come inside."

The surface underfoot was wood, though to Ishara's feet it felt as hard as stone. The Storyteller went straight into her hut. Ishara had to stoop to go through the low door. The hut was like a miniature long house: the room they entered held a sleeping pallet along one wall, leather cushions stuffed with soft dried grasses against the other. A curtained doorway led back into another room. On a perch hanging from the ceiling, something stirred in the dimness, grumbling in hoarse caws and croaks. "An Oji!" Ishara exclaimed. "Is he yours?"

"He is his own," the Storyteller replied in a dry voice. "Sit, child."

The Storyteller sat on her bed, Ishara on the cushions opposite her. In the narrow hut, their knees almost touched. Gray light spilled through the doorway and through the high, small windows under the eaves. "You're the King's daughter," the Storyteller said. "How is it with him?"

Ishara's voice was unsteady: "He is very ill."

"And the boy? The one who helped you climb? You are to marry him?"

Ishara returned the Storyteller's gaze. "I hope to."

The eyes burned from their wrinkled nests of flesh. "But he is Atu, is he not?"

Ishara raised her chin. She had had the same argument with members of her own clan. "Atu marry Tagu now."

The Storyteller chuckled. "But Atu have never married Tagu royalty. Well, well, the world changes, or a tree would remain a seed forever."

Ishara was looking about her. The hut seemed part of the Wall itself, fully as ancient. "Who built this here?" she asked. "Why a house on the Wall?"

"The makers were our ancestors. And the dwellers here were the keepers of the Wall, who watched and warned of any dangers. But then it became clear that the Wall would hold out all threats, that no watchers were needed, and so the hut was abandoned for many lifetimes, until I took a notion in my old head to live here. What do you think of the Wall?"

The question surprised Ishara. "That's like asking what I think about the sea. The Wall has always been here. It saves us from the beasts of the world, and we couldn't live without it."

The Storyteller leaned close. In almost a whisper, she said, "And yet . . . ?"

Ishara could not meet the challenge of her old eyes. She looked down at her own knees instead. "Sometimes," she heard herself confessing, "I think the Wall cuts us off from the past. From knowing who we are. From our . . . " she took a deep breath. "From our souls," she whispered.

The Storyteller abruptly stood, with a grace and energy that seemed too young for her. The Oji fluttered and croaked. "Come," the old woman said.

They went to the large triangular window opening to see a sky flying long, ragged pennants of straggling gray cloud, though blue was breaking through. Ishara sniffed. The air had the clean smell of rain, and from up here the metallic tang of blood could not be detected. The Storyteller stood looking out over the far edge of the Wall at the dark green jungle glistening with raindrops. Ishara stood just opposite her. On either side, like a perilous bridge, the Wall receded into the mist. No, not like a bridge, more like a dam holding back the green flood of the forest. Ishara stepped back.

"Come and look," said the Storyteller. With her head feeling as if it were spinning again, Ishara took timid steps back to the window to stand behind her. She was relieved when the Storyteller sat down. As if sensing this, the Storyteller motioned Ishara to sit beside her. The young girl nestled across the old woman's lap as though she were a long

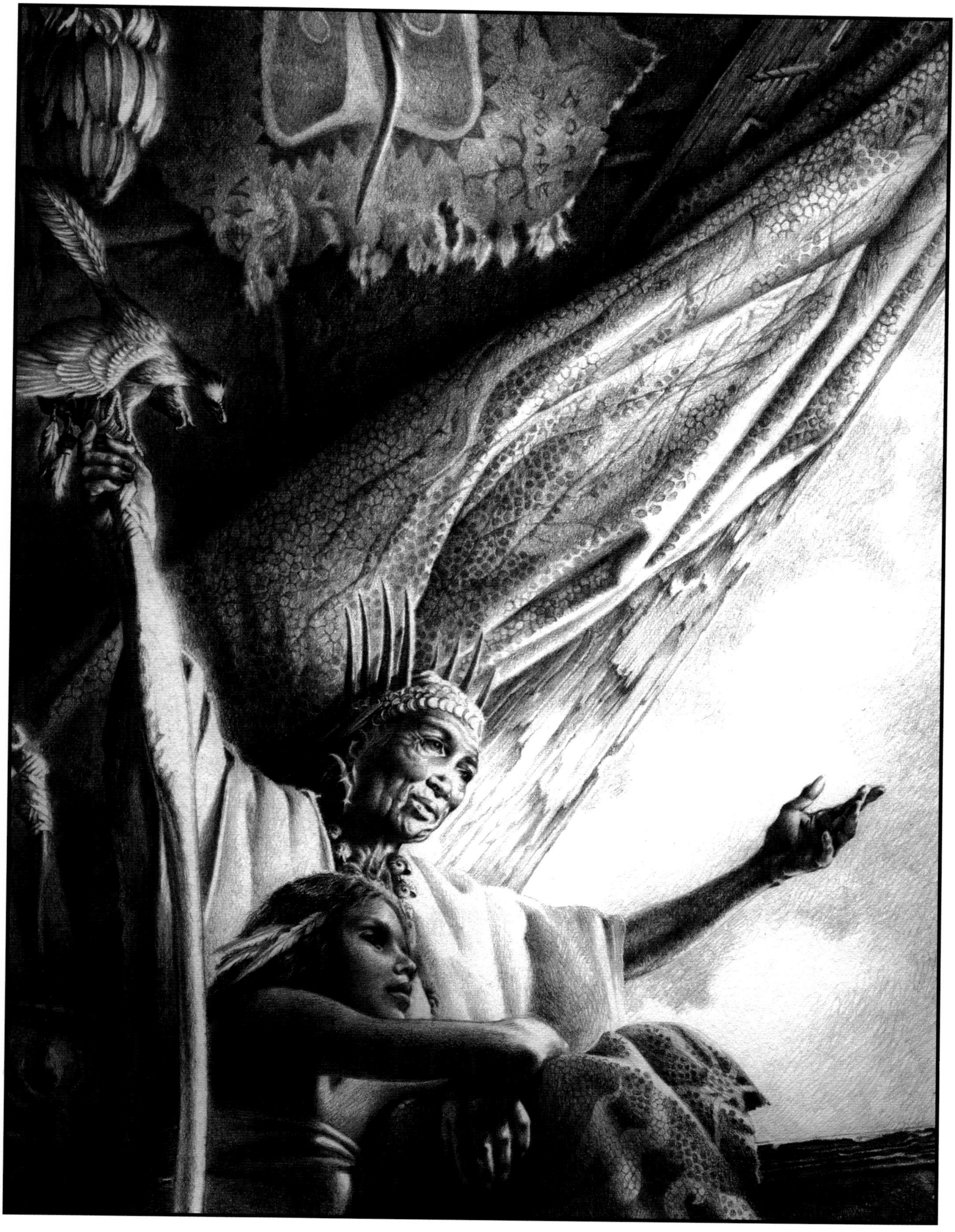

lost grandmother and gazed out at the world. What unfurled before their eyes awed her: deep green trees growing in a canopy glistening and glazed with rain, and beyond that misty distances of pale purple mountains, brooded over by the rounded skull gazing balefully over all, nightmarish in the rain-hazy air. Ishara had seen the mountain before, from the lagoon, but never this clearly. Shapes wheeled in the sky around the bleak stone skull, pterosaurs soaring and dipping. The forest canopy faded away into dimness at the feet of the mountains, and off to the right lay a sliver of ocean, blue and streaked with silver. The storm lay on the far horizon there, dancing on legs of lightning.

The Storyteller did not look around at her. "Is the world beyond the Wall so terrible?"

Slowly, Ishara answered: "It is beautiful."

"But you fear it."

"Yes."

"When knowledge leaves, fear comes to take its place." The Storyteller raised her staff and pointed with it. "There's the course of the great river. You see the break winding through the trees?"

As if a gigantic snake had crawled through the jungle, yes, Ishara saw a twisting, turning dark gap. Pearly mist rose in a cloud from one part of it far away. "I can see it. What's that, like steam rising?"

"There is a chasm. It leads from the mountains to the sea. There where you see the rising haze, the river tumbles down the chasm walls in a waterfall that sends the mist high into the air. But look closer to us, to the place where I point. Do you see the hill there, where the river winds out of sight behind it before coming back into view?"

"Yes."

The Storyteller leaned on her staff. "That's the Old City. Have you heard stories of it?"

Ishara's heart thumped. "I've heard that the people lived in a citadel on the far side of the Wall once. Bar-Atu says that the Tagu angered the gods by their arrogance when they built the city. That's why the gods sent the beasts to punish us."

The Storyteller snorted. "Bar-Atu has more words than the sea has fish! He is from the Atu clan, whose leaders refused to acknowledge the one God of the Tagu! He does not believe in the gods he speaks of—he uses the fear of them to control his followers." The Storyteller laughed. "My child, pay no attention to his lies. They are purely to serve his own ends. Our people did build a great city there, but we built in the midst of the beasts. They were always here, and no gods sent them as punishment. For age upon age our people knew how to control them. And we kept the dangerous beasts away and even walked among others with no fear."

"Magic," Ishara said. "Evil magic, Bar-Atu says. That's what we used to kill the creatures of the forest."

"We killed only what we needed, and it wasn't magic," the Storyteller said quietly.

"But to hold back the predators—there must have been magic."

"Knowledge," corrected the Storyteller. She sighed with a smile. "There were herbs that could be burned, sending up a smoke that repelled or tamed the beasts. We had a stronghold in the middle of the island, and from it we had underground paths that gave us safe passage throughout the land. Our ancestors made walls of memory, where the images of our history lived. And we had our helpers, the giants. They worked with us."

Ishara shook her head. "Children's tales. If we could do those things, our people would never have retreated behind the Wall."

"Well, well, Storytellers tell stories," the old woman said. "There's an end to this children's tale, of course, for stories have endings as well as beginnings. Do you want to know?"

"Yes."

"You asked about the mist of the waterfall, and I told you. How the great rift came to be I don't know. The earth split itself there, maybe in an earthquake before we even came to the island. Or perhaps it is a symbol for what happened to us, in the days when we lost the City. For as the chasm splits the island, so in time a chasm split the people. The Tagu and the Atu tore apart from each other. The Tagu searched for self-control, while the Atu tried to control everything but themselves. This contradiction could not last. The two sides broke into war. From that evil came many more. From that split of the heart, the Wall came to divide the island."

"I don't understand."

"It's a long story, and not one to tell while standing atop the Wall. But one day you shall have it whole, beginning, middle, and end. Or rather beginning, middle, and beginning, since one story gives birth to another. Maybe that will be a story for you to tell. Still, the City did end, and we now live behind the Wall."

Ishara stared out over the jungle at the hill. It looked like any other part of the forest canopy. No buildings, no trace of human works, showed on its rounded surface. "Then the City no longer exists at all."

"Yes, it does. In pieces." The canny old face turned. "Storehouses were there, child, with the seeds of the herbs carefully kept. They may still be there, waiting. Waiting for a healer of the island to repair the great rift in our hearts. Who knows? Someday seeds may sprout. Change is the way of the world. Now it's time you returned to the village. Everyone will be worried about you. And the answer is yes."

"The answer?" Ishara asked.

"You were going to ask if you could return here to visit me."

And Ishara realized that she had been on the verge of asking exactly that.

The stories wore on Vincent Denham. He dozed, he woke, he ate what soft foods the scowling Kara brought him, and he listened to the Storyteller's voice until sleep claimed him again. Now he could not say whether he had been in this cavern for days or weeks. He woke and found that, instead of the Storyteller, Kara sat on the stool, her knees drawn up, her chin propped on her hand, staring at him. "How do you feel?" Her voice was not friendly.

"Better," Vincent said. "I think I'm getting some of my strength back."

She spat. "If I had the choice, I would have let the lagoon monsters eat you!"

Vincent struggled to sit up. "What do you have against me? What have I done to you?"

"I've heard of men like you, men from the world." Her voice gave the last word a poisonous twist, as if she were pronouncing an obscenity. "Before I was born, men like you

41

came to the island. What did they bring my people? Death! Destruction! Now look at you, you come to *study* the island, to *help* us, you will say. But I know you, Vincent Denham. You come for selfish reasons! You care nothing for us!"

Vincent felt hot blood rush to his face. "That's a lie," he said harshly. "And you—do you think your people are the only ones hurt? Because of them, because of your islanders, my family was broken! I lost my father! My life—my mother's life—was ruined!"

The effort exhausted him, and he fell back. Kara's gaze mocked his weakness. Vincent drew deep, gasping breaths. How did she know just how to probe his frailty? He had always prided himself on his control, a man of science who kept his emotions in check, but now he felt a keen pang of despair at how easily she had provoked him into anger.

"What is the trouble?" It was the sharp voice of the Storyteller.

Kara rose from the stool and in a quick burst of her native language, pointing at Vincent, she made what he thought were accusations. The Storyteller listened with a stony face. Kara's voice grew shrill, and she stamped her bare foot.

The Storyteller's face became stern, and she snapped, "I told you to speak in English when we are in his presence, Kara! We will give him our trust . . . and time."

"She's lying," Vincent croaked. "Whatever she's telling you, she's lying."

"We can't trust him!" exploded Kara in English. "Can't you see that? He will destroy us!"

"You will give him time!" The Storyteller's voice was like a lash. It made Kara gasp and fall quiet. The old woman continued calmly, "Vincent Denham does not know the whole story, Kara. Neither do you. You are gifted, but you are young. There are many lessons for you to learn. One is to be patient enough to wait. Another is to be humble enough to listen."

"I don't have to—"

"You do!" The Storyteller's eyes flashed. "You want to be the savior of the island, do you? You think the two bloods that mix and flow in your veins alone make you fit? No! Not unless you learn! Not unless you are patient! Do you wish to unsay the vow you made to me?"

Kara met her gaze for a few seconds, but then lowered her eyes. "I will not unsay it."

"Then sit beside the bed. Listen to me."

Vincent felt the old woman's hand on his forehead. "Why does she hate me?" he muttered.

The Storyteller didn't answer. "Are you ready for more of the story?"

Vincent nodded, though he secretly wondered what use all this was. What was worse, deep down inside he was afraid that Kara's accusations just might be true, after all.

"Ishara!" The King's chief serving woman, Adila, embraced Ishara, then held her at arm's length. Adila was a tall Tagu woman, not pretty but handsome, even as her years shaded toward old age. "We were worried about you."

"I was safe enough. Father?"

"He's been asking about you."

Ishara went into the King's House, a round structure at the center of the village. Her father lay propped up in his bed. Illness had wasted him, hollowing his cheeks, but his eyes lit at the sight of her. "Daughter! They said you went to fight the slashers."

Ishara knelt by his side and took his hand. "I climbed the Wall, father. I was safe with the Storyteller."

"Safe enough," her father said with a smile. "She's the oldest of us, and if anyone knows how to survive, she does." He lifted his free hand to stroke her hair. "But you shouldn't lift spear and shield, daughter. That's man's work."

"Survival is everyone's work," Ishara said gently.

From outside came the rhythmic sound of drums. "What's that?" asked the king. Then, recognizing the pattern, he answered himself: "Bar-Atu is calling a feast."

"A feast of victory," said Ishara.

"You must be there," her father said. "Until I am well enough to stand and speak for myself."

And so that evening, as the meat of the slaughtered dinosaurs sizzled on spits over a fire pit, Ishara sat cross-legged next to Kublai. They were on the raised stone platform at the end of the fire pit, along with the King's advisors. Bar-Atu had gravely welcomed them, but now as he strode back and forth before them, addressing the villagers, it was as if he had forgotten all about them.

"We have refused the sacrifice too long!" Bar-Atu was shouting. "And so the god sends his messengers of death through our very gate!"

Kublai stirred uneasily beside Ishara. "Look at them," he muttered. "Half the people are on his side now. Half of them believe this unholy monster, Gaw, is a powerful god that needs our blood dripping from its jaws."

Ishara stared out at the villagers. With their faces lit from below by the fire, they looked like a band of tormented souls, or like demons on the verge of revolt.

Bar-Atu raised his arms. "Yet we have a chance! The god took only six of our men. And the god gave us ten slashers and a deathrunner to feast upon! How much more would the god prosper us if we gave to him of our own will! I call upon the god! I call upon Gaw!"

And at least half of the villagers echoed back, "Gaw! Gaw!"

Ishara shivered, despite the heat of the fire. Stories told of a time when a king predator —another "god"—stalked the island, a beast of unimaginable destructive power. But the Atu would appease him by giving him one of their own, and the god in turn protected them, allowing them to hunt and to kill in the jungle. Stories. Stories that she had no more believed than she had those of a time when a city flourished in the heart of the jungle, a city prospering amidst the creatures of the island. Now she was no longer sure what she believed.

The drummers had picked up their pace, their instruments thrumming to accentuate Bar-Atu's words. "The Atu know! The Atu remember! The Atu worship!"

"The thing to do," growled Kublai, "is to kill these creatures, not worship them. Give me a hundred spearmen, and I'll tame the island! Why crawl when you can stand like a man?"

"Hush," said Ishara, noticing nervous eyes darting their way. The King's advisors, all Tagu, were uneasy enough already, with this hotheaded young Atu sitting among them. And they knew that Bar-Atu's followers were growing in influence and power.

Now, like a man possessed by a spirit, Bar-Atu stood before the fire pit, a silhouette to Ishara. His arms were spread, his head thrown back in a kind of rigid ecstasy. "Gaw!" he shouted, and his followers repeated the word. "Gaw! Gaw!" Bar-Atu flung a handful of something into the fire, and the flames blazed a brilliant crimson for a second, sending up a billow of smoke.

Ishara's heart was beating fast, perhaps in sympathy with the drums. Part of her wanted to leap up and shout that Bar-Atu was wrong, that Kublai was equally wrong, that there was a third way. But that part was timid. The chant went on and on, throbbing in her head. A burning log in the fire pit collapsed, sending a flight of red sparks swirling up into the night sky.

Bar-Atu was moving around the fire, stamping his feet, as if in a trance, and shrieking even more loudly as he called upon his god.

And then, from somewhere, from everywhere, came the overpowering roar of a gigantic animal.

And Bar-Atu turned, his skin glistening with sweat, his eyes gleaming in triumph. "The god answers!" he shouted. "Hear the god!"

And then again came that terrible, hungry roar.

CHAPTER SEVEN

UNDERGROUND
June 30, 1957

Jack Driscoll ate a meager breakfast of C-rations, took a drink of water from his canteen, and lit a match. He needed no torch now.

The walls began to glitter, as if glow worms were firing up here and there. Pale spots of green at first, then yellows and blues, and then whole patches of color—reds, oranges, spread across both walls of the tunnel as if someone were spilling luminous paint. The process needed light to trigger it, but once the luminescence had begun, it spread for hundreds of yards and lasted for more than an hour.

And it formed pictures.

Driscoll shook out the match. "Who did this?" he asked himself.

He learned that the tunnel walls were overgrown here with what looked like fungus, thin enough to scrape off with his fingernail. But something in the layer responded to light, generated its own glow and colors. The first patches had been just disorganized swirls of color. But as the patches grew denser, pictures emerging. Most of them were fogged, as if the shapes were watercolors that had been dampened. But some were sharp, almost three-dimensional images. And they told a fantastic story.

Driscoll had walked past scenes of immense sea craft, teeming with people and animals, leaving behind some scene of destruction. He had seen these— Arks, maybe?— reach what had to be Skull Island, though the mountain was only a rounded dome with the indications of the skull less evident.

The few sharp pictures gave way to long passages lit by shapeless glows, and Driscoll could not make much of them. But to think of the kind of knowledge that could produce this glowing, nearly living story— "Couldn't have been the savages," Driscoll told himself, and concentrated on threading his way through the endless passages.

He stopped now and then, when the pictures were clearer, when a great beast of the island appeared in colors so sharp and bright it might have been put there yesterday. At times he noticed cruder pictures, as if the makers had found their skills slipping away.

Then Driscoll heard the cries of creatures on the surface.

The tunnel had seemed so safe that he had holstered his pistol. He drew it again.

SKULL ISLAND
Date Unknown

"For the luvva Mike!"

Vincent swallowed the last of his dinner and scowled at the Oji. "Back where I come from, there are birds called parrots that mimic people fairly well. But not like this thing.

Sometimes I get the feeling he's really talking to you."

"You say that as if it were impossible," the Storyteller told him calmly. "There are some creatures that don't understand, and there are some creatures that—may."

Vincent looked at the woman quizzically, then asked, "Where did it—"

"Oji," she corrected.

"Where did *Oji* pick up that saying of my father's?"

"Many, many years ago."

"Then my father—"

"The last time Oji heard your father speak those words was after he had captured what he came to find," the old woman said. "Ojis can live for a century or more. Their memories are long. They bring the words of the dead from the past, though they speak them without real understanding."

Vincent swallowed his disappointment. He handed his empty wooden plate to the Storyteller. In a voice made gruff by emotion, he asked, "Where's Kara? I haven't seen her today."

"She has other things to do. She will be here soon. Anyway, as you say, she doesn't like you." The Storyteller set the empty plate aside. "Very good. You ate all the fruit. Perhaps tomorrow we will give you a little broth, then the next day meat."

"What did you mean when you said that Kara has two bloods in her veins?"

The Storyteller sighed. "She does. One day she will be the guide for our people. And our people will follow her, for she has the blood of the Atu and the Tagu in her. But on what path will she lead them?"

"I shouldn't have argued with her," Vincent said. "She knows how to make me angry. If I'd had strength, I might have—"

"Hurt her? Yes. But you did not. She feels the injuries done to our people over many years, Vincent Denham. Fear and anger do not lead to good judgment."

"But she's been—" Vincent broke off as the Storyteller raised a silencing hand.

"Here you are," the old woman said as Kara emerged from the darkness, carrying two earthenware jars. She glared at Vincent, as if she had been listening.

"I have brought what you asked," Kara said shortly.

"Medicines," the Storyteller said. "Good. Put them down and sit."

Kara did, but her accusatory gaze again swept over Vincent. He thought, *She would kill me without a single regret.*

Oji flapped to clamber onto the Storyteller's shoulder, and the old woman settled back on her stool. "Do you want more of the story now?"

Vincent said, "Yes. You were speaking of the two sides in the war, the Tagu and the Atu. What happened to them?"

"In their arrogance, the Atu took control of the Citadel and the rest of the island. They acted without regard to what their actions could bring, as though they were gods themselves. Rather than go along with them, the Tagu chose to return to the safety behind the Wall," the Storyteller replied. "And with their remaining skills and knowledge, they strengthened and enlarged the Wall. For generations, they followed two different paths. The Tagu survived by not reaching beyond their grasp. As for the Atu, they gradually became base, deranged, drunk with power and killing. Many behaved more like animals than human beings. They unnecessarily killed the creatures of the island, and even killed their own.

In all the years of indulgence, their attention to their own defenses grew lax. They took for granted the hard-won standoff with the dangerous creatures of the island, and the deathrunners grew in slyness and number."

"What are the deathrunners?" Vincent asked. He knew they were some kind of dinosaur, but the old woman's descriptions made them sound like nothing he had ever studied.

"The masters of the slashers," she said patiently. "Never many in number, always dominating the lesser creatures, the deathrunners are different from the other beasts of the island. They have more cunning. They observe their prey and learn from them. They were even thought to understand some of our words and use them against us."

"No reptile could do that!" protested Vincent.

"So you say," answered the Storyteller with a knowing stare. "But the tales of my ancestors say differently."

If that is true, Vincent thought to himself, *they must have been some super race that evolved over millions of years—*

Still trying to come to grips with such a reality, he asked, "What was their prey?"

"Us," responded the Storyteller with a faraway look.

Vincent shivered, unsettled by the implications of what he was hearing. But he settled back to listen to her tale, recited in a voice that rose and fell like a slow song of memory.

There arose amongst the deathrunners a breed of enormous size, power, and intelligence. Under the orchestrated attacks of the deathrunners by this new threat, the proud Atu culture finally collapsed. The relatively few survivors fled to the only place on the island that offered safety: the Wall. Unable to save themselves, they begged the Tagu for help, and this was granted.

But these seemingly pitiful stragglers brought with them a hidden contagion: the last followers of Seth-Atu. Seth-Atu had formed a cult called the Shaitan, which glorified the worst manifestations of Atu thinking and were instrumental in the eventual downfall of the Atu culture. These Shaitan followers hid like sheep among the others. They were the ancestors of Bar-Atu.

Gradually the Shatain of the Atu undermined the well-ordered faith and practices of the Tagu, ensnaring more and more of the islanders in their web of deceit. In time the Tagu forgot most of their hard-won knowledge. As knowledge slipped away, so did their confidence. Their vision became clouded, they grasped at the straws of the Shaitan fanatics, and unwittingly most Tagu became enslaved as their traditional faith was replaced by a cult of fear. At last, only the Storytellers were left to remember the old ways.

SKULL ISLAND
The Past

In the days after the slasher attack on the village, the mood shifted. At the gathering that night, the islanders completely surrendered to that fear and turned to Bar-Atu for help. They had fallen into his trap. They agreed to offer the first human sacrifice to Bar-Atu's god, Gaw. Preparations began. . .

The next morning, early, Kublai had come to awaken Ishara. They had walked beside the sea. "This will never end with one sacrifice," Kublai said grimly. "There'll be more.

And all of them will be drawn from your people, the Tagu, until only the Atu are left, or those who will join the Atu."

"There may be another way," Ishara said, touching his arm. She spoke to him of the Citadel she had glimpsed from atop the Wall, past the mountain with the skull's face. "The Storyteller says the old people had ways of controlling the island beasts, and that perhaps the seeds are still there. If we could find them—"

"We could keep the slashers and the other animals away, and no longer live in fear behind the Wall." Kublai finished. "And there would be no need for sacrifice."

"I know the way," Ishara told him. "But first, take this," and she handed him a small pouch that gave out a pungent aroma.

"What is it?"

"The Storyteller gave me one for each of us. She said to roll the pouch in our hands first to crush what's inside and then rub the pouch on our arms and legs—anywhere we have skin exposed. She instructed us to tie them to our waist and warned to never let them leave our side while we are beyond the Wall."

Kublai sniffed the mouth of the leather pouch, wrinkling his nose. "Are these some of the herbs she spoke of?"

"Yes, but these are ancient and there are very few left. There are different kinds for different needs and after all these years she hopes they are still effective."

"So you already knew I would follow you?" taunted Kublai. And then he smiled at her. "King's daughter," he said with gentle mockery and affection mingled. "I know better than to argue with you. And I guess listening to the old Storyteller can do no harm. But I go for my own reasons as well. There are weapons of old my people used that will be more effective than your Storyteller's plants. Come. There's one way into the jungle other than the Gate."

They picked up spears and shields and slipped away to the lagoon. The Wall marched straight across the peninsula, ending at sheer cliffs on both sides, too vertical for the beasts of the islands to climb. But on one side a ledge, awash with the sea at high tide, was just wide enough for two humans to pass. Kublai led the way, with Ishara coming close behind him. They faced the volcanic stone, hugging it, finding handholds in the pits and crevices. At one point they were directly beneath the Wall, and Ishara could look straight up at its edge, built to the lip of the cliff. It towered upward to the sky, to the broad top where she had stood. It cut all across the island here, curving against the jungle.

Then they were past, and Kublai again led as they climbed up the cliff, finding footholds and handholds in the stone at first, then grasping roots and creepers that spilled over the top. At last they stood high above the rolling sea. "This way," Ishara said, and now she led the way.

They once had to climb a tree when a young carnivorous dinosaur came stalking by, tracking some plant-eater. It did not notice them. They reached the sluggish stream that widened here and there into sinuous lakes. The longnecks occasionally emerged from the forest and ventured into the water here, dinosaurs whose heads rose above the trees as they called to each other with reverberating honks. But they were plant eaters and paid no attention to the humans who skirted their domain, following the course of the river.

The sun sank and vanished, and Kublai and Ishara climbed another tree. Kublai fashioned a sleeping platform from branches bound with creepers. "A hunter's stand," he said proudly. "My people made these in the old times."

That night Ishara slept in his arms, glad for the warmth of his body and for the reassuring steady rhythm of his breathing. With the dawn they set off again. Their pace was steady, even though at times they had to hide when a crashing in the trees told them one of the island beasts must be near. Whether by luck or by the power of the herbs in their pouches, none bothered them. A second night they spent in a hunter's stand built by Kublai, and on the third day they began to near the base of Skull Mountain itself.

The sun was well past its zenith and Kublai and Ishara had covered a great distance when they came over a rise of ground and halted, gasping.

Before them lay a deep cleft. Perhaps it was a place where the earth had partly collapsed during an earthquake. It was many paces across, and it cut into the stone like the place left from the blow of a giant's axe.

A stench of decay roiled out, and the air hummed with the sound of scavenger insects. Bones lay scattered, most bare, others with clots of rotten flesh clinging to them. Multi-legged creatures as long as Ishara's forearms crawled over the bones, attacking the putrid meat. Raising her eyes from the carnage, Ishara found herself staring at the grin of Skull Mountain. The gorge of death was cut into one of the ridges that led to the base of that grim landmark.

"Gaw's lair," whispered Kublai. "It has to be. Look." Ishara saw, nearly hidden behind a craggy overhang, the mouth of a deep, gaping cave. Giant, three-toed tracks came and went in all directions. Criss-crossing them were the odd, two-toed tracks of the death-runners and slashers, whose third toe left no impression because it was hooked into a horrible claw that was raised above the ground. Kublai knew that with a powerful kick, a deathrunner could use such a claw to rip a man in two.

"Let's get away from here," Ishara said, fighting the impulse to retch at the carnal stench.

They left the lair behind and crossed the stony ridge. "There," Ishara said, pointing, as they reached the summit of the next ridge. Not far away the hill she had seen from the Wall rose from the jungle. Looking back, she could see the Wall now, a dark bastion that showed clearly above the green jungle.

Another hour brought them to the hill. With the midday sun glaring down, they passed first a ruin of great, fashioned stones that no one man could lift. The structure was overgrown with tendrils and creepers. A standing stone, as tall as a tree, supported a basin of some kind. Not far from it a similar edifice had been cast down, the basin shattered. The place was quiet in the sweltering heat. "This can't be the Citadel," Kublai said doubtfully.

"No. It's too small." Ishara realized that from the Wall, the distance had been deceptive. The green hills of the Citadel lay far away. This, at most, had been an outpost in the ancient days.

A few buildings still stood, though Ishara did not at first recognize them, even when standing next to them. They blended in almost perfectly with the stone outcrops and the vegetation. The streets had long since become avenues of thick growth. Roots had thrown stone down from stone, spilling walls and spoiling enclosures. Here and there, though, empty doorways could be seen, or hollow windows.

Ishara and Kublai crept in and out of these. Little was left. The few intact rooms had no furniture, no sign of human habitation. Hours passed, and they found nothing. "We'll stay here for the night," Kublai decided in one building. They had found a stairway to a second floor, and there a room was free of debris, the stone floor soft with dust but in one piece. And no predatory footprints showed in the dust.

Four tall, oddly-shaped windows looked out from the round room. Ishara went to the nearest and looked out, trying to imagine what this place must have been when it was a home of her ancestors. What sort of people had raised it, lived in it, worked in it? And what wonders had they done, and where had they hidden the secrets?

She caught her breath. Something was moving on the outskirts, something large and dark, far darker than a dinosaur. "Kublai!" she called as loudly as she dared.

He was at her side in a second. "What?"

"Something there. See?"

They stared through the opening. Whatever was moving was half hidden by trees and brush. It seemed to be following the line of the wall that had run around the structure they were in before time had overthrown its stones.

Ishara grasped Kublai's arm. The shadowy thing was coming to a clearing. It moved slowly into the afternoon sunlight.

"A kong!" Kublai exclaimed. "I thought they were all dead! My people say they all died generations ago!"

The creature was humanlike but gigantic, well more than twice the height of a tall man. Covered with graying fur, it stooped at the shoulders but for the most part seemed to walk upright. It—no, *she*, Ishara saw, a female—lifted her head and sniffed the air. She had an air of dominance, as if she feared nothing that could find her, and to Ishara she seemed at home here. Her whole demeanor was that of a guardian visiting a place she knew and stood ready to protect. Then, apparently satisfied that no threat was nearby, the kong gave a surprisingly soft, chirruping call.

And again Ishara gasped as a second animal, an adolescent male, followed the first into the clearing. The older one nudged the younger. The younger stood to its full height and looked around. For a moment, its eyes were turned toward Ishara, and she almost believed the creature had seen her.

No. In the strange vegetation-choked window, and from that distance, that was impossible. The kong's gaze swept on.

Ishara shivered. For that one instant, the moment when she had stared into the young one's eyes, she had felt an uncanny wave of sympathy. The young kong's eyes were filled with curiosity, a deep melancholy, and with something else.

Intelligence.

Ishara could only call what she had seen intelligence.

CHAPTER EIGHT

SKULL ISLAND
The Past

"**L**ook!" Kublai pointed to a ridge beyond the trees.

At first Ishara didn't know what she saw there. It was dark, huge, and . . . moving. Then the shape stood, and she felt the breath catch hard in her throat. It was a third kong, an enormous one. "A male!" she said.

"Must be the father," Kublai replied. "I thought all the kongs of Skull Mountain were dead. They used to live there ages ago. That's what Bar-Atu has told us—"

The female kong was rooting in the underbrush, the younger one taking something she offered and eating it. Ishara couldn't tell from this distance whether the mother was finding insects or some kind of fruit. Her skin tingled as she took in the scene. This was something she had viewed only in the old sculptures and carvings still to be found around the village, jutting from odd places or half-buried. She had also seen an unusual picture in the Storyteller's hut, one that the Storyteller said came from the days of the ancient islanders. But no representation could give her a true sense of these creatures' size. The mother was as tall as a fiber palm, almost as tall as three men standing one on the other's shoulders. Nearly the same height as its mother, the younger kong already was broader at the shoulders with the beginnings of massive arm and back muscles shifting beneath its fur. Both of them walked upright, though on occasion they leaned forward on their long, powerful arms.

As for the distant male, Ishara could only guess. But it had to be head and shoulders again as tall as the female. Its long arms were the size of large tree trunks. But it was the confidence with which it moved that so impressed Ishara. There was something about these creatures that she could not fully understand. Ishara wondered how her ancestors could have tamed these gigantic—

A shriek ripped from the female kong, cutting Ishara's thoughts short. Instinctively, both Ishara and Kublai lowered themselves, staring out the ruined window but trying to hide at the same time. The brush thrashed in the distance. The young kong scrambled toward its mother's voice, the dark hair on its shoulders bristling. It hooted in concern or alarm. The mother backed as quietly as she could into a stand of tall ferns. On the distant ridge, the huge male kong had dropped from sight.

"What is it?" Ishara whispered, craning to see more.

"Keep down. Something that could frighten those animals must be dangerous." But Kublai was raising himself higher, too, trying to penetrate the screen of brush, palms, and ferns. The atmosphere was electric, the stillness deafening. Ishara suddenly realized that nothing protected them from what was out there—nothing more tangible than the pouches they wore, which now seemed as foolish as toys. She felt suddenly very vulnerable, as though something was looking over her shoulder, but she dared not turn around.

The kongs were keeping so still that it was all but impossible
to see them. Their bodies, half-glimpsed through the foliage, were
simply a more solid blackness than shadow.

But the disturbance in the undergrowth was coming closer.
Whatever it was had to be huge, as large as the kongs or even larger.
A longneck, possibly, straying from its herd? But when Ishara
whispered the thought, Kublai shook his head. "No, I think not.
Whatever it is seems to be stalking. Longnecks are dangerous only
if disturbed or if their young are threatened. It is a flesh-eater,
but what kind?"

The roar that burst through the jungle made Ishara clap her
hands over her ears and grimace. It sent a clatter of small flying
reptiles spiraling into the air. It was harsh and as sickening as the
grate of blade on slate, and it seemed to go on forever.

"Gaw!" exclaimed Kublai, opening and clenching his hands.

And then Ishara caught a hint of an enormous reptilian body
in the brush, only partly seen but as indelible as a nightmare.
A glinting eye, a hint of prognathous jaw. A form wasp-waisted
and barrel-chested, a handlike claw—but the size of a hunter's
large shield!—grasping a tree trunk. And movement, movement far too fast for something that size, movement toward
the hidden kongs.

Gaw, whatever it was, seemed to sink down to the earth.
Then, surprisingly far ahead of where it had vanished, there it was
again, stealthy and fast. Ishara found she had been holding her

breath. And just as she let it out, the female kong roared in defiance and charged!

The impact of massive bodies sent a tremor through the crumbling walls of the old Citadel. Ishara grabbed Kublai's arm, felt its muscles corded and tense. Out in the green maze, branches snapped and thrashed, leaves spun in dizzy whirlwinds. Snarls and growls accompanied the thuds of blows given and received. And then a terribly human-sounding death cry, almost like human words. The sound died bubbling in her throat, and the female kong pitched from a thicket, falling on her back. Her fur was soaked with dark blood, her throat torn open. She stirred feebly and lay still, half in and half out of the thicket, arm extended, reaching toward something unseen—

The juvenile kong burst from its hiding place, but as he raced toward his fallen mother, a swarm of slashers boiled over him. The creatures leaped at him, clung to him, ripping his limbs with razor-sharp teeth and claws. The young kong whirled wildly as he tried to rip them from his body until he fell backward over a gnarled root, writhing into the undergrowth amid a cacophony of animal shrieks and breaking branches.

And then a shattering roar, coming from the depths of the jungle. "It's the father!" Kublai said in Ishara's ear. "He's coming from the mountain!"

Gaw answered with a saurian challenge of its own, and the monster dropped low and raced through the brush. Its path converged with that of the gigantic kong. Now both Ishara and Kublai stood and leaned out the window.

The two beasts met in a clearing where the ridge met one side of the mouth of Skull Mountain. Gaw was the largest killer on the island, but it was different from any meat eater in other ways. Its trunk and front limbs were manlike, the arms ending in dexterous hands, each armed with three powerful, clawed fingers. It was far faster and more intelligent than the other large predators, and as it challenged the kong, its stance was confident and threatening.

The kong charged, and the dinosaur dropped low, striking upward as its foe closed. The kong was almost its match in height, but the force of Gaw's attack sent the kong reeling back. The silver-coated kong, clearly ancient, was battered, and one eye was missing, a jagged scar cutting across its orbit and down the cheek. But age and wounds could not diminish the kong's fury, and it lowered its head and struck again, pounding Gaw with its fists.

Gaw gave ground before his onslaught. Ishara clenched her hands, trying to will the kong to defeat this deadly enemy. Breaking away from the kong, Gaw spread its arms in a strange gesture. It bobbed, screeched and clicked like some grotesque, giant bird of prey. A pack of a dozen or more deathrunners, bigger and deadlier than the slashers, came wheeling in from the forest in answer to Gaw's summons.

Ishara could not help shouting a warning as six of the creatures stabbed in on the kong's blind side. The struggle was too far away for her voice to be heard, though Kublai instantly put his hands on her shoulders, as if he were preparing to flee and drag her with him.

The kong bellowed in anger as he struck at the deathrunners. Their bodies spun through the air, broken. Gaw charged, only to meet a barrage of hammering clouts as the kong fought all his foes.

Gaw reeled from the blows, but managed to keep its balance. The monster twisted, and smashed at the kong's legs with its tail. The kong evaded the swipe but left himself open for a stabbing thrust of Gaw's teeth. They closed on the kong's left arm, near the shoulder, and the dark beast threw its head back and howled in anger and agony. Three deathrunners hung by their jaws from the kong's right arm. When Gaw jerked its head away, a chunk of flesh came with it. The kong shook off its smaller enemies and lunged forward, reaching with its good arm, trying to find Gaw's throat.

The reptilian monster feinted, then struck forward with the speed of a snake. Its jaws clamped on the kong's throat, and again Ishara heard the almost human shriek of a dying kong. The earth shook as the two struggling beasts fell into the underbrush, and for some minutes, Ishara could not see what was happening. Then she heard the triumphant roar of Gaw.

"It's killed them," Kublai said.

Ishara felt numb. "What is Gaw?"

Kublai drew a deep breath and whispered: "It is said by my people that in ancient times, it was this kind of monster that caused the final downfall of the Atu. Bar-Atu claims it was Gaw himself, that Gaw cannot die. But I have heard from elders that from time to time a deathrunner is born that is different from all the others. It lives many times the lifespan of a normal animal. It grows in size, in cunning, in ferocity, and it is somehow necessary for their survival. There is never more than one, and now that one is Gaw. If we

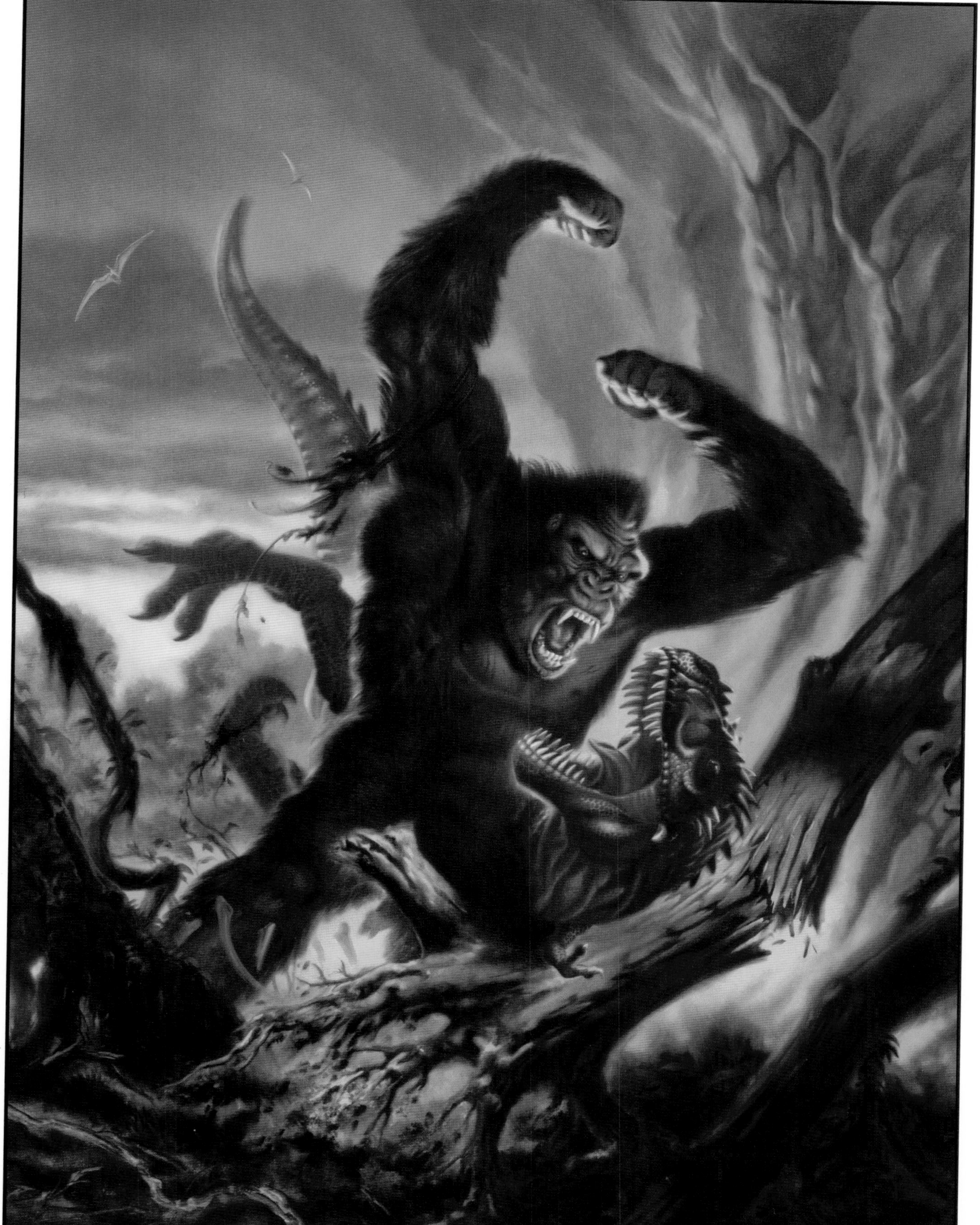

could kill Gaw, I think, we could defeat the deathrunners. Gaw thinks for them, leads them, herds them, as they herd the slashers."

Kublai stared without moving until finally he relaxed. "There it is, on the ridge," he said. "It must be hurt. It's retreating."

Ishara caught only a fleeting glance of Gaw, the deathrunners following, now so far away that it was only a fast-moving shape.

She and Kublai crept down from their hiding place. "I'm going to look at the dead female," Kublai told her.

"Kublai, no!"

"It's all right. They are gone."

Ishara followed Kublai. The setting sun cast a blood-red light over the battlefield. Ishara stared at the few scattered buildings, if buildings they were. They seemed to be a mixture of mortar, intertwined with living trees whose growth must somehow have been arrested ages ago. Someone—their ancestors—had shaped these into semblances of dinosaur frills and other skeletal forms that from a distance blended into the landscape but which on close inspection proved to be a hollow fusion of many trees. It was as if the earth had given birth to them. Ishara could only wonder what they must have looked like before being deserted and overgrown.

They left the outpost behind and climbed a low rise. Kublai dropped to his stomach and urgently signaled Ishara to do the same, but she crept beside him. "Oh!" She pressed her hand against her mouth to keep herself from crying out.

A great two-legged meat eater had emerged from the jungle with one of its young, still feather-clad. The parent bowed its massive skull down and then scratched it with one of its tiny arms before letting out a sharp barking hiss. It then sniffed the air and grunted, a low, guttural sound. The two predators looked directly towards the dead kong. Fearlessly they strode forward, skirting the ravine as they neared the gaping mouth of Skull Mountain. They paused now and then to look around them with baleful glances, then arrived at the lifeless body of the father kong. Both creatures buried their snouts in the carcass and tore free glistening, dripping gobbets of flesh. With a toss of their heads, they snapped the meat down, grunting to themselves.

Ishara saw again how different these dinosaurs were from Gaw. This beast's puny front legs ended in two small claws. Gaw's were much longer and brawnier, ending in large, powerful hands. And the king dinosaur's eyes, while certainly fierce, lacked the look of terrible intelligence that shone in Gaw's eyes.

A furious roar! The larger meat eater leaped back from its feast as a dark, hurtling blur slammed into it. Ishara felt the rubble hard against her belly and chest as she tried to flatten herself into the ground. The young kong was not dead—and it clearly thought this creature had killed its parents. It rained thunderous blows on the flesh eater, slamming its body against a tree and smashing its fists hard into the creature's head and chest. The dinosaur fought back, but the young kong grappled with it, and they tumbled toward the gaping maw of Skull Mountain. The dinosaur rolled free, roared, and kept the enraged kong away by wildly snapping its jaws and kicking out with its massive hind legs.

The great meat eater snarled, its jaws dripping saliva streaked with blood as it rose to its feet. The kong again pressed his attack, but the predator quickly turned and caught him across the midsection with a crushing blow from its tail that sent him sprawling. Ishara heard its body crash to earth somewhere and realized it had fallen into the ravine which snaked into Gaw's lair. The king dinosaur gave the fallen foe no more attention, as its juvenile came bobbing and hissing from the undergrowth. They proceeded to greedily rip back into the dead kong's body.

Ishara grasped Kublai's arm. Kublai looked at her, and she knew that he, like she, was absolutely exhausted, as though they themselves had been in a battle. The sun was low in a crimson sky and they resolved to stay where they were. They had seen enough. They needed time to think—their original plan now seemed like madness. As quietly as they could, they retreated to the outpost and climbed back to the room from which they had watched Gaw's battle with the kongs. Kublai said, "We'll never make it to the Citadel and back."

"Not with Gaw and the deathrunners so near," Ishara agreed. "It's still a long way to the Citadel."

"We will decide tomorrow," Kublai said. They shared a sparse meal from the rations he carried and then spent an uneasy night sleeping in that strange room. Each time Ishara dozed, she dreamed of the monster Gaw and of the deathrunners sweeping in a wave over the embattled kong.

In the morning, each of them kneaded the leather pouches of herbs the Storyteller had given them and rubbed them on arms, shoulders, neck, face, and legs. The scent was becoming faint. They set off with the sunrise, beneath wheeling, raucous pterodactyls flying from the empty eye sockets of the mountain's face far overhead. The father kong's body had been reduced in the night to scattered bones and rags of fur. Scavengers were always ready for those who fell in the jungle.

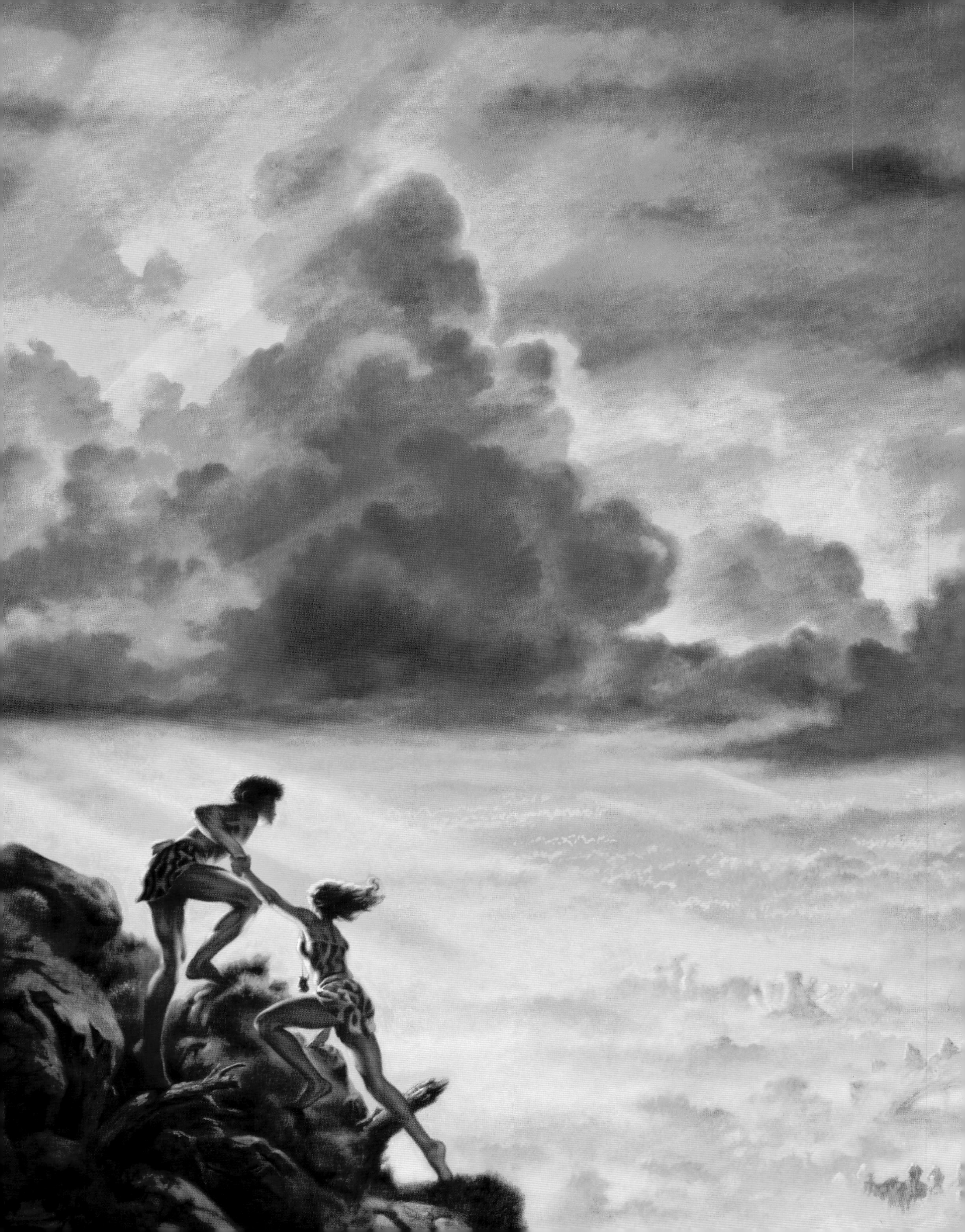

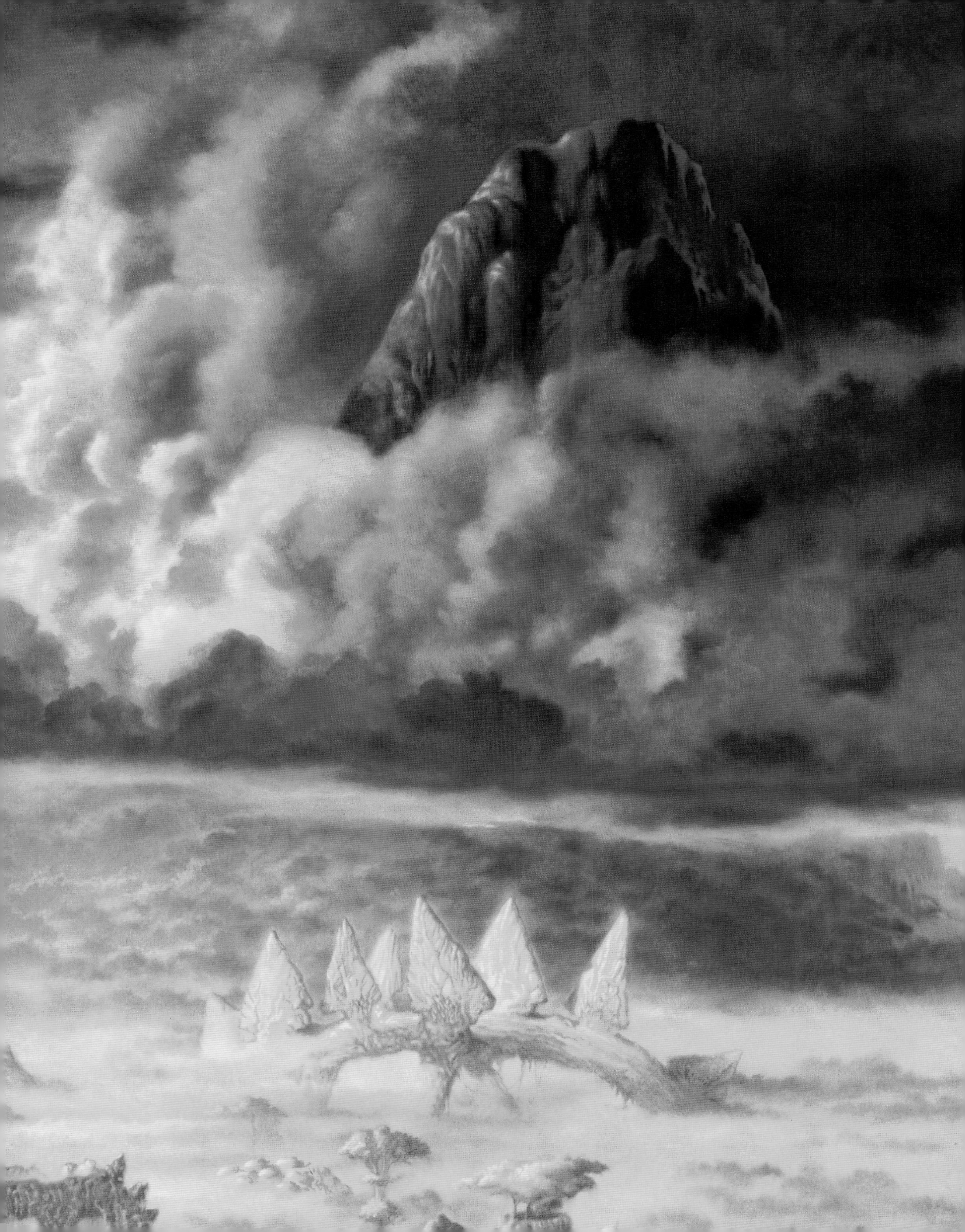

It was a clear morning. They woke before sunrise and set out, passing through wisps of ground fog but able to see the stars overhead. All seemed peaceful, though they knew better. Somewhere nearby Gaw lurked, and there were other dangers, too, like the king dinosaurs. "Do we go back?" Kublai asked.

"No," Ishara said slowly. "We can't. If we fail, everyone will be at the mercy of Bar-Atu and his murderers. We have to try to reach the Citadel."

"Then let us start." Kublai, with the stealth of a hunter, led the way along a rising, rocky path that skirted the base of Skull Mountain. Just after sunrise, they reached a high point on the pathway, and Ishara cried out in wonder.

There, below them and still a long way off, lay the Citadel, emerging like a dream through billows of fog. Shapes of the ancient structures lay half-concealed, half-revealed, lit to glory in the slanting rays of the early sun. Ishara could not take it all in. Her heart swelled.

"We can't get there," Kublai said, his voice despondent. "Look."

He pointed downward. A dozen slashers flashed in and out of the trees far away, at the base of the ridge on which they stood. The creatures had not noticed them, but they were hunting. Ishara looked from them to the Citadel, so promising and yet still so far away.

"We can pass through the slashers. This will protect us," Ishara said, fingering the pouch of herbs.

Kublai replied grimly, "We can't trust in that, not with slashers on the prowl. Come, let's see if we can find a different path."

And so, instead of heading directly toward the Citadel, they traveled far along the ridge as it drifted to the south. In time they caught the first refreshing breaths of cool, salty air. Slowly, they descended into the jungle before finally emerging onto a pristine, crescent beach that cradled a quiet lagoon. They were far away from the slashers, far away from the gruesome experiences of the day before. The dreamlike clouds and soft, rolling waves beckoned. They both walked to the edge of the water and, kneeling down, listened to the rhythmic sound of the surf. "I wonder if swimming could wash all memory of yesterday away," Ishara said.

"Is the water safe?"

"Yes. Look, there is a school of sleeks."

Kublai relaxed. Sleeks were reptilian and superficially similar to the dolphins that occasionally sported in the village bay. They were playful, toothless, large-eyed—and they never appeared when dangerous sea creatures were near. Maybe their senses warned the sleeks to stay out of the way of predators, or maybe the predators themselves were wary of the sleeks. Either way, their presence meant the water was safe. Kublai waded in, then plunged forward.

Ishara followed him in. She sensed that, like herself, Kublai had to feel cleansed after the blood and death they had witnessed. The salty water was warm and clear. Ishara felt the sting of salt in her eyes, tasted it on her lips. It was clean, and that was what she needed. The sleeks kept their distance, for they were always shy around humans, but Ishara could hear the puffs of their breathing and their high-pitched squeaks.

She and Kublai swam lazily, then just floated in the warm water. "What path do we take next?" Kublai asked. "We can't go over, or even through, Skull Mountain. It would take a giant to do that."

It was true. The far side of Skull Mountain showed ramparts of vertical cliffs, rearing up from deep jungle. Somewhere beyond them lay the Citadel, but how to get there? She began, "Maybe, we should—"

"Ishara! Behind you!"

Ishara turned, her heart leaping into her mouth. A fin cut through the water, racing toward her, a long dark shadow beneath it. And then another and another! Suddenly the water erupted and something leaped beside her. Her outflung hand brushed the leaping creature's side—

Something happened.

What it was, she could never afterward explain. But for a moment, as the sleek's slippery body passed beneath her palm, she felt a connection, like nothing else she had ever experienced. And then, the creature that had raced past them, perhaps trying to see if they were food, returned, more slowly. It raised an inquisitive head from the water and gazed at them with eyes as big as Ishara's hand.

Surprisingly, it then playfully rolled on its side and nudged her with its long, slender snout. Ishara could clearly see its lack of teeth.

And its touch told Ishara she was safe. "It's all right," she said to Kublai, whose face had turned pale.

"Sleeks never let us near them," Kublai objected. "They—what did you say? How do you know we're safe?"

"I—I just know it," Ishara said. "Look, they're friendly!"

Kublai started as another sleek's head broke the surface near him, and beyond that two more.

As the sleeks swam closer, so close that she could reach out and touch them, Ishara could see the difference between them and dolphins. They were similar, so similar that at a distance they could easily be confused with each other. Sleeks were air-breathers, just like dolphins. But they had an extra set of flippers toward the rear of their bodies, and their tail fins were vertical, not horizontal: unlike a dolphin, which undulated in an up-and-down motion, a sleek swam with its tail moving side to side, like a fish. And their minds—How did she know that? Somehow she did—their minds were sharp, curious, and strangely protective. They crowded around Ishara now, as if eager to make contact with this land creature that had touched their leader.

Ishara cried out in surprise rather than alarm as one surfaced almost beneath her. She grasped its fin without thinking, and then the creature leaped with her, clean out of the water, and for a moment she was flying, feeling inside her the joy of play that the sleeks knew. Then she plunged back into the water, only to emerge in a spray of foam, laughing. "I told you they're friendly! Grab on with me!"

The hunter had surfaced in Kublai. "But they never come close! Are they going to attack?"

Not even acknowledging his question, Ishara insisted: "Here they come. Quick! Take hold!"

Kublai couldn't resist. With an eager grin, he quickly grabbed the surfacing sleek and slipped right next to Ishara. But as soon as he joined with her on the dorsal fin of the leader, she laughed and let go to grab onto another as it passed close by and dived under water.

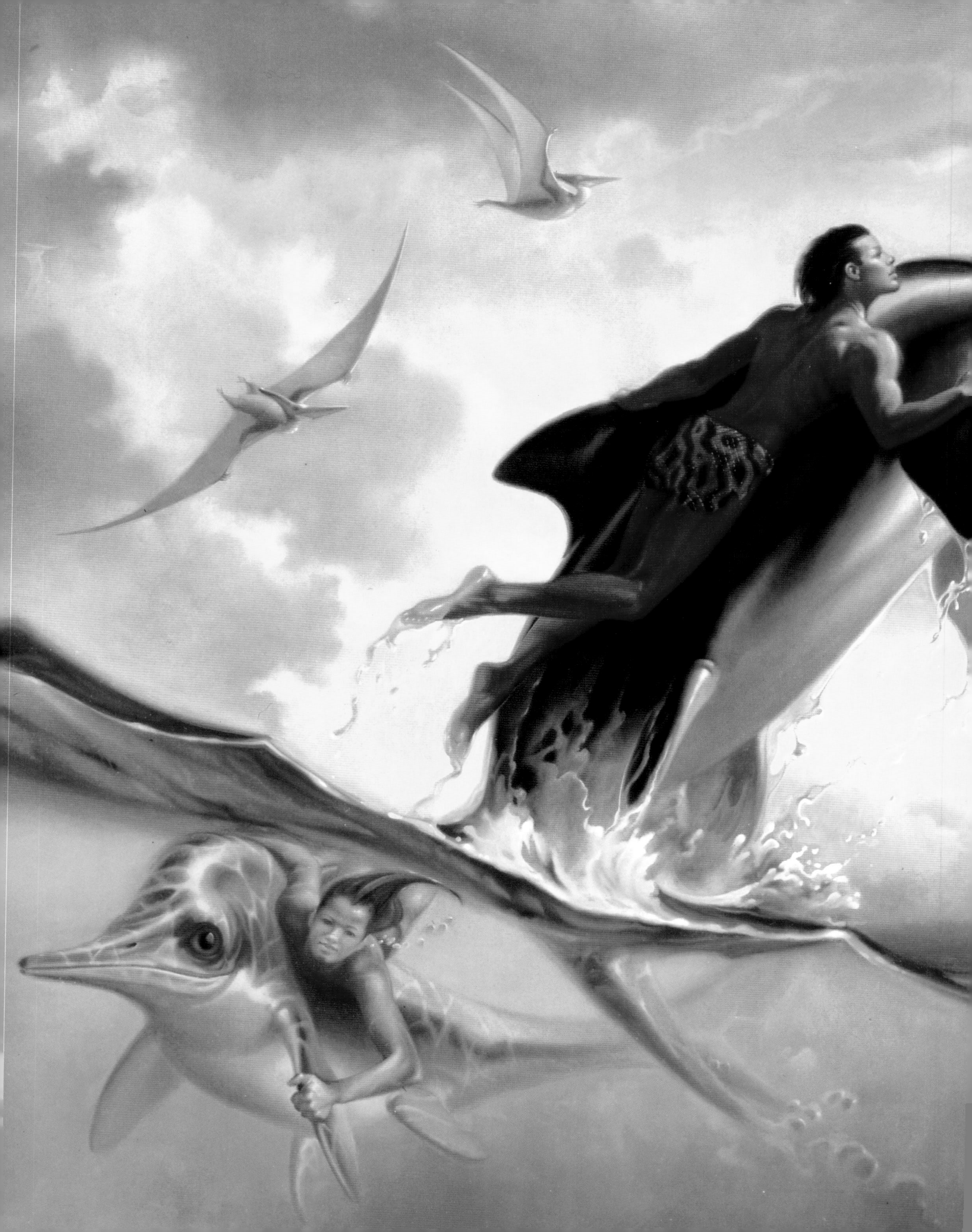

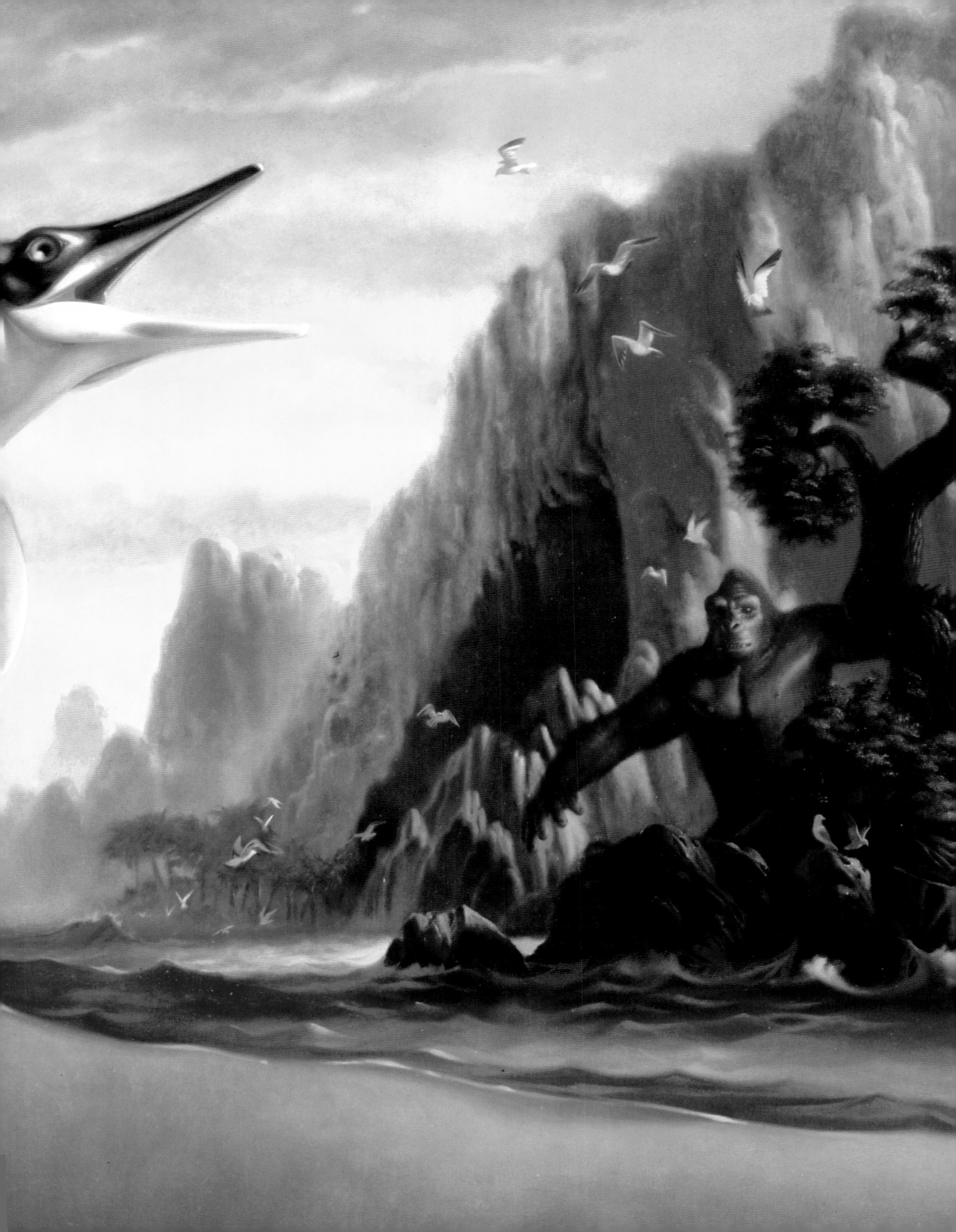

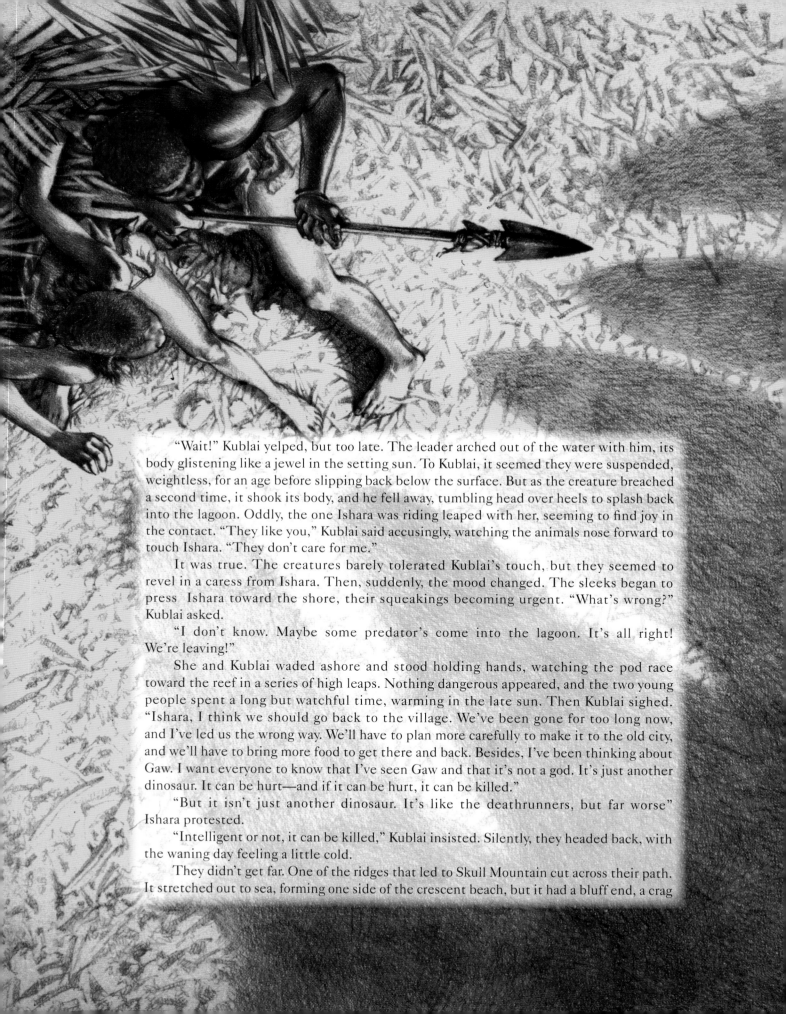

"Wait!" Kublai yelped, but too late. The leader arched out of the water with him, its body glistening like a jewel in the setting sun. To Kublai, it seemed they were suspended, weightless, for an age before slipping back below the surface. But as the creature breached a second time, it shook its body, and he fell away, tumbling head over heels to splash back into the lagoon. Oddly, the one Ishara was riding leaped with her, seeming to find joy in the contact. "They like you," Kublai said accusingly, watching the animals nose forward to touch Ishara. "They don't care for me."

It was true. The creatures barely tolerated Kublai's touch, but they seemed to revel in a caress from Ishara. Then, suddenly, the mood changed. The sleeks began to press Ishara toward the shore, their squeakings becoming urgent. "What's wrong?" Kublai asked.

"I don't know. Maybe some predator's come into the lagoon. It's all right! We're leaving!"

She and Kublai waded ashore and stood holding hands, watching the pod race toward the reef in a series of high leaps. Nothing dangerous appeared, and the two young people spent a long but watchful time, warming in the late sun. Then Kublai sighed. "Ishara, I think we should go back to the village. We've been gone for too long now, and I've led us the wrong way. We'll have to plan more carefully to make it to the old city, and we'll have to bring more food to get there and back. Besides, I've been thinking about Gaw. I want everyone to know that I've seen Gaw and that it's not a god. It's just another dinosaur. It can be hurt—and if it can be hurt, it can be killed."

"But it isn't just another dinosaur. It's like the deathrunners, but far worse" Ishara protested.

"Intelligent or not, it can be killed," Kublai insisted. Silently, they headed back, with the waning day feeling a little cold.

They didn't get far. One of the ridges that led to Skull Mountain cut across their path. It stretched out to sea, forming one side of the crescent beach, but it had a bluff end, a crag of volcanic stone rearing above the surf. Beyond that the land dropped to yet another beach. And in a narrow inlet on the far side was something that neither Ishara nor Kublai had ever seen before.

It rode on the water, though it leaned to one side. It seemed to be made of wood, and it had—what?—brownish-white wings of a kind. And on the beach were boats, not shaped like the canoes of the islanders, but rather shield-shaped. A man stood over the boats, carrying something like a long black stick. He wore outlandish garments that covered most of his body, and his skin was the palest human flesh that Ishara had ever seen.

Kublai again led the way, ducking into the underbrush, giving the stranger a wide berth. "What is that?" he asked, pointing at the floating vessel. "A—a boat? It must be the biggest boat in the world! And who are these men? I've never seen anyone like them!"

"Outsiders," Ishara said. "They might not know about the dangers. We should warn them."

"I don't think so," Kublai responded. "They may be dangerous themselves." He found an animal path through a thicket of spiky brush and stooped as he led Ishara along it. It curved away from the sea.

But soon they emerged from the thicket into a clearing and froze. Opposite them, obviously just having come from the other way, were five men, as pale as the one on the shore. They all carried the long black sticks. The one in front was tall and broad-shouldered. One of the others leveled his stick toward Ishara and Kublai, but the leader struck it down with his hand and said something quick and sharp in a foreign language. Then he gestured, motioning Kublai and Ishara forward.

Kublai said, "Stay behind me. Be careful." He took a step forward, spear at the ready.

The tall, pale man spoke. His language sounded to Ishara like the twittering of the flying reptiles, but in a deep, booming register. When Kublai didn't react, the tall man said something to one of the others, a shorter, heavier man. The man spoke several times, words that Ishara could not understand. Then a distorted, odd-sounding word: "friends."

"Who are you?" Kublai asked. "How did you get here?"

The man shook his head. Kublai repeated himself slowly. The short man jabbered to the tall one. The tall one shouldered forward and gestured toward the ship. His expression was not threatening, but his demeanor was urgent. Slowly, Ishara began to understand that the vessel had a hole that let water in. These strangers had come to the island seeking aid.

"Tell him we'll help him," Ishara said.

Kublai gestured for her to be still, but the tall, long-faced man had noticed her. He smiled, a smile like the sun coming up. He tapped his chest and said "Mag-wich."

"Mag-wich," Ishara said, imitating the sound.

The tall man laughed and nodded. "Cap-tain Mag-wich," he said slowly. He pointed at Ishara and raised his eyebrows in query.

"Ishara," she said, understanding. She touched Kublai's arm. "Kublai."

"Ishara," Captain Magwich said immediately, soberly. "Kublai." He came forward, still smiling. He wore strange clothing: soft tubes that covered his legs, leather covers on his feet, and covering his arms and chest a garment so pale that to Ishara it looked like the face of the moon. He reached into the garment and produced something, which he held out, offering it to Ishara. She took it in her cupped hand. It was a ring of gold, glowing in the sun. He nodded, smiled, and closed her fingers on it. And to Kublai he held out a gleaming knife with a jeweled handle. As if moving by its own will, Kublai's hand took the weapon from him.

"They're telling us they will pay," Ishara told Kublai. "If we help them, they will pay us with gifts."

"What should we do?" Kublai asked, his voice worried.

"They will die here," Ishara replied. "They are strangers. They don't know they're beyond the Wall."

Kublai turned the knife, sending flashes of reflected light into Ishara's eyes. "I've never seen anything so fine."

Captain Magwich put both of his hands on Kublai's shoulders. "Kublai," he said. He gestured toward the ship. "Help."

Smiling despite himself at the big man's beaming face, Kublai nodded. "Kublai . . . help," he repeated. He pointed to the ship and mimed its moving. "Kublai help."

The tall Magwich laughed and nodded. Kublai tried to explain that they had to move to the village. Ishara stepped forward and pointed to herself and to Kublai, then lifted one finger, two fingers: the two of them. She pointed and held up all of her fingers, opening and closing her hand. More people there. Magwich seemed to get the idea, and when Ishara gestured for the strangers to follow, he said something to them and they fell into line.

The seven of them walked along the ridge, but despite Ishara's and Kublai's efforts, they could not get the men to understand the dangers of the island. When they tried to mime an attack by a dangerous animal, he shook his long stick and laughed.

Their trail had to take them close to the great hollow under the gaze of Skull Mountain, where Gaw's den lay. Near the ravine feeding into it, Ishara remembered that this was where the body of the young kong must have fallen. If it had attracted scavengers like the king dinosaurs, they would have little chance. Of them all, only Kublai carried a spear.

They were making their way across a jumble of scree, fallen blocks of stone, when Kublai stopped and shouted a warning. A lanky man that Magwich called Skeets had drawn ahead of the others, and he looked back, not ahead, when Kublai called out.

He did not see the slasher.

The man-sized creature leaped from ambush, landed atop a pile of tumbled boulders, and then onto Skeets's back. Its vicious bite snapped his neck, as its sickle-like toe claw nearly sliced him in two.

The four other strangers quickly brought their sticks up to their shoulders, and Ishara cried out in alarm as they spat fire and thunder! The slasher reeled back, blood spouting from two wounds, soaking its stiff, sharp feathers. The lifeless body of Skeets fell face-down—

Behind the slasher, something dark reared. It was the adolescent kong coming from the jungle on the other side of the lagoon, Ishara saw, still alive, though torn and bleeding. The slasher, turning to flee from the thunder-sticks, ran straight into it. The kong, its eyes mad with pain and anger, grabbed the dinosaur, lifted it clear off the ground, and broke its back. It flung the body against the rocks, and then turned and faded into the underbrush, not seeing, or not caring about, those who witnessed the confrontation from behind trees and bushes.

As they slowly emerged from their hiding places the strangers were pointing and gabbling. Magwich strode over to the dying slasher. He reached to his belt, drew a knife that dwarfed the one he had given Kublai, and cut the dinosaur's throat. As the body twitched, he knelt beside it, his eyes rapt. He rose and said something to the men.

They took the useful things from Skeets's corpse, his thunderstick, his knives, items from his clothing and belt. Then, hastily, they piled stones on the body. Ishara looked at Kublai. Didn't they know that the larger scavengers would have no trouble digging it up again?

Magwich gestured back toward the path they had followed. The others, clustering close, started back toward the sea. Kublai and Ishara followed, relieved to be leaving the scene of slaughter.

They reached the shore, and then Magwich pointed at the distant, huge boat. Magwich stooped and drew an irregular circle in the sand with his finger. He tapped it, then poked a finger beside it. He pointed to the hole he had made, then to the boat. "It's the island. He's asking us to show him how to get to the village in the boat!" Kublai said with sudden understanding.

Ishara knelt, touched the hole Magwich had made in the sand, then traced a line a quarter of the way around the map. She tried to indicate the peninsula and bay. Magwich pointed to the two of them, then to the boat. "He wants to know if we will come," Ishara said.

Kublai looked at her. "It might be safer than the jungle. These men have no pouches of herbs to protect them. Do you trust them?"

Ishara looked at Magwich. His big, pale face was solemn, but not threatening. "Yes," she said slowly.

The men rowed out to the big boat in their smaller ones. Ishara and Kublai scrambled up the side, marveling at the huge thing, bigger than a long house. Magwich opened a hatchway and showed them water far down, shaking his head. Some men worked a device that brought the water spouting up and over the side, and others raised a weight from the sea. The great wings unfurled, filled with wind, and the craft began to move as Kublai pointed the way.

Ishara felt a strange mix of elation and fear. The island fell away behind them. A man at the front of the boat threw a weight on a line, calling out something, and the vessel slowly threaded its way through the shallows. Slowly, but faster than they could have walked, they moved toward the peninsula and the village. Already the Wall was there, dark above the jungle.

Ahead of Ishara, Magwich followed the direction of Kublai's pointing finger. There. The roofs of the village, still small in the distance, but clear. Ishara realized the stranger was trying to thank Kublai. The big man reached out and patted Kublai's back. Kublai was visibly pleased at the gesture, but Ishara knew him too well. Kublai was not only taken with the friendship of the strangers, but with the size and power of such a strange vessel and the weapons the men possessed. She knew he was already calculating their effects on the island's people, and on Bar-Atu. Suddenly, she had a strong desire to warn Kublai to be careful, but it was too late. The mysterious, pale man stood imposingly at the front of the ship, side by side with Kublai, and she could see her people were already gathering at the shore.

SKULL ISLAND
Date Unknown

"Too much!" Kara shouted.

The Storyteller fell silent, her old eyes gleaming. "What do you mean?"

Vincent watched the two of them. Kara had leaped to her feet, frowning, holding her fists clenched. "He's an outsider! You tell all our secrets! He wants to be a great man in his world. He wants to bring more like himself here to take, to steal, to kill and call it study!"

Vincent felt himself flinch from Kara's accusation. An angry response rose in his throat, but a gesture from the Storyteller silenced him.

"He *must* know the story," the old woman said simply. "And so must you. Without knowledge, there is no choice. Without choice, there is no hope of freedom. Do you understand?"

Kara did not answer, but Vincent did. His voice sounded strange even to himself, low and humble, the voice that as a child he had spoken with in the confessional.

"I think I do. If we learn from what you have to teach, if we are wise enough, then we will choose well."

A slow smile began to appear on the Storyteller's lips, but Kara turned on Vincent, crouching in her anger. "You!" she shouted, scorn dripping from the word. "What do you know of right and wrong? You don't have the gifts I have! You don't see what I see! You think you will learn all about the island, do you? Take back pieces of it for your people to stare at? Fool! You are weak, and you'll never live to get off this island! Even in your sleep you cry and moan like a coward. You don't deserve to live!"

The Storyteller touched Kara's face, and the younger woman jerked away from the touch. Firmly, the old woman said, "So you choose who should live and who should die?" Kara remained silent. The old woman's gaze embraced Kara as she continued, "Such arrogance is born in pride, the bane of the Atu. You have great gifts, Kara, that is true. But you are infinitely less than the Infinite. Are you humble enough to admit that to yourself?"

Kara panted as if she had been running. "I know only this," she said in a low, seething voice. "This man is a threat to us and to our people. And if you can't see that, you're blind as well as old and stupid!"

The Storyteller raised herself to her full height. Her stare was imperious, Vincent thought, the stare of an offended queen. Clearly, without anger, she said, "The Atu thought as you do, Kara. They taught that power was all that mattered, but strength is measured in many ways." Then her voice took on a tone of command: "Now you will be silent! And you will listen—and learn!" The Storyteller's rebuke had an ageless authority, and Kara stood transfixed. She glanced toward Vincent and in a softer voice she added, "And as for Vincent Denham, I tell you that he will live. And learn. As can anyone with an open heart."

But Kara's expression told Vincent that at the moment, whether his heart were open or closed, she would have liked nothing more than to rip it hot and beating from his chest.

CHAPTER NINE

SKULL ISLAND
June ?, 1957

Jack Driscoll snatched sleep when he could. His waking time passed in intervals of making his way forward through what had become a maze of tunnels, sometimes in the glow of those strange wall-pictures, sometimes in the ruddy glare of torchlight. Once he had to wade through knee-deep flowing water, surprisingly cold, but drinkable. He constantly paused to consult the map and compass he carried with him, struggling to maintain his progress toward the Wall. Three or four times he realized he was in a blind tunnel, the ends bare rock or tumbled boulders. Then he backtracked, looking for the sooty marks he had left to blaze the trail. Now and again he lost his footing and fell.

In one of these falls his outthrust hand had clashed hard against a stone, and he had shattered his watch. "Great," he muttered. "Just great."

Sometimes he came to places where the ceiling had fallen in. The jungle overhead had filled in so completely, however, that the little daylight that filtered through was murky and greenish, as though Driscoll were underwater. With what he had, Driscoll could not cut through the maze of lianas, roots, and fallen timber. Still, if he could judge from the slanting tight beams of sunlight, he was still heading roughly toward the Wall.

And then at some point, hours, days, after he had fallen into the first tunnel, Driscoll caught the moist touch of above-ground air on his face and the constant scent of decaying foliage that he remembered so well from his first visit to the island. A few moments later, he heard the sound of animals.

Slowing to a careful shuffle, with one hand thrust out against the rough stone wall, Driscoll edged forward. At first he thought he saw another of those mysterious living paintings. Then he realized that he had come to the brink of an arched opening that looked out onto a moonlit night.

Driscoll balanced himself, every nerve tingling. He could not at first clearly understand what lay before him. Then a cloud that had been partly obscuring the moon drifted away, and Driscoll felt his eyes widening.

The tunnel fed into the wall of a great bowl-shaped opening. A rim of stone ran around the top, casting deep shadow beneath it. Across from him, perhaps ten or twelve feet from the basin's floor, was another arch, leading away into darkness. He could see two more, lower, smaller arches. With some surprise, he realized that the basin had been filled with years of fallen leaves and branches. At least one man-made level, perhaps several, lay buried beneath the detritus of eons. Driscoll carefully lit a torch and leaned far out. Once, ages before, a graceful bow of stone had run up to the tunnel's end, but most of that had fallen. Nothing stirred on the surface of leaf mould beneath him. With a grunt of resignation, Driscoll doused the torch and dropped it. The thud sounded reassuringly solid.

"Here we go," he told himself. He lowered himself from the broken edge of the stone walk, held on for a moment, and then let go. He dropped more than his own height, felt his boots crunch into springy earth, and sat hard. He scrambled up again at once, holding his rifle at ready. His heart thumped hard, and from the sky above he heard the melancholy screech of pterosaurs.

When nothing attacked, Driscoll groped for his torch and found it, still warm. He lit it and stood near the center of the stone basin.

At one time it must have been a sizable room, perhaps the foundation for a round tower. The opening above him showed more stone arcs, all broken, like the ribs of a gigantic skeleton. Judging from the inward slope of the walls, Driscoll estimated that the place had once been at least forty feet deeper. How many millennia had it taken for the upper structure to crumble and for the foundation to fill with forty feet of leaves?

The walkway to the far tunnel opening looked scalable. Driscoll made his way toward it, felt something snag his toe, and stooped to clear away what he thought was a twig.

It was a human skull.

To the left of it was a hand, held together by a mummified covering of flesh. The two parts protruded from the leaf mould like a dead man digging upward from his grave. Kneeling, Driscoll scraped away more and more layers of the leaves. He found three different bodies, as far as he could judge. And he found ivory buttons and metal belt buckles. There was also an ugly, rusted bulldog of a pistol, its grip long gone. Driscoll was no expert, but the pistol, which bore the almost unreadable name "Eley," looked to be of nineteenth century vintage.

But one thing was clear. Driscoll had found the remains of more Europeans.

"I wonder how many they murdered," he thought aloud. "Savages."

The sky overhead was growing pale with dawn. That told him which direction was east, and that, in turn, told him that the Wall lay in the same line he had been traveling. His compass readings had been on the money. Maybe he was even within sight of the Wall, he thought. It was worth a look.

He scrambled up the eroded walkway, found hand and toeholds, and, with his rifle slung on his shoulder, he pulled himself up to the verge of the pit. "Getting too old for this," he panted. But he hauled himself out into the open and stood upright.

The stars had vanished in the pale pre-dawn sky. Insects rioted all around, a good sign. They would have been silent if something large were moving nearby. Driscoll selected a likely tree and began to climb it, pulling his way from branch to branch, pausing to rest every few minutes. The sun broke over the rim of the world, and the sky overhead turned to pinks and blues.

At last, on a stout limb that was almost as high as he could climb, Driscoll stood and looked around him. Skull Mountain, off in the distance, part of its dome ruddy with the rising sun, part in deep purple shadow yet. A glint of the ocean. And, yes, not as far away as he had thought, the Wall, a dark, sinister barrier glimpsed above the tree canopy. Overland, maybe four or five hours march. Underground—well, who could tell?

Driscoll descended, dropped to the earth, dusted his hands. Could he risk the march through the jungle? Maybe the big creatures were scarcer close to the village. Or maybe they liked to stay close to a source of food.

He felt a tingling on the back of his neck, the hairs rising in that primitive reflex of growing fear. But why?

Then he heard the silence.

The insects were quiet.

And something, he felt sure, something between him and the tunnel entrance, was watching him with hungry eyes.

SKULL ISLAND
The Past

Kublai led the men around the point and into the lagoon near the village. Ishara watched the sleeks until the great boat glided to a halt, the men dropping a curiously shaped thing to hold it in place—an anchor, she later learned it was called. The shore filled as the islanders flocked down to see this strange new thing, crying out in surprise and alarm.

Then Kublai, Ishara, Magwich, and six of the strangers climbed into the smaller boats and rowed ashore. The people of the island saw Kublai, and though they fell back, they did not flee. Kublai was first to step out amid the murmuring crowd, and he called to the people, telling them not to be afraid. He told them the strange pale men were friends. Still the crowd jostled and the islanders pointed at the newcomers, asking questions, exclaiming in their excitement.

Bar-Atu stood silent as the procession filed toward the king's house, watching them with hooded eyes. Then he stepped forward, barring their way. "You!" he shouted at Kublai.

"Where have you been? Who are these strangers? Explain yourself!"

Kublai drew himself up. "I have been beyond the Wall," he said sternly. "Though I owe no explanations to you. I am a hunter, Bar-Atu! I am a prince of the island!"

"The king has been fretful and worried!" Bar-Atu shot back. "How dare you take his daughter into danger?"

Kublai's anger ran high. "Who says Ishara was in danger, as long as she was with me? I go where I wish, Bar-Atu, and do as I wish. I ask no one's permission!"

His air of command was unmistakable. Ishara saw Magwich glance at Kublai with a smile and a nod. The man might not understand the words that Kublai spoke, but clearly he gathered that Kublai was a leader, not someone to be ordered around. Magwich took a step closer to the young man.

Kublai said, "As for the strangers, they came here over the sea in a great boat, and they need our help. I have sworn to give it to them. Will you say I cannot?"

Bar-Atu glared, but with the people of the island clustered near, many of them shouting agreement with Kublai, the priest did not press his point. He stepped aside, with no hint of graciousness, and the procession passed him by, the strangers chattering among themselves in their own language.

All of the other villagers came out to see these creatures, as peculiar to them as anything on the far side of the Wall. Attendants brought Ishara's father from his house, and sitting on a carved wooden throne, he received the men gravely. With difficulty, through sign language and with Ishara's help, they told him of their plight, and On-Tagu agreed to consider the situation. Meanwhile, he ordered the villagers to feed the visitors. He rose and walked back into his dwelling unassisted, but when Ishara tried to follow, one of Bar-Atu's servants moved to block her way. Bar-Atu instead went inside to consult with the king.

The strangers appeared to enjoy the food the islanders brought to them. Ishara and Kublai stood a little apart and watched the festivities. "They have great power," he said admiringly. "Perhaps they have been sent to save the island."

Ishara felt troubled without exactly knowing why. She noticed that as Larana, one of her cousins, bent to offer the men fruit, one of the sailors grabbed at her. The younger one, the one Magwich called Charlie, leaped up and struck the man's arm away. The other sailor turned on him with a snarl.

Then Magwich spoke sharply in the strangers' tongue, and the sailor relaxed, laughed, and bowed to the frightened Larana with exaggerated courtesy.

He laughed, as if to say it was only a joke. But none of the islanders joined him in his laughter.

When the feast ended, On-Tagu sent Bar-Atu with his decision: The villagers would help the strangers. And so over two months a fleet of canoes assisted as the strangers built log huts on a knoll above the beach, then emptied their vessel of everything it carried. Crates, boxes, strange constructions of metal and wood, they carried ashore and stored in the huts, keeping men on guard the whole time. There were many, many more of the pale strangers than Ishara had believed, but Magwich took care to see that they did not mingle too much with the islanders. The young one called Charlie, though, spent much time with

Kublai and Ishara, learning more and more of the island speech and teaching them some words of English.

Charlie learned their language rapidly and as work progressed, he explained what had to be done. The men had to patch the ship's leaks and mend something called "ribs" and "knees," although Ishara could not imagine what these might be in a boat. It would take time, Charlie explained, much time. Weeks, or even months.

But during those calm weeks, worries seemed pointless. When the time came to haul the ship ashore, the islanders made a game of it, each canoe taking a line from the huge vessel. They towed the helpless craft behind them. Kublai's eyes shone. "Like hunters bringing down the greatest of the beasts," he said to Ishara. "See what we can do!"

It took well over two days of towing and hauling before the big ship was safely beached. Through Charlie, Magwich explained that the men would sleep in tents near the beach, to watch over the ship and to be handy for the work that had to be done.

That began after one day of rest. Wood was a problem, because the man who seemed responsible for cutting the timbers did not care for any that grew close to the shore. Parties went out along the peninsula to look for more. Charlie, who was younger than the others and evidently not of much use to them, spent his time with Ishara and Kublai.

Kublai was not much interested in the strange English tongue, but Ishara found it enchanting. Charlie seemed to enjoy teaching her how to pronounce the odd words. Kublai had not the patience for the lessons, and soon he deserted them to join the working party and learn more about the ship and about the weapons that spoke with a voice of thunder. Every evening Ishara and Kublai spoke of what they had done during the day. When three more weeks had passed, with little more done on the repair work to the ship than the cutting and hauling of some trees, Kublai said sadly, "On-Tagu's illness is worse. He can no longer sit at all."

"Yes," agreed Ishara softly.

"Tonight is the ceremony of the full moon," Kublai continued. "Bar-Atu plans to speak of something. He has been asking me about what we saw beyond the Wall, and he has been talking with Magwich and the others of their weapons. I don't know what he's planning, but with the king so ill—I am worried."

The sailors always seemed happy to take time off from their labors, and the prospect of a feast cheered them up amazingly. That evening, everyone on the island assembled on the hillside between the shore and the village. The sailors kept apart, a small group of nearly a hundred among the thousands of islanders. Kublai and Ishara sat together near the strangers, so their view of Bar-Atu was from a distance. His voice rang out strongly enough for all to hear, though, and behind her, Ishara could hear Charlie translating the speech into English for their captain.

With torchlight gleaming on his face and chest, Bar-Atu first talked of the coming of the strangers, and then of the beasts of the island. "Gaw strides the forest as a god!" he cried. "But On-Tagu says he is not a god. Very well. Since the Tagu of old boasted that they controlled all the animals of the island, let On-Tagu show us! We thought the kongs were dead and departed, but now we hear that one or more still live. If On-Tagu believes Gaw is not a god, let him capture a kong! Let him train the kong, as his ancestors did! Let the kong slay Gaw, if Gaw is not a god! But will On-Tagu do this?"

Ishara put her hand on Kublai's arm. Her father was so ill that he could not stir from his bed. "What is he doing?" she asked.

She felt Kublai's arm trembling beneath her touch. Suddenly, he jumped to his feet. "Bar-Atu!" he shouted, pushing forward.

The crowd parted for him. Bar-Atu, standing on a platform between two torches, waited grimly. Kublai reached the platform and leaped easily up onto it. "You ask the impossible!" Kublai said, pointing toward the king's house. "On-Tagu has the illness and weakness of age on him. But your idea is good. I have the blood of the Tagu and of the Atu both in my veins. Since the King is too ill for the task, I tell you all this: I will do it myself! I will capture the kong!"

A cheer rose from the people, and behind Ishara, Charlie tried to translate all that had happened. Ishara bit her lip. In the firelight, Kublai stood tall and proud—too proud for his own good, she thought. "The Tagu wouldn't do this," she said fiercely.

"What?" Charlie asked. She had not realized she had spoken so loudly.

In her despair, she said, "Kublai thinks he could lead our people if he can get their respect. He wants power for himself. But Tagu would avoid killing."

Magwich came and sat beside her, in the place Kublai had been. In English, he said, "Sometimes it's a question of killing or being killed. The animals on the island—they're monsters."

"I don't understand that word."

"Not natural," Magwich said, his voice kind. "Thirsty for blood. It isn't right that you and your people are kept to this end of the island. You should rule the whole of it, not be walled off here like prisoners. Your young man is brave. Accept him for what he is."

Ishara understood much of it. She looked beyond the platform, beyond the village, at the Wall—and saw a dim light there. Troubled, she rose and skirted around the crowd. The small doorway to the stair up to the Storyteller's hut was unguarded, and she slipped inside and climbed up.

The Storyteller sat cross-legged outside her house. "You are troubled," she murmured as soon as Ishara reached her.

"I have seen the kong," Ishara told her. "Now Kublai says he will capture one. But the young one is hurt, and I don't know if it could stand against Gaw even if it were full grown."

A wind came from inland, bringing with it a sulfurous smell, the breath of the hot springs and geysers on the shoulders of Skull Mountain. It was a warm wind, but still Ishara trembled. "Is it possible?" she asked the Storyteller.

For a long time, the old woman did not reply. At last she said, "I don't think so. The Tagu trained the kongs ages ago. They protected the kongs, and the kongs protected the people. But the secrets have been long lost. And lore says that even when they were known, the methods were dangerous to use."

"Bar-Atu does not protest. Why would he want a kong in the village? The Tagu were the ones who tamed them!"

"Bar-Atu has his own reasons," the Storyteller said. "I think he does not believe Kublai can succeed. If Kublai fails, then his power is diminished. If he captures the kong, then Bar-Atu will claim his gods are behind the capture. It is a dangerous game."

"Kublai could lose his life," Ishara said.

"He could lose more than that," the Storyteller murmured.

The hunt for the kong would not be undertaken soon. Kublai spent many days gathering and training a party of hunters. He spoke less and less to Ishara, and Ishara found herself often in the company of Charlie. Her English improved, along with his grasp of the island language.

Magwich was everywhere during those weeks. He visited On-Tagu with medicines that did no great good, though they brought no harm to the old man. He supervised the work on the ship, and he spent hours talking to Bar-Atu. Ishara could not help liking the man, who had a deep laugh and a ready smile. He was old enough to be her father, and he treated her with a kind of indulgent amusement that a father would show a clever daughter.

One day Magwich had his men fire their weapons for Bar-Atu and Kublai. Ishara covered her ears and winced at the explosions. The blocks of wood that were the targets fell over, splinters flying from them. The stinging smoke drifted in a cloud that made her cough.

"We could help in your hunt," Magwich told Kublai, and the young man's eyes shone.

"You must not harm the kong!" Ishara cried out.

Magwich looked at her with evident surprise. His strong face had been darkened by work in the sun. She shivered as she realized that one reason she thought of him as fatherly was that he resembled her father—as he used to be, when Ishara was a child. "I don't mean to use the guns against kong, Ishara. But past the Wall are other things that our weapons can discourage." He clapped a hand on Kublai's shoulder. "Your young man is brave—brave as any I've seen—and I like him. You wouldn't want him hurt."

"No," Ishara agreed.

"Then my men will be glad to protect him. We owe you something for helping us with the ship. This is little enough reward." His smile was reassuring.

But behind him, Bar-Atu was holding one of the rifles, listening as Charlie explained how it worked. Bar-Atu's eyes were those of a hungry man who spies a meal.

Another few days, and then on a morning that Bar-Atu had announced as propitious for success, the hunting party assembled in the space before the Wall. Fifteen young men of the island were chosen for their strength and skill. The ship supplied another fifteen men, each armed with a rifle and a pistol. Kublai was the leader of the party, and he named Magwich as his lieutenant. "If I die, follow him as you would me," he told the islanders.

Magwich, beside him, raised his voice. In English, he said, "Shipmates, on this voyage we take orders from Kublai here. You do what he tells you. And if I run into something that eats me, why, you follow Kublai and don't worry about seeing to my funeral. But I expect we'll be bringing home some meat for tonight!"

Then, to Ishara's surprise, he repeated the speech in the island tongue, flawlessly though with an outlandish accent. Charlie must have been teaching him, too. The entire party cheered.

Ishara was able to speak to Kublai only once, just before Bar-Atu's followers opened the Gate. "Don't do this," she pled softly.

"I have to," he told her. To Bar-Atu, he called, "See that Ishara stays here!"

All that day Ishara waited for news, but none came. She visited her father, who now slept for most of the time, and held his hand for hours. With the coming of night, she climbed to the Storyteller's hut atop the Wall. She slept there, and at daybreak the next morning she stood looking out into the forest. "Kublai will not return just because you wish him to," the Storyteller said kindly.

At noon, Ishara heard gunfire, faint and distant, a rattling volley. Then nothing more.

Until the late afternoon. With the red sun low, Ishara heard a crashing in the forest, not far from the Gate. She called the Storyteller to her side, and they stared downward. "There!" Ishara said, pointing.

The Storyteller gasped and took her hand. "It really is a kong!" she said.

Behind the kong came a mixed line of Europeans and islanders. The islanders kept pikes at the ready, and from time to time a sailor fired a gun into the air. The kong, still limping, flinched away from the strange explosions and came nearer and near to the Wall.

Then Ishara heard Kublai shout, "Now!"

From hidden perches in trees men dropped nooses of rope down. Some missed, but half a dozen looped around the kong's neck. Immediately the men leaped down from the trees and hauled on the ropes. Others joined them. The kong reeled, clutching at its throat as the ropes cut off its breath.

"No!" Ishara shouted.

The weakened, injured kong staggered, swept a threatening arm, but finally crashed to the earth. The men cheered, and the Gate swung open.

Then Ishara was running down the narrow stair, tears stinging her eyes. By the time she reached the bottom, the men had dragged the kong inside and the gates had swung closed. Excited islanders crowded around, and Ishara could not see what was happening. She could tell only that the men were dragging the body to the massive trunk of an ancient tree, the largest there was behind the Wall. "Let me see! Let me see!"

They ignored her, and she pushed her way slowly through. When she finally saw what had happened, she was weeping, sobs shaking her whole body. The dazed kong was tied to the trunk, his head lolling, his eyes unfocused. Bar-Atu was handing Kublai a whip. "No!" Ishara screamed again, her voice lost in the cheers of the islanders. She turned as the whip cracked and fled to the sounds of its repeated blows.

"It's wrong!" she told Kublai late that night. They were on the beach, at the far end from the Europeans' ship. Waves came rolling in, black against the darkness, then creaming into white. The sound was like the earth breathing. "Kublai, you know it's wrong!"

"It's a beast," Kublai replied sullenly. "It doesn't understand anything else. The whip and starvation—those are the only ways to break its will. Bar-Atu knows."

"Bar-Atu lies!" she said fiercely. "This isn't the way of the Tagu! You saw the kong when it tried to defend its parents. It's more akin to us than to beasts!"

"I know what I'm doing!" Kublai seized her arms and stared into her face. In the faint light, she could see the intensity of his gaze. "Your father will die soon. What do you want? Do you want Bar-Atu to become the only leader? I can stop him!"

"Not by becoming him!"

He pulled her toward him, but Ishara broke away and ran. Halfway to the village, she turned and looked back. Kublai stood, a dark silhouette against the white surf, his stance angry and proud.

Two months passed, then three. More and more, Ishara stayed with the Storyteller, looking down into the village. The Europeans refloated their ship, but anchored it in the bay. They remained on the island, keeping to their own small village of huts on the knoll overlooking the beach.

And every day Kublai beat Kong, as Ishara now thought of him. Kublai fed him only when Kong was submissive. The great creature was becoming gaunt. Without telling anyone, not even the Storyteller, Ishara sometimes slipped away in the dark of night to bring a few morsels of food to the captive, or give him a drink. At first Kong drew back from her in a way that wrenched her heart, but gradually he came to trust her. She spoke softly to him and wished she had the courage to cut his bindings.

And slowly her feeling of dread grew. She spoke of it to Charlie one evening. "Tomorrow is one of the nights of sacrifice," she told him.

"What? Chickens and such?" asked Charlie, with a grin. It was meant as a joke. There were no such things as chickens on the island, though the Europeans had a few scrawny hens on board their ship, a source of wonder to the islanders.

"One of our people," Ishara said.

Charlie looked at her, his young face startled. "Go on."

"Bar-Atu remembers the days when the Shaitan offered humans to the wild gods. Now Bar-Atu says the offerings must begin again. This is the moon of the first sacrifice. His priests will choose a woman from the people and tie her outside the Gate. Then they will sound the gong on the wall until Gaw comes. If Gaw takes the sacrifice quickly, then he approves of Bar-Atu's teaching. Or so Bar-Atu says. Gaw has never refused any flesh."

Charlie looked uneasy. "Maybe with our guns we can—"

Ishara shook her head. "It's too dangerous to open the Gate when Gaw is near. Gaw has attendants, deathrunners, many of them. Even with your rifles, you could not kill so many."

The young man frowned. "But Kong isn't trained."

"No. He may never be ready to fight Gaw. His parents weren't, and they were much larger and stronger."

The next afternoon was overcast, with a threat of storm in the dark sky. Bar-Atu's priests brought out the chosen sacrifice, a girl called Ashanta, and performed the ritual of bathing her, anointing her with oil, clothing her with flowers, of purifying her for the sacrifice. At sunset they dragged her drugged, listless body outside the Gate and tied her to the altar of Gaw. As the light died and torches flared, Bar-Atu gave a signal, and atop the Wall two men began to swing hammers at the gong atop the Storyteller's hut. The old woman never stayed there at such times. She had come down and was sitting with On-Tagu, rocking back and forth and crooning softly. Ishara heard shouts and hurried outside to see what was wrong.

A roar pierced the twilight, a hoarse saurian roar from beyond the Wall. Gaw was coming. Up on the Wall itself, men had kindled fires, and cauldrons of boiling oil, rendered from the fat of dinosaurs and kept here for defense, steamed and billowed. Near the fires, spearmen pointed into the distance, shouting as they did. Ishara knew that sometimes Gaw came with an escort of deathrunners, and that they often tried to force the Gate. At times Gaw's coming had taken in death more than just the intended victim. Now the men took every precaution, just in case Gaw should find the sacrificial offering not to his liking.

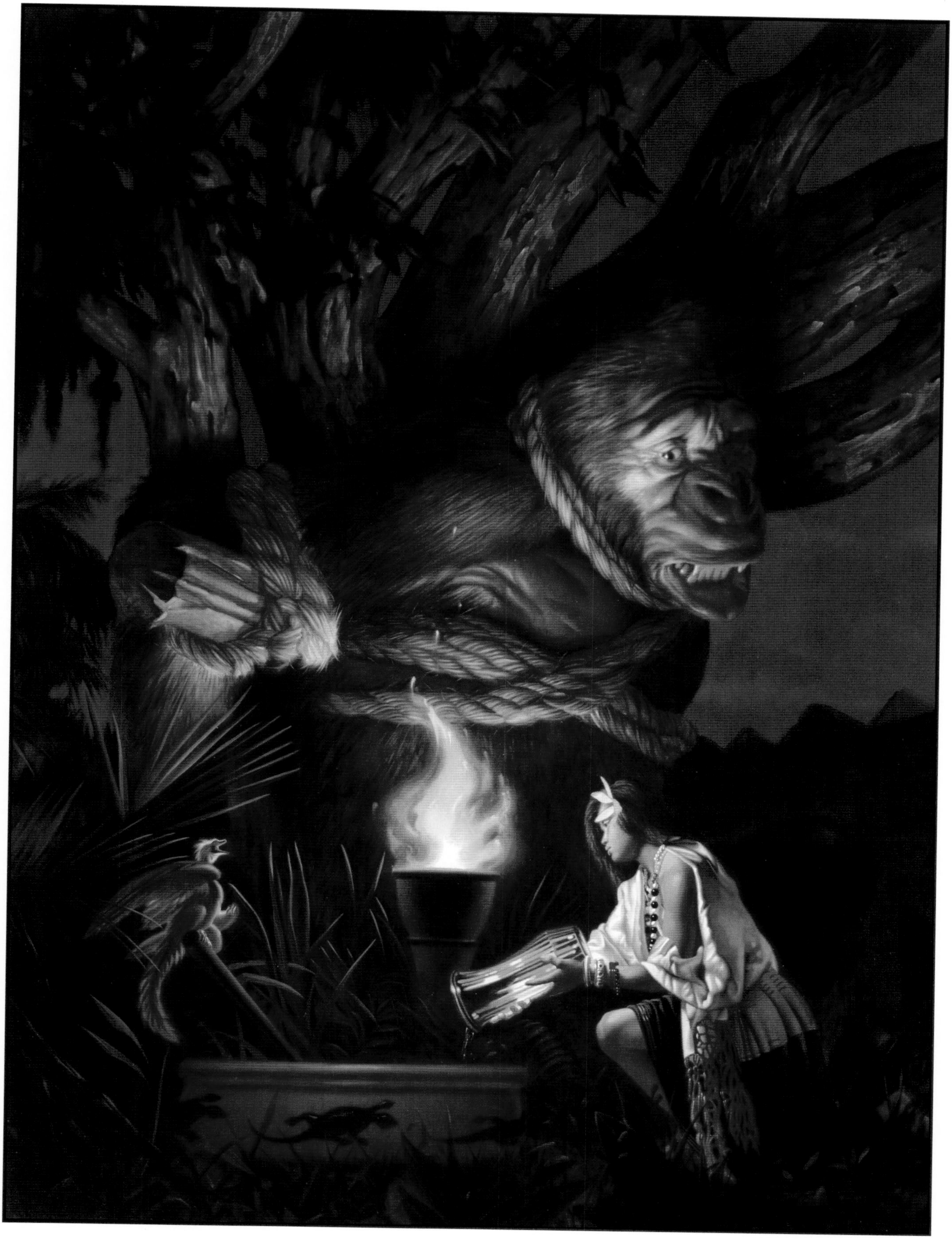

A shriek of rage, inhumanly loud even though it came from far beyond the Wall, made Ishara's flesh crawl. She ran through the village and came to Kong's clearing. Kong struggled to stand, tugging at the ropes that bound him. "What is it?" Ishara asked, but no one was there to answer.

And then she understood. Kong had heard Gaw's cry from beyond the Wall. "You can't," she said soothingly. "No one can help—"

Another shriek and a guttural roar tore through the air. The world seemed for a moment to hold its breath, too terrified to move. Then from the dark clouds overhead the first bolt of lightning seared the sky. Thunder rolled across the island. In response, Kong threw back his head and howled defiance. Ishara took a step back, sensing Kong's anger. Kong's seemingly wasted arms heaved, the sinews and muscles cording with effort.

The tree around which Kong's arms were bound swayed, rustling, and then the wood gave a sharp crack. Kong's eyes grew wide and wild, and his shoulders knotted as the ropes holding him parted with a twang, whipping the air. "No!" Ishara shouted again.

His shoulders flexed as he redoubled his effort. Ishara ran to find Kublai. Behind her she could hear wood splintering.

She had not gone far before a priest of Bar-Atu came running toward her, brandishing the great braided whip. "What is it doing?" he shouted. He did not live to hear an answer. A sweep of Kong's arm shattered the man, sending his broken body tumbling, the whip flying. Ishara could have touched Kong as he hurtled past. She ran behind him, shouting a warning.

Kong burst into the torchlit clearing before the Gate. He rose to his full height, well more than twice that of the tallest man, and his huge fists thumped his chest. Ishara stopped at the edge of the clearing. To her, time stood still as Kong gave out an ear-splitting roar and leaned forward to pound the earth. The impacts made her stagger, and the men in the clearing, stirred from their shocked inaction, stumbled as if their knees were buckling. Ishara stared at Kong in horror. His primal rage transformed him, changing his features. Instead of the suffering face of an intelligent creature, he now wore a mask of fury terrible to behold. Recoiling in fear, Ishara remembered what the Storyteller had said: a kong aroused to anger was exceedingly dangerous. Ishara's mind whirled, her emotions torn between the empathy she had felt for the young Kong and her terror at this raging creature.

Suddenly Kong lunged toward the Gate, striking those who stood before him, sending them tumbling like broken dolls. Kong slammed into the doors of the Gate with such force that they groaned and creaked, but for the moment the great beam locking them held. The men on the beam platform began to haul for their lives, realizing that their only chance was to let the rampaging Kong out before he destroyed everything on this side of the Wall.

Kong seemed to grasp their purpose. As soon as he saw the beam begin to slide between the two huge skull-like forms which held it in place, he grabbed it with both hands and wrenched it free, flinging it to one side. It slid, sweeping half a score of men from their places. Now nothing held the Gates shut but their immense weight. They began slowly, slowly, to move.

And to her horror, Ishara saw the doors were not opening outward under the force of Kong's strength, but inward! With a crash the doors sent even Kong sprawling backward. The great hinges groaned as both sides of the colossal Gates swung open under the force of Gaw's huge clawed hands. The last of the bravest who had rushed to try and close the

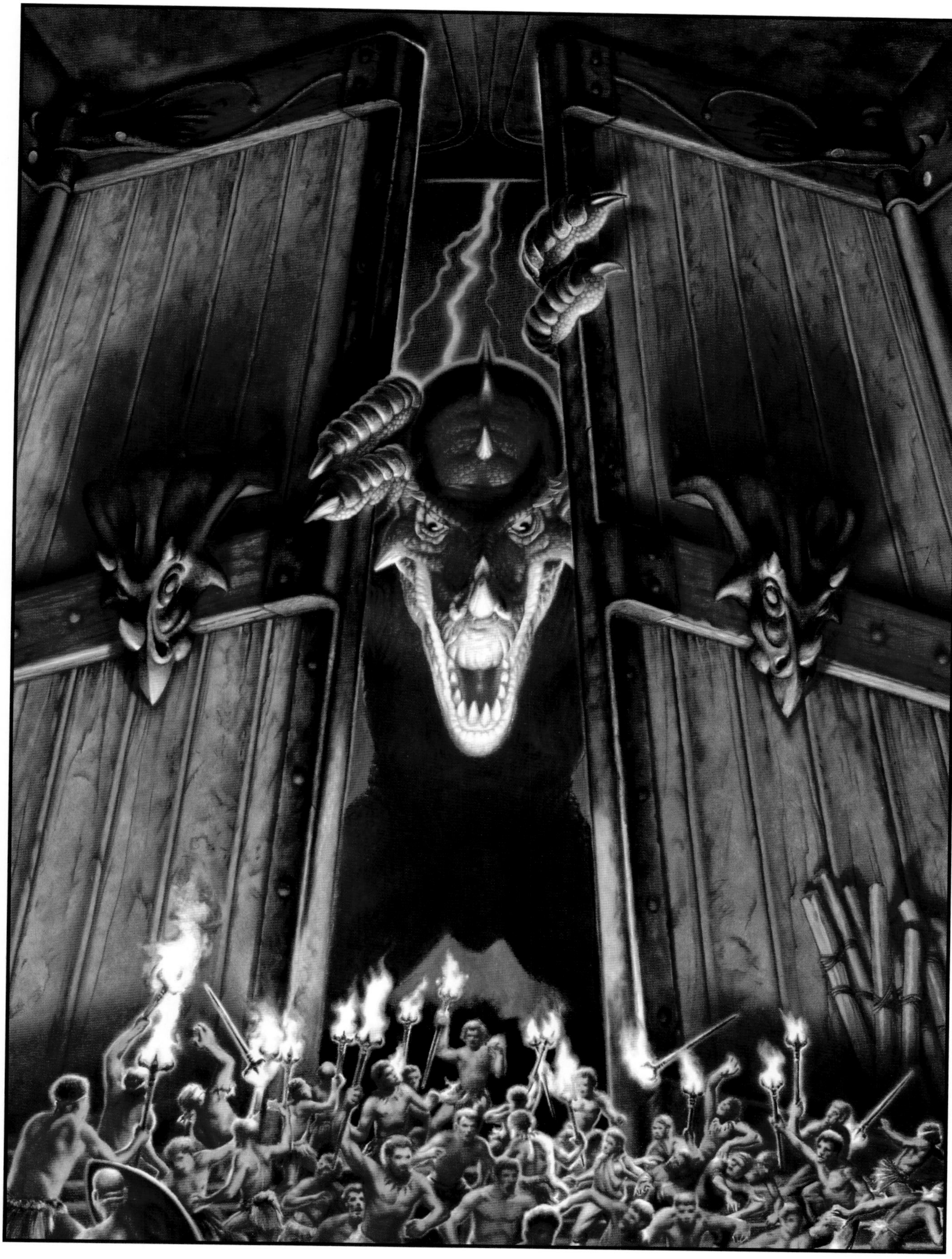

Gates began to scatter like flies. Torches dropped and flew as the huge, malevolent face of Gaw leered above them.

The islanders fled in all directions. Ishara saw Magwich and half a dozen of his sailors pushing against the flow. One of the men leveled a rifle at Kong, who was painfully rising again to his feet. Magwich struck down the sailor's weapon. "You fool! That beast is all that stands between us and death!

Kublai was shouting orders from atop the Wall. Just as Gaw raised his massive limbs to eviscerate the dazed Kong, ribbons of hot oil steamed down, searing Gaw's back. Bar-Atu was baying his disapproval, but Kublai's warriors ignored him and poured more oil from the cauldrons.

Gaw's back arched, and he reared with a roar of pain and anger. "Fire!" Magwich cried, and from the rifles of his men tongues of flame erupted in the dark. If the bullets found Gaw, they made no impression.

But a cascade of fuming oil splashing across his head and into his eyes did. Gaw reeled backwards, screaming in agony. At that moment, Ishara suddenly felt — somehow knew — that Gaw was a female. Gaw screeched, then turned and ran back into the forest. From the dark space outside the Wall, an untold number of her minions rushed, chattering and hissing, following their queen into the jungle.

Ishara saw Kong charge through the open Gate, leaping over a pool of smoking oil. He roared once, pounded the earth again, and then seemed to pause in thought for a moment before taking a different direction from Gaw, fading into the darkness. "The Gate!" Kublai yelled. "Close it now!"

"Ashanta!" screamed Ishara. Before anyone else could move, Charlie drew his knife and ran outside. Ishara followed immediately, feeling the heat from the pooled oil rising around her bare legs. With quick movements, they cut Ashanta's bonds, and the three of them stumbled back inside just as the men began to shove the Gates closed.

"He's gone," Ishara gasped to someone in the dark.

Hands led Ashanta away, and Ishara found that the Storyteller was embracing her. "Yes," she said in her old voice. "Kong has escaped. The men will never get him back, not now. He will go to Skull Mountain to heal and grow strong."

"Gaw will kill him," Ishara said numbly. "She is twice Kong's size, and swarms of deathrunners are always with her."

The Storyteller looked off into the darkness. "Never repeat the mistake that almost cost you your life. Kong is no longer the helpless young creature you first encountered. If he survives, in time his body will grow as large as his spirit. In rage he will be far more terrible than what you saw tonight."

Ishara shuddered at the thought. "Has he changed forever? You should have seen his face when his parents were killed. I cannot imagine the young Kong growing into the creature I saw tonight. He would have killed me had I been in his way, though I was the only one to show him kindness."

The Storyteller patted her shoulder. "Ishara, when we help, it should be for the other, not for ourselves. Life is not always fair, nor do we always know what is best to do. I cannot see the future, but I know that Kong will be Kong. His spirit is too great to be anything but a king. The next time Kong encounters Gaw, their struggle will be to the death."

CHAPTER TEN

SKULL ISLAND
Date Unknown

Vincent Denham lay awake, not knowing whether it was night or day. In this strange cavern, there was little difference. He idly wondered what day it was and how long he had been here. It seemed a long time.

And yet, it couldn't have been that long. A week? That much? He wasn't sure.

He had been puzzling over the Storyteller's tale for some time now. When had Ishara's story taken place? The late 1800's? Was the kong of the story his father's Kong? He suspected it was. The Storyteller had once said that the kongs lived half again as long as men. If Kong had been just a juvenile, then by the time of Carl Denham's visit in 1933, he must have been in the prime of his strength, a fully-grown creature of power and force. He had no real way of knowing.

But the Storyteller couldn't be that old. If she had been counseling Ishara sixty-seven years ago, that would make her well over a hundred. She looked ancient, Vincent thought, but surely not that old! Yet he could not deny her uncanny sensitivities, and those of Kara too. He could not explain them scientifically, but he could not deny their reality, either. He comforted himself with the theory that in his weakened state he was more susceptible to their suggestion. He didn't mind the Storyteller, who emanated an overall calm and peacefulness. Kara, though, was beginning to frighten him, and he was still too weak to fight the feeling off.

Vincent dozed, and when he woke, it was because Kara was beside him, shaking his shoulder. His injured shoulder. He could not tell if she had done so innocently or if she wanted to wake him with pain. "Here," she said shortly, offering him a shallow cup.

He took it and sniffed its contents suspiciously. The odor was bitter, ashy. "What is this?"

"Medicine." Kara tossed her head. "*She* said you are to have it. Drink it all."

It was tepid, slimy, and tasted worse than it smelled. Vincent got it down without gagging and handed the empty cup to Kara. "Where is—" he began, but the young woman turned and left him without a word.

He drowsed again, and when he woke, it was to the raucous screech of Oji. The Storyteller sat near him, her chin resting on one hand, her eyes speculative. "What are you seeking, Vincent Denham?" she asked him.

He frowned. "You know that. News of my father."

"You still have not learned what you seek." The old woman sighed. "No matter—you will in time, I think. But you begin to see a little, do you not? You see what your father took from the island when he took Kong?"

"If it was the same one."

"It was the same. Oh, yes, it was the same. The last of the Kongs, and the greatest of them. Shall I tell you more? Shall I tell you happened after Ishara's father died? That she married—and not of her own choosing? Shall I tell you what happened the next time Kong met Gaw?"

As if taking his silence for a "yes," the Storyteller closed her eyes. "The Europeans did not leave the island. Not then, not for a long, long time. Months passed, and some of them took brides from the village. Magwich was always helpful, always kind. He it was who buried On-Tagu that summer, when the old man's spirit finally left him. An honor guard, he called his men. And they raised a stone to the dead king, after their own custom. . ."

SKULL ISLAND
The Past

On the longest day of the year they buried On-Tagu atop a low hill overlooking the ocean. Charlie and some of the other sailors had carved the name, in letters of their own alphabet, in a spire of black volcanic stone, and this they set at the head of the grave. Ishara wept and scattered flowers, as was the practice of the island. Her father had slipped away at the end, sleeping deeply until one night when he simply ceased to breathe.

Death came to him the day before the second sacrifice of the year. Bar-Atu, who had vanished some days before the old king's death, reappeared just after the funeral, though he refused to take part in it. The ceremony of naming Kublai the new King came the following day, and a glowering Bar-Atu assisted in that. Kublai, perhaps not sure of his power yet, allowed Bar-Atu to send his own servants onto the Wall, and they lit the fires and prepared the cauldrons. A sacrifice was chosen, was bound to stout new pillars many steps farther from the Gates than the old ones. Gaw came, with a guard of deathrunners, and she snarled at the men atop the wall. Clearly she remembered the heated oil, and she warily kept her distance from the doors. Then she charged toward the sacrifice and with a roar of disdain ripped the screaming victim from the altar. She turned and disappeared back into the jungle.

For a week Ishara visited her father's grave every day. On a quiet evening, she placed a perfect seashell on the grave and sat looking down the slope, toward the village. Children were playing some game of their own far down the grassy hill. Ishara realized that any one of them, all of them, might be chosen as sacrifice. "I swear," she said in a fierce, soft voice, "I swear, my father, that I will never let Bar-Atu, no, nor the Wall itself, cast the shadow of fear over my spirit or my people."

Hours later, toward evening, she saw a figure striding up the hill: Kublai. She waited stoically.

He slowed as he approached, as if she were surrounded by a forbidding circle. He crouched next to her. "Ishara. I come to tell you of my sorrow at your father's passing."

Ishara nodded but did not speak.

After a moment, Kublai reached to pick up the shell. It was whorled and delicate, and three small holes had been drilled in its body. "A musical shell," he said. He lifted it to his lips and played a little melody, haunting and simple. "Why put such a thing here, Ishara?"

She took it from him and replaced it on the grave. "My father gave me this when I was a little girl. If you really loved me, you would not need to ask such a question."

Kublai's expression grew stern. "Ishara, I do honor your father's memory, and I will, but not with children's playthings. My honor will come through this!" Kublai drew a knife, one that Magwich had given him. "And with this!" With the other hand, he held out his spear.

Ishara shook her head, her eyes on fire. "You understand nothing, though you are our king. I tell you, Kublai, there is more power in this shell than in all of your weapons."

Kublai replaced the knife. He took Ishara's hand, stood, and helped her to rise, too. "We will not speak of such things. I came to tell you this, Ishara: We are to marry."

Ishara studied his face and saw shame deep in his eyes. He was still the same handsome youth she had known, but now she saw cruelty in the set of his mouth, determination in his expression. "Is that truly your wish?"

"Bar-Atu says we must," Kublai returned firmly. "And we will unite the Atu and the Tagu people in a way that has never been done before. The kings have always been Tagu. Now the people will have an Atu king in me—and you are Tagu. Our children will be true Tagatu. Our son would be the first ever to lead our people."

"I would not marry you because Bar-Atu said I should!"

"I would not ask you for his sake," Kublai said. "Don't you see? Bar-Atu is wrong. Our marriage would destroy his cause, now or when a son is born. It is a weapon to use against him!" Perhaps he even believed it. Without speaking, she reached for and held Kublai's hand, and so accepted him.

The wedding ceremony was held at the full of the moon, and that night Kublai took Ishara into the king's house as his bride and queen. And now would he expect her to bear him a son? Their son would be the first leader of their people to ever have the blood of both lines in his veins, that was true. But would he be a pawn of the Atu and lead the island to ruin, or a king who would have the strength and conviction to restore Tagu tradition?

More weeks passed, with Ishara feeling as if she were battling for Kublai's soul with the subtle and scheming Bar-Atu. At times Ishara stood gazing up at the great Wall, noticing that late in every day its shadow crept out to claim the village and everyone in it. On one such evening, Ishara stared up to the hut where the Storyteller lived and realized that in truth it was late in the day for her people. And yet beyond the Wall, the Storyteller had said, an answer waited. Ishara closed her eyes and her mind went groping into the darkening jungle, searching for the answer, praying that there was a way to find it. . .

On the night of his escape, Kong had rushed out headlong to battle the gigantic saurian. His kind had always borne a great enmity against the flesh-eaters of the island, and instinctively, he felt the challenge and the fury of imminent battle. But once beyond the great gate, once he had seen the scalded Gaw flee, Kong's own weakness after weeks of captivity took hold. He took a different path through the dark trees.

The cries of the humans back within the wall still echoed in his ears when the first deathrunner attacked. The small creature, moving in silence, leaped for him, jaws snapping, claws flashing. With a roar of anger, Kong dashed it to the earth, shattering its bones. He burst into a clearing as lightning flashed and a sharp rain stabbed down from the clouds. Three more of the deathrunners leaped for him, coming from the shadows of the undergrowth. In a terrible silence, Kong seized them, slapped at them, struck them. Over the trees he could see the red reflection of the fires beyond the Wall, but otherwise he struggled in darkness. He crushed the skull of one attacker, felt more leaping at him, tearing at his flesh, stamped on another, seized another in his teeth and bit down, breaking the spine.

Breathing deeply, tasting blood, Kong ripped at the dead deathrunner's flesh, feeding. His captors had kept him starved. Now he ate the meat of the three fallen deathrunners, filling his belly, finding strength in the bodies of his enemies.

But he could not rest. From behind, two more of the deathrunners attacked him. The wily creatures had circled, then had attacked from his blind side. Kong snarled, hurling himself backward, falling to the ground, crushing one beneath him and scrambling back up again at once. Wind lashed him, and he could smell water, not rain, but the standing water of a lake. Snarling, tearing off the last of his tormentors and flinging it aside, Kong lowered his massive shoulders and hurtled into the forest, heading toward the scent of water

More of the deathrunners chittered in the darkness among the trees. A scout had found him, had summoned others, and now they were pacing him, running him down, waiting until he was too weary to defend himself. Or waiting for their queen, Gaw, to come and finish him off.

Kong seized a massive fallen branch and used it as a club, striking down any deathrunner he could reach. He ran for a long time, his enormously powerful legs propelling him faster than a man could run. Another clearing, and the storm had swept past, with a pale full moon now showing between ragged flying clouds. It gleamed on the backs of ten or twenty more of the deathrunners, closing in. Kong struck at them, took out four with one blow, sending them flying through the air, broken-backed and dying.

The ground sloped downward. Ahead, through the trees, moonlight reflected back in points of light from the lake surface. The chattering deathrunners slowed, dropped back, a sharp, urgent warning note creeping into the cries they made. Kong reached the edge of the lake, and the two bravest or most foolhardy of the deathrunners made a rush at him, leaping high, trying to reach his throat, his jugular. He struck one down, clutched at the other, staggering, splashing into the shallows. He ripped the deathrunner free and plunged it beneath the water, feeling it heave and squirm as its lungs filled and it drowned. He left it floating and waded into the water, sensing that the deathrunners would not follow him there.

Holding his head back, Kong waded deeper and deeper into the black water, until he was far from the shore. He did not know just where he was, but far ahead the moonlight shone on a rounded stony shape that had to be Skull Mountain. Kong's mother and father had always made their home in the mountain heights, secure from the large predators, who could not climb. For Kong, the mountain spoke of safety, and it drew him forward. He stayed just close enough to the right-hand shore of the lake to touch the bottom with his feet, half-wading, half-swimming as the moon sank low and the night wore on.

Ripples hit him now and then, coming from the unseen distance, raised by he knew not what. He persisted, not seeing the great long dark shape in the water that was slowly creeping toward him, closer and closer.

Dawn was on the way when Kong came to the marsh on the far side of the lake. The earth here was soft, slimy, and it sucked at his feet. He searched for a place to leave the water, saw an outcropping of stone, and made for that. Skull Mountain lay closer now, its craggy forehead lit with the rising sun. Leathery-winged flying creatures launched themselves from the great empty eyesockets and spiraled up into the morning air.

Kong reached the jumble of fallen boulders and wearily hauled himself out of the water. He was weak and chilled, his wounds aching, his muscles near their limit. His sodden fur lay heavy on him, and his limbs could hardly support his own weight. In the dimness, he rested for a few moments on the stones, then dragged himself back to his feet.

A fallen tree lay on the far side of the boulders, on a slope leading down into the lake. As Kong neared it, the tree stirred, lunged forward: it was a crocodile-like monster, thirty feet long, torpid from the coolness of the night but insatiably hungry. Kong backed away as smaller animals with snake-like necks and tails made strange noises as they ran in all directions. The monster lurched closer, its great mouth gaping. He had no chance against those jaws, those fangs.

And then the thing that had followed him reared from the lake with an outraged bawl, dripping water. It was a longneck, a plant eater, not normally dangerous unless something ventured too close—or threatened her young. The sauropod burst from the

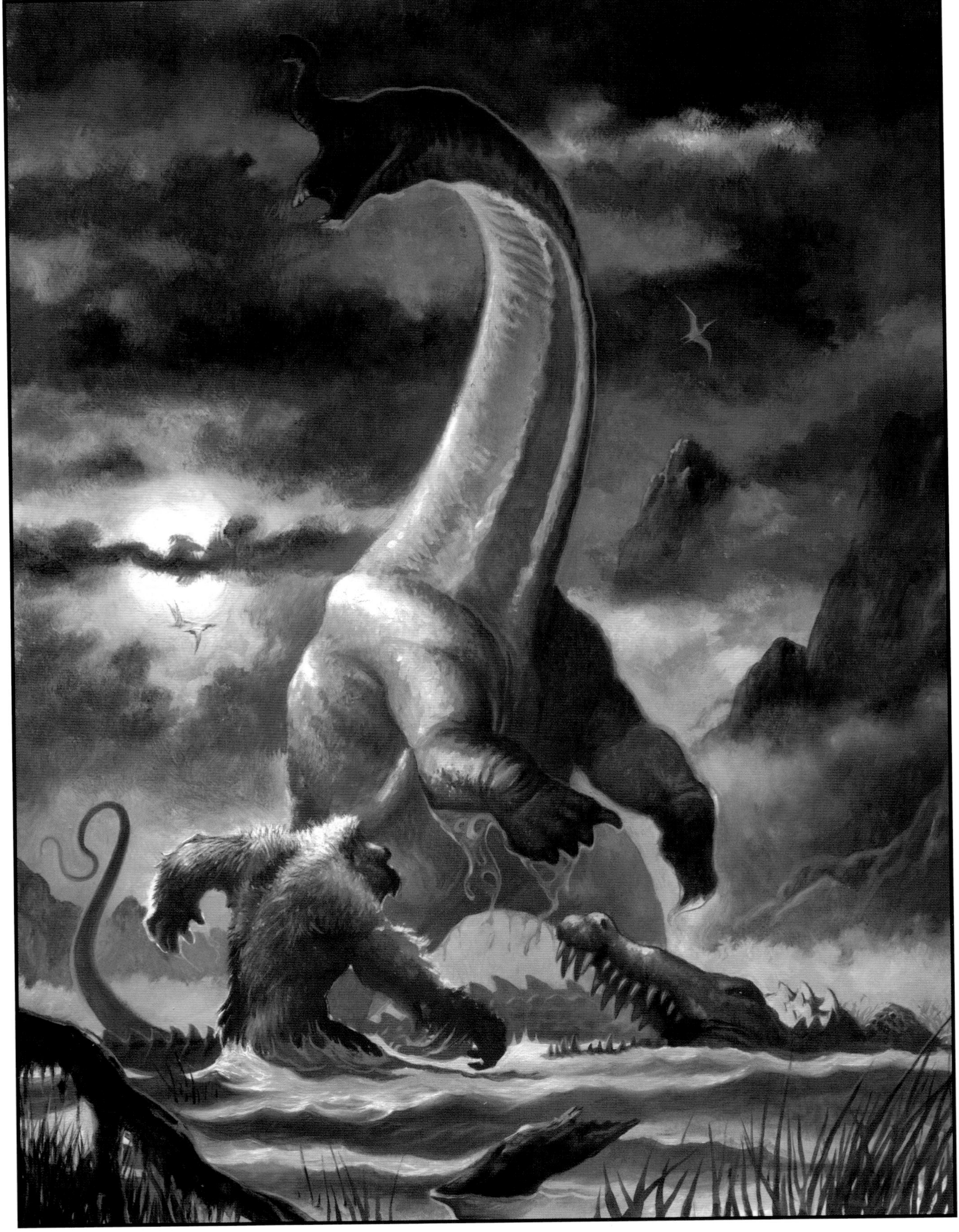

depths, reared on her hind legs, towering up, impossibly tall—and then it came down with a world-shattering crash, its front legs crushing the life from the flesh-eating phobosuchus, the monster crocodile.

Kong fell sideways, saw the angry sweep of that great neck as the plant-eater searched for him. It bawled again, now completely out of the water, and swept its long, deadly tail, snapping trees off short. The monster dwarfed Kong; he had no hope of surviving combat with the creature. It lumbered forward, hunched at the shoulders, sweeping its neck from side to side as it looked for him.

Only one chance. Kong leaped, seized the base of the neck, and clambered up onto the creature's back, just where the neck joined the torso. The plant-eater went berserk. It shook, screeched, trampled everything as it tried to dislodge him and crush him. Kong hung on, desperate.

And then the monster reared again, sweeping Kong high into the air. It came down hard on its front legs, jolting Kong loose. He fell to earth, landing on his shoulder, feeling a stab of pain. Kong scrambled to his feet. The sauropod had shattered a tree, and Kong seized one of the limbs, prepared to strike at the creature as he had at the deathrunners—but how could he injure this mountainous beast?

The sauropod could not focus on him, a dark thing against the dark background of mud and foliage. Its head swept toward him—and Kong swung, swung with all of his strength. The club connected with the head, the small head on the end of that huge neck. The head snapped away, and the sauropod's knees buckled. It crashed to earth, with Kong leaping to club the head again, then again. The plant-eater's body was out of control. The legs brought it up, staggered, reeled, and then the creature fell sideways, its collapse like an earthquake. The sides were heaving—it was not dead, but stunned. Kong dropped his club and fled again, skirting the bed of the river that fed into the lake.

The land rose, and soon he was on the lip of a ravine. His nostrils twitched at a scent of death and decay ahead, and the smell of many deathrunners. Kong veered, climbing over rising, broken ground. By midday he had come to the base of Skull Mountain, to the side away from the sea. Cliffs rose here, nearly vertical, gradually becoming the rounded overhang of the skull's cranium. Height. The predators could not climb.

He hauled his weary body up, hand over hand, up the sheer cliffs. His breath rattled in his bruised and aching chest as fatigue threatened to loosen his grip and send him tumbling.

At last Kong came to a ledge far above the jungle. From here he could see the lake, and beyond that, on the edge of the world, the unbroken dark line of the Wall. His lips curled in a sneer of anger and defiance. The ledge slanted upward, and he followed it, seeking for the safety of height. At last he could force himself to go no farther. He crept under an overhang. Above him and to his right loomed the high mountain, pierced with caverns and resembling nothing so much as a skull. An image of death, but perhaps a place of safety, a place to rest, to recuperate.

A place to gather his strength for revenge.

CHAPTER ELEVEN

SKULL ISLAND
The Past

A year passed, and part of another. Though Charlie became Ishara's trusted friend, now he could not be alone in her presence. One of her serving women always had to be there as chaperone. Ishara chose one who knew no English, and she and Charlie spoke in that language. He told her strange stories of the world outside, stories of fighting aboard ships and of the men he called pirates.

She had the impression that Magwich and his crew had fought off some of these men in a desperate battle before coming to the island. But surely by now they had repaired all the damage done to their ship. Why did they stay?

"Ah," Charlie said in answer to that, "that's the Captain's way. He's a curious sort of fellow for a seaman. Likes to know everything. Take the way he picked up the island lingo so fast. He's always been like that, learned the tongue of every place we've traveled. And old Bar-Atu is full of stories. He says the whole island's full of treasures—and that's something that communicates in all languages, if you get my drift. But Magwich knows he needs a plan, a way to find the loot and take it without being eaten alive by monsters."

Monsters. Ishara now knew what the word meant.

She thought of it every sacrifice. Four. Six. Eight of them, and it had been two years since her father's death. Nine. Ten. Eleven. And never did Gaw refuse the sacrifice. Sometimes she allowed the deathrunners to have the victims. It tore at Ishara's heart to see the hideous creatures torture and kill people she knew. Those of Tagu lineage muttered against the custom, but Bar-Atu overruled them, knowing exactly how to exploit the islander's fears. The Storyteller was held a virtual prisoner, and once she had been silenced, any hope of freedom disappeared. How could they all be so blind? Ishara's father had pointed out the end result of Atu treachery, disguised as compassion, and he had sought to unite the people of the island with the Storyteller's advice—and then he had fallen ill, and now he was gone.

As for Bar-Atu, he became more and more implacable. Three, four times a month he retreated into his hut, where he used herbs that gave him visions, put him in trances. He would always come out saying he had been in communication with Gaw, the island's god, and that Gaw demanded more obedience from the people. More blood.

At first Ishara pleaded with Kublai to reject Bar-Atu and to follow her father's ways, but he refused. Ishara fought with her husband more and more. "Won't you do this?" she asked in despair.

Kublai had become terse, speaking to her rarely. "I will take a party of hunters out," he insisted. "We will kill as many of the deathrunners as we can. No one has any love for them, not even Bar-Atu. With them dead, Gaw is not as great a threat. Perhaps even Gaw can be killed. That is the way to break Bar-Atu's power—to show that I am even greater than his god. Then I would hold absolute control over the island and everyone on it. I could force them to live as you wish them to live. I thought that was what you wanted!"

"The true danger is not outside the Wall—it's inside you. That's what terrifies me! Kublai, haven't you wondered why the people are so easily misled by Bar-Atu's lies?

"Often. But I am a ruler, Ishara. I must accept that Bar-Atu wields great power, and I must find my own way of dealing with him. With the help of Magwich, I have a chance of weakening Bar-Atu. His men are not afraid of that cunning murderer. With their weapons to pit against Bar-Atu's fanatics, I have a chance of winning—if I choose my time well."

"Are you deaf to the Storyteller's words? She—"

"Is an old woman, Ishara. Her way might have worked in the past, but not any longer.

She has no force to equal Bar-Atu's fire and determination. He touched her hand and leaned closer. "The time is coming soon. Magwich will come with me, and together we will put an end to Bar-Atu's treachery with force—the only language he understands."

"Do you trust him so much? Why do he and his men linger here? What do you offer them? Why don't they leave?" Ishara's frustration was palpable.

Kublai turned away from her. They lay in bed together, but they rarely even touched these days. "Some want to go, but their voyage is a long one. They have none of their own provisions left. If we bring in enough meat and other food—"

"That could have been done long ago."

"I don't know, then!" Kublai snapped. "I am king, Ishara, but a title means nothing without power behind it."

"But the kind of power you seek, Kublai, is the wrong kind!"

"We will speak no more of this! I have a plan. I must do what is best," Kublai snapped.

"Kublai, our people—your people—are slaves under Bar-Atu's whip of fear. He has them sacrifice their own children, like animals, to gods who are animals. It is madness, and it comes of fear of what lies beyond the Wall. We are human, Kublai, we are not helpless! But you must teach the people that fear is dangerous only to those who surrender to it. You must—"

"What I *must* do is decide what is right," Kublai said in a tone of finality. "And that decision is mine alone!"

The first great hunt took place a few days later. It lasted for three days, and at the end of that time the party returned jubilant with three dead deathrunners and the meat of one of the great plant-eaters, a kind they had never killed before. The people feasted, but there was far too much meat, and much went to waste, cast into the sea as it began to decay. The Europeans smoked long strips of meat on wooden frames, but the islanders who tried this food found it revolting in taste.

Still, the villagers cheered Kublai as the greatest of hunters, as a king who brought them food in abundance and who promised more. Bar-Atu smoldered in his anger, shouting "Gaw gives the meat to the hunters' weapons!" He glared at all those who celebrated and sat without eating for the rest of the evening.

Ishara had no stomach for the festivities. On the third night she climbed to the Storyteller's hut, above the shouts and cheering of the great feast, and listening to them as she ascended, she wept.

For a long span of days, Kong roamed the high forest beyond Skull Mountain, a plateau with sparser trees than the lush jungle. In the time that had passed since his escape from the village, he had grown. And he had learned.

He fed well. When his parents had been alive, they had found fruits, grains, leaves to eat. Kong still did that. He knew which trees bore fruit, and he knew that old rotten logs were full of insects that could be gathered and devoured. But now he ate flesh as well. The deathrunners never came to this side of Skull Mountain, for the nearly vertical cliffs defeated them, but plenty of other smaller animals roamed the plateau. Kong had taken pterodactyls from their perches on the cliffs, and he had learned how to track and kill the armored plant-eaters almost half his size. Their defense was to tuck in legs and head, so they looked like humped boulders, but they could be turned over, and their bellies were softer, less defended. Kong had learned to raid nests for eggs, too.

He grew stronger, more muscular. In his memory the days of his captivity sill smoldered, a dull pain relieved only by his recollection of Ishara's tenderness. From the cliffs and the plateau, Kong looked down on the forest below. Sometimes he saw the great reptilian creatures that dwelled there. Once he caught a sight of a king dinosaur, like the one he had fought, and the fur on his neck and shoulders bristled. In his mind a creature of that kind had killed his parents. He witnessed its ferocity from his high place, and in him ferocity awakened. The strong survived; the weak died. The fierce prospered and ruled. Kong learned.

He became at home on the bare stone cliffs, climbing them with practiced ease exercised and broadened his already prodigious strength. At last, driven by curiosity and restlessness, he moved along a narrowing ledge until he reached the face of the mountain. He found handholds and toeholds that no other creature his size could have used, edged around until he hauled himself, at last, into one of the eye sockets of the skull face itself. The space inside was a vast vault, dry-floored but reeking from the droppings of pterodactyls. Ledges and pathways led Kong to the far eye socket.

Venturing to the opening, Kong stared outward. And looking down, he saw—

Gaw.

Far, far below. Kong hissed and stared. A ledge led from two ridges on either side of the mountain to the mouth opening of Skull Mountain. Beyond that, a great crater opened in the earth, and in this crater was Gaw, at rest in the sun. Around her wheeled a herd of deathrunners, fighting over scraps of flesh and bone. Plaintive cries came from other creatures, juvenile ceratopsians. The deathrunners had herded them into the mouth of a ravine and would not permit them to leave. One had been slaughtered not long before—the deathrunners were contending for what remained of its meat.

Kong's eyes narrowed. It was possible the deathrunners could come into the mouth of the mountain. They would have to climb out of the crater some distance away, but they could follow the ridges, then the ledge, as he had done. But could they get from the mouth to this cavern?

Kong spent hours exploring and finally found a passage downward, one leading to the lower cavern of the mouth. It could be blocked with boulders easily enough. And then what? He would be trapped up here.

Or would he? If he came from the cliffs, he had a back way in, one that the dinosaurs could never use.

Over the next days, Kong made many journeys from the plateau into the caves. He blocked the steep passageway down into the mouth, using stones pried out of the cavern walls. He brought soft grasses to make a bed. He found a water supply in the depths of the cave, warm, brackish water, but drinkable. And he brought food, enough for days if he needed it.

The first night he spent in the cavern was . . . profitable. The pterodactyls coming home to roost were easy prey, snatched from the air, their necks broken, and the next morning stacked in the sun to dry. Two nights, and the pterodactyls did not return, but flew to more remote cliffs.

Kong brought lianas into the cavern, tough, thick vines. He found ways to loop these around a strong stalagmite. He could toss these from the eye socket and have a way of descending and ascending.

Then he heard sounds from outside, the shrill trumpet-call of a maddened adult ceratopsian. Kong climbed down the vines and sped along the ridge until he stood on a boulder-strewn ledge, looking down into the crater. He instantly grasped what had happened. The deathrunners had rounded up more juvenile ceratopsians, but this time the mother had been close enough to follow. She had burst into the lair in fury, and now she charged the deathrunners that were nipping at the heels of two of her offspring.

One leaped at her, but a snap of her great beak bit the predator in half. She lowered her head and skewered a second with a brow horn, tossing her head to dislodge it, snorting in anger the whole time. The small deathrunners fell back from her—

And then a deeper, louder challenge split the air. Gaw had come. The triceratops spun, confronting the larger menace.

Another deathrunner sprang at her, but she trampled it and circled warily, lowering her head. Kong noticed the gleam in Gaw's eye as she took a careful step forward. The triceratops charged, bellowing, but Gaw spun away from the horns with surprising ease. The infuriated mother turned at once and lunged, and Kong saw how careful Gaw was to avoid those horns, how menacing they were. He would remember that.

Staccato, hissing chirps echoed from Gaw, and a horde of deathrunners leaped at the triceratops from behind. It grunted and snorted as its massive body and horned head quickly pivoting toward them. Immediately Gaw rushed forward and seized the plant-eater in her powerful front arms. With a roar of effort, Gaw threw the heavy dinosaur on its side, and then struck again and again, viciously snapping her jaws.

Kong growled as he watched Gaw rip open the plant-eater's throat, remembering how his own mother had died. Kong snarled, seized a boulder, and hurled it. It crashed down the face of the ledge and smashed to earth beside Gaw. The startled creature leaped back, its screams echoing throughout the cave. Kong threw another boulder, not at Gaw, but at the pack of deathrunners. The impact killed half a dozen of them. Another boulder rained down on them, then another. Gaw roared in rage. The killers swarmed up the sides of the crater.

Kong had already retreated. He climbed the lianas, then hauled them up after him. The snapping, chittering deathrunners arrived at the mouth of Skull Mountain, only to be greeted by more deadly stones. The harsh, furious voice of Gaw called them away. She stalked the distant crater, lashing her tail, staring up at Kong, secure, safe, beyond her reach. Kong beat his chest and roared a challenge. Gaw answered with an unearthly shriek.

So began a siege and a war. Kong struck when he could, always killing a few death-runners, sometimes even bringing a body home with him for food.

Gaw chose more inaccessible places to sleep for herself and the remaining death-runners, the pack was thinning. Enmity was stoked to a fever pitch.

And in the lonely evenings, Kong found things in the caves, things that reminded him of his father and his mother.

Things that reminded him that he was the last of his kind.

Hatred burned.

Loneliness grew.

The years had not changed the Storyteller. She was strong for all her wrinkles and apparent frailty. Ishara visited her less frequently, but whenever she did, the old woman welcomed her warmly. One evening the Storyteller said, "Come, my queen. Let's sit and talk for a while.

"I'm sick of it all," Ishara told her. "Kublai is making the old Atu mistakes all over again. I can't bring him to see the truth. He is becoming Bar-Atu's puppet."

The Storyteller put her arm warmly around Ishara's shoulder. "We must all choose a great path to walk: either for good or for bad. All the paths in between lead eventually to one of the two, depending on what a heart truly desires."

"Why are we in such trouble? Why has Bar-Atu seized such control of our minds and hearts?"

"Because lies are often easier to follow than the truth. Bar-Atu calls the bad path 'good,' and the good one 'bad' and his lies deceive many, so they follow him. But the great paths go where they will, no matter what name he gives them. You, and Kublai, must not be fooled if you are to save our people." The Storyteller touched her cheek with a calming hand. "Be at peace, Ishara, and do not worry. The learning is in the journey. Listen to your old Storyteller. Have faith and never give up hope. You will find that your eyes will be opened when the time is right. When it seems darkest, the stars shine brightest," she said.

"I want to choose the right path," Ishara said slowly, "and I want Kublai to choose it as well. I wish there were a way to show the people they're being fooled by Bar-Atu's lies."

The Storyteller was staring at her with a strange light in her eyes. "You have the blood of the Tagu Storytellers in you," she said. "Yes, you have that in full measure."

From that day life changed for Ishara. She spent all of her time with the Storyteller. Oji, the Storyteller's pet, became her constant companion and refused even to accept food from the Storyteller. "He is yours now," the Storyteller said. "And he knows that."

There were days when, sitting quietly she felt the same connection with Oji, and other animals, as she did with the sleeks in the sea. Creatures did not seem to have any fear, or react to her as they would to anyone else.

Frightened at first of the sensations, Ishara only slowly told the Storyteller of what she was experiencing. The Storyteller nodded solemnly. "It is in your heritage," she told Ishara. "It is a gift of the spirit, given to the Storytellers."

"Then you have these feelings, too?" Ishara asked.

The Storyteller inclined her head. "Yes, but in a different way. Each Storyteller, it seems, is given a different part of the story. Little by little we add what we learn, and we pass it on to others. One day our people may know the whole story," she added with a smile.

Thinking about this, Ishara gazed down from the Storyteller's hut. From here she could see both sides of the island. She felt her skin prickle strangely as she suddenly realized something: if she could climb higher, higher even than the Wall that had arisen between her and Kublai, she could see, she could understand both sides. Then she would know clearly what she must do. Ishara gasped and heard the Storyteller murmur, "Yes. I know. You want the best for our people. Kublai wants to be a strong king."

Ishara swallowed, feeling her throat tighten. Her mind raced as she blurted out, "But what can I do to help him? I know now he needs me more than ever, and I should be there beside him!"

With a slight smile, the Storyteller said, "You give me hope, Ishara. You have taken a larger step than you know. I cannot guide you to where you must go, but I can tell you this: your gifts are given you to discover answers to the problems of the island and to your own troubles."

"I don't know how," Ishara said.

"You will. Understand that Kublai must find his own path without your gifts of perception. If you lead him, you will take what he needs away from him. With Bar-Atu and his followers ever present, Kublai must now use the gifts he has been given to accomplish the tasks before him. You each have a part to play. And then there is the stranger, Magwich. On whose side does he stand, other than his own? You must watch him and decide that."

"It is a heavy burden," Ishara said meekly.

"I know it is, and you are the only one who will listen to a mad old woman like me. We have very little time to act, and we may have only one chance. We must succeed."

The Storyteller gently caressed Ishara's face. "Listen to me: Bar-Atu and his men are about to usurp the power of the King. Kublai is with them. Unless you help him, he will not survive."

"How do you know this?"

"I am old, but not blind. I see more from my perch atop the Wall than Bar-Atu ever suspects."

Ishara sprang to her feet. "But Kublai will not even talk to me!"

"He still loves you very much," the Storyteller said. "But his heart has been wounded by pride and misunderstanding."

Ishara felt as if her own heart was being torn in two. "How can Kublai's way give us hope? He follows the old Atu path, and you know where that will lead!"

"Life is not always so simple. There is more than one way to tame a beast. At times you must give before you can receive, and answers may be found in the most unexpected places. There are bonds I can feel between the two of us, and between you and Kublai. Nothing can be solved when we build walls between ourselves and others. There is one Wall on this island, and that is enough."

Ishara felt weary. She leaned against the Storyteller. "I will try to understand and to find the way. How must I begin?"

"Your hope is to find the secret places in the Old City, the vaults where the ancients stored seeds, formulas, and knowledge. If this knowledge is properly used, fear of the creatures beyond the Wall can be conquered and our people can once again become their own masters. This can rekindle their hope by offering them a choice other than Bar-Atu's cult of blood and death. If our people can master the beasts of the island with knowledge, then Kublai may expose Bar-Atu's lies and restore a proper balance to the island. You must go with them, Ishara, and search for the secrets of our ancestors while they search for treasure."

Ishara felt fear and confusion, but she fought to master the feelings. Dimly she began to realize that the Storyteller was right, that her destiny and Kublai's might work out in a way she could not now even suspect. In the midst of evil and darkness, light could find a way to shine through.

A brilliant day came, with only a few lazy white clouds, a day of heat and promise, and the hunt was to take place on the next morning. As the day passed, Ishara was restless until sunset, when she found Charlie and asked him about the hunt, though he couldn't tell her much. "I'm no great hand with a rifle," he said. "And our ammunition is beginning to run low. Captain Magwich takes only the best shots." He shrugged. "I'm glad *I'm* not going. I think they're crazy! The villagers who stay away from those monsters, they're the smart ones."

"Where are they going?" Ishara demanded.

"I don't know," Charlie said, looking miserable. "Into the jungle, that's all."

Ishara could not control the beating of her heart. "Charlie, I need your help. Because I *am* going."

They had been sitting on a rocky outcrop, staring out over the western sea, toward the sunset. Charlie sprang up, his eyes wild in the fading light. "Are you cracked? Besides, he'll never let you. It's too dangerous." He rubbed his arm, as if he were cold, and growled, "They're dangerous."

Ishara stood. "Still, I will go. Kublai needs my help, and my heart tells me this is the final hope of our people, our last chance. I need you to go with me, Charlie."

Fear flashed in his eyes. "Your people, not mine. Look, I'd like to help, but—listen, Bar-Atu don't know it, but your Kublai, he's out to kill Gaw. I've seen that thing close up. I don't think any of the men are likely to come back. Ishara, I like you, but I spent years in shackles, praying for rescue. I don't want to get gobbled up by monsters. I never wanted to join Magwich's crew, but it was that, death, or slavery, and at least sailing with Magwich was a kind of freedom. But to go up against Gaw—what good's freedom to a dead man?"

Ishara swallowed hard. "Then I will go alone. You can still help me if you will. Stay here and watch after the Storyteller. Now she is the only one standing between Bar-Atu's lies and the souls of our people, and you're the only one I can trust to protect her." Ishara saw relief flood Charlie's face, and taking that as her answer, she turned on her heel and walked away.

"Wait—how can you survive out there alone?" Charlie called after her. She pretended not to hear.

And before dawn the next day, Ishara left the Storyteller's hut, a soft leather bag of the precious herbs tied around her waist. As she set out, she was aware of the irony of her plan: Her journey would begin in the dark. She did her best to put all doubt out of her mind and to proceed with the conviction of one who had already succeeded. She followed the Wall to its end, intending to creep around it and wait on the far side. Then she planned to follow the men at a distance.

Dawn had just broken when she heard a footstep behind her. Giving no sign, Ishara continued on her way, but when she reached a thicket of brush, she quietly stepped aside. A moment later, a thin figure crept past. Ishara touched his shoulder and felt the man start in surprise. "Charlie?"

"I didn't want you to go alone," he said miserably.

"I asked you to look after the Storyteller."

Charlie grunted. "Yeah, well, she don't need any help. I went to talk to her, but she waved me off. 'You know where you have to go,' she says, and I did, by thunder. I didn't want to, but I knew." He grimaced. "Or maybe she didn't say it at all. The voice was more in my head, like, and I somehow knew which way you had gone, and I trotted right along after you, and here I am. That's a strange old lady, Ishara. She gave me this." He held out a leather pouch, like the one Ishara wore.

She didn't tell him of its power over the beasts of the jungle. "You said it was crazy to go into the jungle."

"I know," Charlie admitted. "I still think it is, and I guess I must be crazy myself. If I end up dying out there, I'm gonna be so mad I'll probably kill myself."

Ishara gaped at him, until she realized that Charlie had just tried to tell a joke. She smiled at him. "All right. If I die, you can kill me, too. Let's go."

"I got a pistol," Charlie said. "Six shots, that's all I have. I hope you know where we're going." He shivered, though the morning was already hot. "I'm scared to death already. But it'd be worse if something happened to you because I was a coward. I'll follow you."

"You're not a coward," Ishara said, and she led the way to the end of the Wall. She worried about whether Charlie would be able to make the climb down the cliff face, across, and up again, but he was a sailor and was agile enough. Being on the far side of the Wall made him nervous, though. In the pale light of dawn, his eyes jerked at every sound.

Ishara stood for a moment with eyes closed. She could feel the clean air laden with morning dew. She heard the chirps of early insects and from everywhere the sounds and singing of the flying things. "There are no dangerous animals near," she said. "They may have learned to stay away from the Wall now."

"I hope they learned good and proper," was Charlie's response.

Before long the Gate opened just wide enough to let the hunters through two at a time. Ishara and Charlie crouched in the undergrowth. Ishara counted silently. Ten island warriors. Twelve armed sailors. And leading them, Kublai and Magwich. As the hunting party strode past, Ishara wondered why the men all carried slings, like bags with loops. It couldn't be for the meat. They always butchered the animals they killed and bore the meat home on spits made from saplings.

But she had little time to wonder. The hunters trotted on in a tireless, long-legged stride, not exactly a run but faster than a walk. They moved with purpose.

As she and Charlie followed, Ishara became aware that previous hunts had left blazed trails through the forest. The hunters knew where they were going and headed there with silent certainty.

The sun climbed higher, sending slanting rays of light through the forest canopy. The men startled small creatures, Ojis and agile little insect-eating saurians, no bigger than one of the European chickens. The hunters ignored these. From time to time, Ishara paused, but she could sense no large animals anywhere near. Charlie did not want to take her word for it. He had the hunted look of a man who was beginning to doubt his decision.

Before noon their path led them out of the deep forest and onto a ridge that snaked toward a distant mountain. Ishara and Charlie dropped farther behind the others, and then realization came to Ishara. With reverence in her voice, she said softly, "The Old City. That's where they're heading."

"I thought the Old City was just a legend of your people." Charlie asked her, swatting at a stinging fly on his neck. "Are you saying it's real?"

Ishara did not answer, though she felt her brow furrow with concern. Why would Kublai take the hunters there? If they were after meat, better game could be found along the streams. What did they hope to kill there?

But the certainty of her own quest cut into her consciousness like a blade. "Come," she said to Charlie. "We have to move quickly."

They left the ridge and plunged back into the forest. After a few moments, Charlie whispered sharply, "Have you ever been this way before?"

"Once."

"How do you know where we're going? There's no trails!"

"I know the way."

"I hope you do."

Ishara knew how anxious Charlie had to be. The jungle had become denser, and they crept along a winding, tortuous way, finding passage through undergrowth, among the boles of ancient trees. She found a stream and they followed its course. They skirted pools where the only danger was from crocodilians, but these were sunning themselves on the far side and paid the passing humans no attention. "Look at that one," Charlie said. "Thirty foot if it's an inch!"

"Only a crocodile," Ishara said.

"Yeah, well, I never thought I'd be relieved to hear that," Charlie grumbled as they hurried past the sunning giant.

They found a place to sleep, and they passed an uneasy night, with Charlie restless on a lower branch of a great tree and Ishara on a hunter's platform above him. Charlie asked, "What's that?" five or six times, but the noises he heard were always wind, water, the faraway cry of a harmless night animal.

They started again before daybreak, and at last they emerged on the very path that Ishara and Kublai had followed on their first visit. This time there were no slashers to be seen, and they had reached the path ahead of the hunters. They passed the outpost from which Ishara and Kublai had watched the death of Kong's parents, then followed an invisible trail toward the distant green hill of the Citadel. They spent another anxious night in a tree and got another early start. Not long after sunrise, they came to a great clearing. Standing in the open, Ishara looked skyward. With a flutter that made Charlie jump, Oji circled down and landed on her shoulder, making an inquiring, purring sound in his throat. "Scared me," Charlie said.

"Oji is guiding us," Ishara told him. "He would warn us if danger came near. We have reached the city."

"This is a city?" Charlie asked, staring about him. Ishara realized how alien it must look to his eyes—buildings that seemed outgrowths of soil and tree, structures that fooled the eye because they did not have the look of built things.

"It's our Old City," Ishara answered. Suddenly they heard the hunters approaching, and coming closer at every step. Oji leaped into the air and vanished into a dark opening. "Follow him. Come on, Charlie. In here."

They climbed through what probably had been a window many years before. Charlie had a hard scramble of it. "If that thing's our guide, tell it to remember that we can't fly!"

This was a place made of living trees, their growth somehow controlled and managed so that even after hundreds, perhaps thousands of years, the structure held its shape still. Ishara found a kind of spiral ramp that led upward, and she and Charlie climbed until they emerged in a single room with many windows, high above most of the City. From one window, Ishara looked back toward the ridge. She could see the hunting party, now coming on at a trot. Charlie craned to see past her.

Something felt very wrong. Ishara sensed danger, not to herself, but to Kublai—but not danger from any animal. What was about to happen? She could not say, but the air was as tense as it was before a thunderstorm.

Suddenly Oji squirmed and scratched at a leather pouch tied around his neck. He chattered something that sounded like the island word for "fear."

Charlie stared at the agitated creature and asked, "Can't you make that thing be quiet? I don't know why we followed a bird, anyway!"

Oji began to peck at the solid stone wall.

"Stop that!" Charlie hissed.

Oji stared at him and in Charlie's own voice chided, "Can't you make that thing be quiet?"

Charlie looked as if he were caught between anger and laughter. "I'll be a—wait, what's he pecking at? Look at this!" He leaned forward, his finger tracing a fissure in the wall beside the window, a crack that did not look accidental.

"I don't know," Ishara said impatiently, sparing it a look.

"It's loose." Charlie could just hook a finger inside the crevice. He pulled, and a section of the wall opened as if on hinges. "It's another room!"

Not a large one—not even the size of a midshipman's berth, as Charlie put it. It was a space where Ishara might have had room to crouch, but not enough to stretch out. And filling it were stoneware containers, straight-sided jars with lids. Ishara took one and found that the lid lifted off easily. Inside the first one was a dark mass of seeds, withered but sending forth a haunting scent. Another held a fine yellow powder, perhaps the spores of some fungus, and another had more seeds, broad and brown. "Oji!" When Oji fluttered to her, Ishara untied the thong that held the pouch around his neck and emptied it into her cupped hand. Her eyes widened.

"What is it?" Charlie asked, craning to see. "You got an expression like Captain Magwich opening a chest o' gold!"

After a moment of silence, Ishara spoke in a whisper: "Not gold, but better than gold. Worth all the gold you could imagine." The contents of Oji's pouch were an exact match for the contents of the jars. "My ancestors used these," Ishara said slowly. "With them Kublai and I could—"

Voices cut her thoughts short. Charlie was staring out the window. She joined him and looked down. Some distance away, the hunting party had paused before a dome-like building. Magwich was shouting orders, and the men were busy with knives, chopping into the surface of the dome.

"What are they doing?" Ishara asked.

One of the sailors struck a match, one of their precious, hoarded supply. "Get down!" Charlie said, tugging at her.

The sailor touched the match to a trail of powder, then scrambled away. Ishara opened her mouth a moment before the blast came, ripping an opening in the ancient structure. "No!" she shouted, her voice lost in the thunder of the explosion. "No! They can't!" She turned and ran for the passage down, with Charlie following close behind.

She threaded her way among the ancient structures. She paused as she came in sight of the dome. A hole, still smoldering, gaped in its side, and from the hole one of the sailors climbed, holding aloft two glinting objects. "Chiefie was right!" the man yelled. "Gold statues! Dozens of 'em!"

"Haul them out," Magwich said.

From this distance, Ishara could see only that the little statuettes were vaguely man-shaped. No, bulkier—statues of kongs, perhaps? Or of a dinosaur?

"You'll remember your promise," Ishara heard Kublai say.

"Of course," Magwich told him. "You see what that blast did to the building. Something like that could easily stop your Gaw. But powder's not so easy to come by here on this blessed island. Such gold as you say we'll find here should just about pay for it."

"They must not do this," Ishara whispered to Charlie.

Charlie put a hand on her shoulder. "Stay put. I've seen the captain when he's after gold. He'll kill anyone as gets in his way."

"You don't know what's in these buildings! It's the last chance of life for my people! We've got to stop them!"

Charlie patted her shoulder. "Lay low." To her surprise, Charlie stepped around her and strode toward the hunters. Magwich saw him before Kublai did. "What are you doing here?" he demanded. "You're no sharpshooter!"

"You can't do this," Charlie said. "Look, this stuff don't belong to you, Captain."

Magwich looked stunned, but then he threw back his head and laughed, a rich, deep laugh. He held a rifle butt-down on the ground, leaning easily on it, both hands on the barrel. "It does now. Kublai here is chief of the whole island, and he says it's ours. Don't you, Kublai?"

"As payment for killing Gaw," Kublai answered.

Charlie turned to Kublai as if he were going to speak, but before he could open his mouth, Magwich whirled the rifle up and clubbed him. Kublai cried out in shock. Charlie went sprawling, his limbs limp, clearly unconscious before he hit the ground. Magwich said, "Same way you tried to train Kong, Kublai. That's how I train my men." Ishara gasped at the change in his eyes, usually full of humor and easy-going authority. Now they glinted in the waning sunlight like polished steel.

They still hadn't noticed Ishara. She backed away, turned, and heard some of the men coming toward her. One of the tree-like dwellings had a low, arched opening. She dropped to her hands and knees and scrambled through. Through the opening she could see legs and feet, both bare and shod. "What was that?" asked one of the sailors. "Look in there. Something went right through there."

Ishara backed away. Then the floor ran out, and she stepped off into space. For what seemed like an age she fell, before landing hard, on her back, in the dark.

CHAPTER TWELVE

SKULL ISLAND
June ?, 1957

Jack Driscoll couldn't shake the feeling that he was being followed. Yet nothing showed itself, and he heard nothing. He knew he was still heading toward the wall, though in the dense forest he could see nothing of it. Then the trees began to thin out, and the underbrush grew higher and denser.

Something shrieked off to his left. Driscoll stopped, backed against a tree, and stared through the green gloom. Nothing.

An answering shriek from straight ahead, then a high-pitched twittering. More sounds from the middle distance. Driscoll frowned. What was making the noise—and how many of the things were there? He could climb a tree, maybe, if he could find one with a low enough branch to give him a foothold. The one he leaned against gave no hope of that. It went straight up, branchless, until a hundred feet up it spread its canopy.

The sounds came closer, and Driscoll retreated, moving not straight back along his track but at a diagonal to the path he had followed. Why couldn't he see the creatures making the noises? They sounded near enough.

Then other twittering voices came from behind him, and he felt surrounded. Light off to one side, an opening, a clearing in the forest. That would give him a better field of vision, anyway. Driscoll made for it, stepped into a startlingly bright pool of sunshine. Knee-high brush was at work reclaiming the open space, a spot left clear when a forest giant had toppled some years before, taking other trees with it.

A breeze made the greenery sway gently. Gripping his rifle, Driscoll squinted, sweat stinging his eyes. What in the—? Something was subtly *wrong* about one brushy plant, at least as tall as he was. It looked different, odd, its movements not quite what they should be. Was something lurking behind it?

Then he saw the two gleams of eyes, nearly at a level with his own. And he felt chilled.

The creature was in front of the brush, not behind it. Its thin body bore feathers, downy feathers that perfectly mimicked the leaves behind it in color and texture, and it swayed as the wind gusted, keeping almost a perfect rhythm. But not quite.

Driscoll heard the rush off to his right. He spun, saw the charging dinosaur, one just like the one standing in wait, and he fired. He missed, but the creature sheared off. Driscoll scrambled back, wondering how many there were, how—

He fell.

Desperately, Driscoll snagged a vine with his left arm. He smacked into the side of a pit, one he had not seen because of the undergrowth. A few straggly bushes grew from its sides, and he came to rest in the branches of one of these, his rifle falling from his reach.

He heard a hissing above him. One, two, three predatory heads, and they chittered to each other. They could not reach him.

Below him, Driscoll saw a scatter of bones. "They herded me," he said. "Herded me like a goat to the slaughter!"

The far side of the drop was not as steep. Already one of the creatures had dashed around and was descending, hopping like a gigantic bird, tilting its head to keep Driscoll in focus. The other two chittered, and it answered.

Driscoll had the uneasy feeling they were *talking*. The one below him circled, looking up. He was in the middle, twenty feet below the ones on the rim of the drop, twenty feet above the one on the floor. He could see now that many of the bones scattered below were human.

The creatures were smart enough to hunt in packs. Smart enough to find places that served as natural man-traps. Smart enough to lure or chase their prey into the trap.

Jack Driscoll felt a chill work its way down his spine. A quarter of a century ago, his shipmates had been chased and killed by enormous monsters. These feathered predators, though, were smaller, about man-sized—and fiercely intelligent, if he was any judge.

"Can't I get a break?" he whispered to himself, or perhaps to Fate. "I've paid my dues. Can't I even have a chance to enjoy my old age?" He chuckled ruefully. "Can't I have a chance to *get* to my old age?" He closed his eyes and tried to imagine what Ann was doing right now.

Self-pity rose in him, and instinctively he fought back. He opened his eyes and slowly unholstered his Colt. The two heads above him ducked back right away.

But the one below him had nowhere to hide. The automatic roared, and a bullet smashed right between the creature's eyes, sending it spinning. It fell, tried to rise, and sprawled dead. From overhead came an angry burst of that twittering cry. Driscoll ignored his emotions, concentrating on his physical sensations. Sweat stung his eyes. His legs and back ached. The branches of the brush scratched him. "I survived once. I can survive again," he said out loud. Then a wry smile twitched his lips. "Then again, I didn't always talk to myself."

There seemed to be only one path that the predators could take down. Keeping his eye on it, Driscoll climbed down himself, noticing that this depression, like the other one, looked more man-made than natural. Across from him, Driscoll could glimpse the nearly-buried tops of three arched doorways leading into darkness. He grunted, wondering whether he had the nerve to trek underground again, heading perhaps to another dead end, with those horrors behind him.

No choice, really. Driscoll retrieved his rifle, then had to duck low to enter the first of the three tunnels. Its floor was a good five feet below that of the hollow. He lit a torch, and followed a narrow path of stairs to a high arched opening. As soon as he entered, a vast space to his left began to shimmer with light in slowly expanding waves. Before he could think, his rifle was at ready and he had flattened his back against the side of the cave. Then he realized that the light was coming from no human source. He took a deep breath. Well, at least his reflexes weren't bad for an old guy. He looked nervously back down the passageway. If the two creatures were following him, they were doing so silently.

As the shock wore off, he observed that the pictures were somewhat sharper than the ones he had seen earlier. He realized he had stumbled upon a scene of the Wall being constructed. Something, a kong it looked like, was hauling an enormous timber up a long slope. A barrier was being erected that cut the peninsula off from the rest of the island.

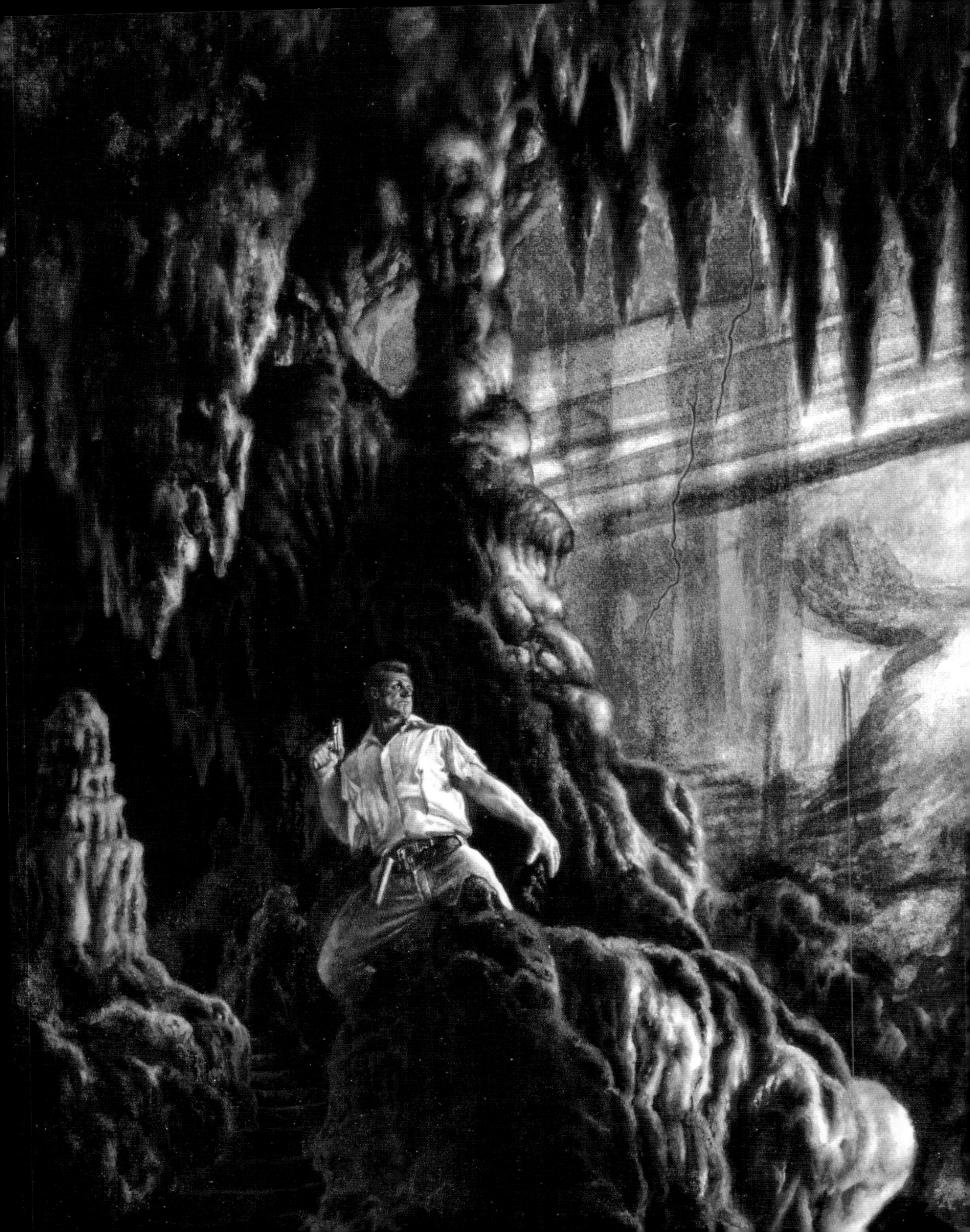

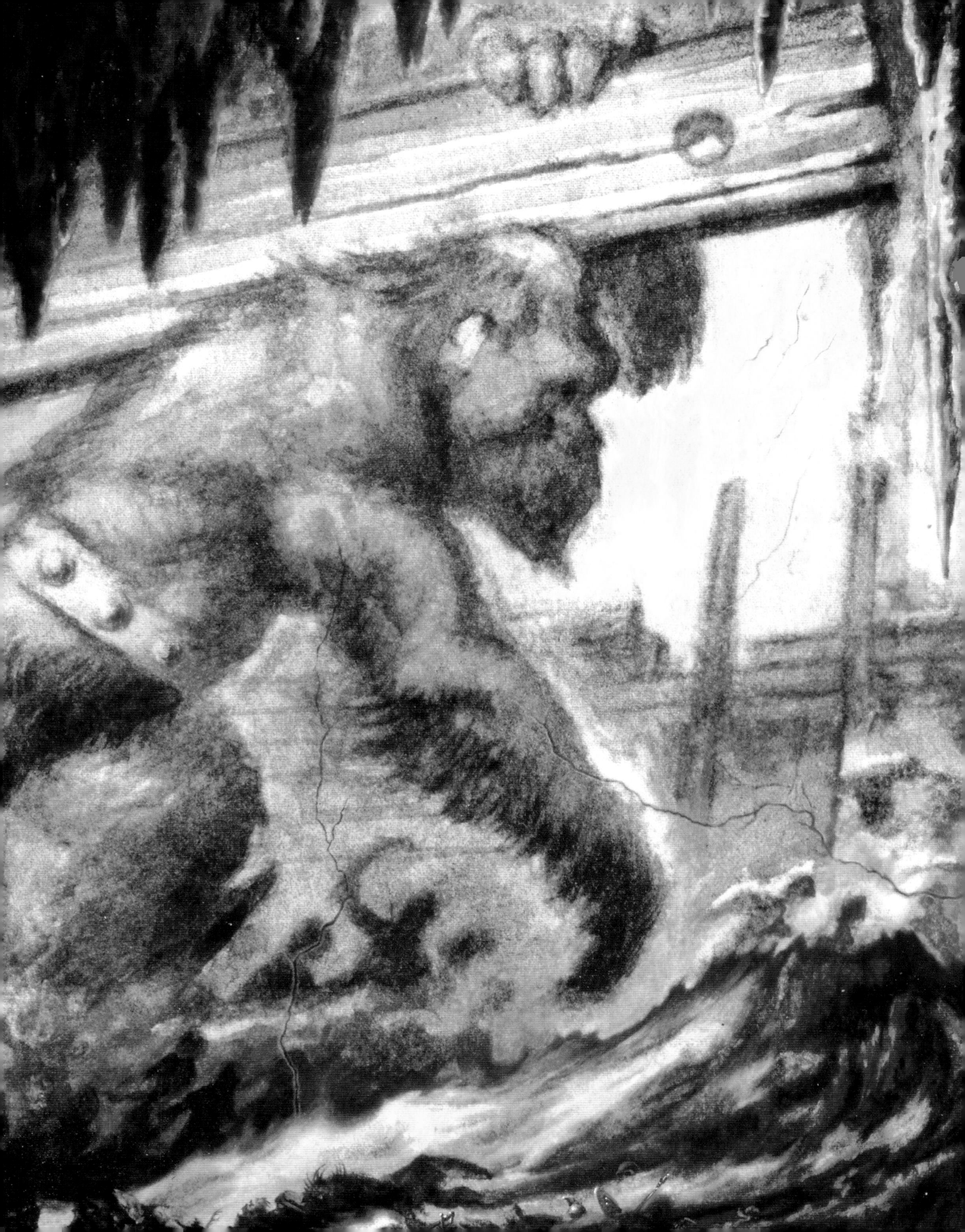

And then it dawned on him: could that have been why the doors were there? Not to keep kong out, but in the distant past, to let them *in*? He had always assumed the doors were necessary to haul in a dead dinosaur, or trap one—a carcass like that could feed the village for months. Other panels across the way showed enormous, half-demolished ships of extraordinary size and something he could not make out: men fighting with each other, or were they man-sized dinosaurs? Something of extreme horror was taking place, but virtually all the images were obscured with unusual markings and scratches. In the hardened mud floor Driscoll saw two-toed footprints all around. In one place he found a broken claw embedded in the solid stone of the wall. Piles of what looked like petrified excrement desecrated what was obviously some sort of memorial. The hairs on the nape of Jack's neck stood on end and chills rippled through his body. He thought of the pile of human bones he had just seen, but refused to make the obvious connection. It was too grotesque to accept and he moved quickly past it, praying the events that took place around him were old. Very, very, old.

Again, as before, the images slowly moved across the great plane of the cave wall. How in blazes had the ancient people of the island accomplished this? The walls were covered with mosaics of minute glowing dots, forming patterns that seemed to move, or flow, across them. There was nothing electronic involved that he could see—not that there could have been—and the cave wall was solid rock. Everything seemed to respond to light alone. Driscoll marveled at the ingenuity. How could savages have built such a civilization—or had he misjudged the people of the island?

A passage turned northward, toward the heart of the island, so he retreated. The central tunnel seemed to lead more or less toward the native village. There the wall illustrations were different. There was no hint of a peninsula, let alone one with a wall across it. These portrayed some sort of structures in what looked like a city, if you could call it that. It was unlike anything he had ever seen, and in his day he had seen a lot.

"This place may be even bigger than Angkor," he thought, recalling the massive Cambodian temple complex, and instantly he remembered something he said to Ann all those years ago when describing the Wall on the peninsula for the first time: "I went up to Angkor once. That's bigger than this. . ."

Could the same people who built the Wall have built this city? Or did some super race live separately from the primitive tribe behind the wall?

He followed the tunnel until he arrived at a low opening. He wormed through it to discover he had gone in a circle. He was again in the vast amphitheater. Looking at it more closely, Driscoll realized that the architecture required to build such a structure was far more advanced than he had thought, and he realized, too, how truly extensive the network of tunnels had to be.

Looking again at the bas-relief on the north wall of the enclosure, he could tell that it represented a war—but what men were fighting, and who, or what, had they fought?

Gigantic ape-like creatures were involved. Kongs? His mind reeled: what would this island be like with more than one of those brutes running amok? The smaller images were vague and eroded—were they people or some sort of bizarre saurian the size of a human? And then he wondered, were even the kongs at risk from something on this island—was there no end to the dangers here? Driscoll imagined that the battles had taken place a thousand years ago, perhaps more. He could not tell from what was exposed and he was not about to dig around and find out more. Leave that to the archaeologists, he told himself—or the art critics.

Driscoll walked a few hundred yards before he came to more, but badly decayed images of something burning in huge pots of some sort. In the foreground were figures—people, he saw—doing whatever they did with gigantic dinosaurs grazing only yards away. Were they pets, or had the humans tamed them or controlled them somehow?

The passage ended in collapsed rubble. Driscoll retraced his steps. The last of the three passages seemed to parallel the one he had left. Its pictures were much cruder, though the colors and lines were brighter, sharper. Hunters brandished spearlike weapons, but more lethal looking, enhanced in some way that he could not clearly define. With these, the hunters felled gigantic saurians. Groups of others turned their backs on the hunters (or soldiers?), while many of the armed figures were pointing their weapons. Following the glowing mosaic, Jack saw that the figures all moved toward a huge wall at the jungle's edge, a wall Driscoll recognized. The stream of humans looked desperate, the unarmed ones carrying jars that looked heavy, filled with something that did not show in the pictures. And the expressions on the faces were anguished, like those on the faces of refugees Driscoll had seen during the world war.

"Okay," grunted Driscoll, trying to make sense of it all. Something caused a war, he thought, and the losers got kicked out. Behind the wall must've been the only safe place, but who went there? Criminals? Made sense, he decided—the city-dwellers had the higher civilization. Maybe they sent all the scum to live behind the barrier. The walled-off peninsula might have been a prison.

Jack remembered how those creeps captured Ann and offered her as a human sacrifice to Kong. Staring at the procession pictured on the wall, Jack found himself hoping that half of them had been eaten before making it to the wall. The island was no different from anywhere else: Every society had its bad apples. While most people went about their lives working and minding their own business, some few thirsted for power or revenge, and they led everyone into war. Driscoll grunted in puzzlement. Maybe the city-dwellers had been too tender-hearted to kill the ones they drove out, but what happened then?

Why would those savages behind the wall still be around while the powerful and advanced civilization that built the city was destroyed? Had it been some kind of plague? The city was in the middle of nowhere—how did it get built? Something went wrong and the dinosaurs ate all the civilized humans? There was no way of knowing.

Driscoll had always held a sneaking fascination with the mysterious cultures he had encountered on his travels. Something in him mourned the loss of those who had built and lived in this now-dead city. And he shivered at the thought that Vincent was now in the hands of the outcasts who survived. God only knew what they could be doing to him. Jack set his jaw. All he could do was try to reach the Wall as fast as possible.

"The keepers of the old ways were the Tagu," the Storyteller said to Vincent. "My people, my ancestors."

"I don't understand," Vincent complained. "Were there always two clans?"

"That is difficult to answer. In the remote days, when our first ancestors sailed here across the ocean in great ships, we were all one people, and all followed the Rules that bound us together. However, even before that they occupied a corner of the world that no longer exists. They may have been of two minds in their own ancient history before they came here. Our oldest stories tell of a great war won by the Tagu that forced them both to become one, the Tagatu. From that war came the Rules, which were to be observed by all equally under the guidance of the Storytellers, whose ancient line was finally acknowledged by all.

"It was as a united people, the Tagatu, that they came to the islands. They brought the ancestors of King Kong with them. They left a dying land torn with fiery mountains and cracking earth to seek a refuge. They found this island, and they found another terrible war, but not among themselves."

Vincent frowned. "With whom? Were others already living on the island?"

The Storyteller's expression was grim. "Others. Yes, that is a good name for them! Tagatu search parties landed here many times before they felt it was safe for all to follow. They spent years developing the scents which could control the great creatures that dwelt here and make their landing safe. It never occurred to them that there were others on this island that did not want to be found!"

Vincent shifted on the side of the bed and felt a shudder shoot through his spine. "The others were not—people, were they?"

"Not people, no." The Storyteller continued: "I call them others because even though they were not human, they were more than animal. They came to be called 'deathrunners.' My ancestors had been on the island for months before the deathrunners began to strike. The provisions from the long journey had long been exhausted, and the ships had been scavenged for building materials and were no longer seaworthy. There was no escape. They destroyed their great ships, using the timbers to build a barrier to protect their settlement."

"The Wall."

"It became the Wall. This was only possible under the protection of the kongs, huge creatures of great strength and great intelligence, trained by a select few of the Tagu. They were indomitable even in the face of death. In time the Tagatu refined their sciences to a point where they were able to better control the island's creatures. Eventually they became the absolute masters of all things that lived here."

"But this was before Ishara's time," Vincent said, trying to work out the history of the island in his own mind.

"Many, many generations before." The Storyteller sat watching Vincent. He was well enough to sit on the edge of the bed now, though he felt miserably weak. The old woman said, "And after that, the Tagu and the Atu together built the Old City, the ruins of which Ishara discovered, as I have told you. For a long time, for many lives of men, the two sides prospered, though their disagreements became more and more heated."

"The Tagatu somehow kept the dinosaurs from destroying the city they built as well," Vincent said slowly. "But how?"

"With the secrets of the plants. Even so, they were never able to completely control the deathrunners, whose minds, being far more advanced than other beasts, were less susceptible to their compounds. Deathrunners adjusted to them quickly, and the mixtures had to be changed constantly. The Tagatu scientists in that area were mostly of Tagu heritage. They had knowledge that they did not always share with the Atu, partly because Atu scientists thought it beneath them, partly because the Atu were not trusted.

They held themselves apart, developed their own traditions. The Atu in time became the chief warriors, and they were necessary. No one knew when the deathrunners would strike, and only the Atu could hold them off. The Atu became arrogant in time, too trusting of their own strength."

The Storyteller spoke of how this arrogance led to trouble. The Tagatu as a whole had gained a hard-won but gratifying stalemate with the island's saurian inhabitants. Over time the Tagatu built incredibly intricate subterranean passageways and studied their world and its inhabitants in great detail. They began, over many years, to gain a sense and balance of their new world that rivaled their understanding of their old world. But certain Atu, descendants of the leaders of that warrior clan, eventually convinced all the Atu to pull more and more apart from the rest.

Throughout it all, the Tagu maintained their observance of the Rules. They revered the Storytellers and their traditions, whose collective wisdom was proven through generations and believed to be a reflection of God. Descendants of the Atu questioned the need to worship anything, feeling they were supreme. Theirs was a philosophy of self. Many extraordinary thinkers rose in their line, but almost without fail they ridiculed the Storytellers for their supposed superstition and sentimentality. The Storyteller sighed and said, "The Atu thought they ruled their world, but it was their passions that ruled and their pride that ruled them. This proved their undoing."

Vincent was leaning forward, trying to follow the thread of this ancient history. "How?"

"My Storyteller ancestors were ridiculed for not focusing what they taught on the natural world. But Storytellers were not as concerned with the secrets of nature as they were with the nature of people. Theirs was the science of the unseen, the study of the movement of the soul. This they knew better than the Atu knew the island. They predicted the result of Atu ways as surely as knowing that a spear, even when thrown by the strongest warrior, will eventually fall to the ground."

Vincent took a deep breath, wondering whether his own philosophy, his own study, was that different from what the Atu had followed. "I don't understand," he said.

The Storyteller patted his hand. "Be at peace, Vincent. Let me continue with my story and you will find out more.

"It was said by some that fanatical Atus still bitterly resented their defeat at the hands of the Tagu centuries before they came to the island. These Atu, no longer believing in the need for Tagu sciences, sabotoged the carefully prepared Tagu seed mixtures. They deliberately opened the way for hordes of deathrunners to attack to show the Atu's strength by fending off the attacks with their own weapons when the Tagu ways seemed to have failed. As time would tell, they were overconfident in their ability to control the chaos that ensued."

The Atu, the Storyteller explained, emerged with power.

They abandoned the Rules and sought to split the people into the two original clans, the Tagu and the Atu. Then the Atu warriors started a campaign to hunt the deathrunners to extinction.

Sadly, many Tagu no longer believed in their leaders and, fearing for their safety, were won over by the Atu lies. The remaining Tagu, their numbers diminished, were in the end too few to fight back. Sensing the inevitable and fearing for their lives, Storytellers led the faithful Tagu on an exodus back to the Wall.

"But Atu dominance didn't last," Vincent said. "You say that by Ishara's time, all the Tagu people were on the safe side of the Wall."

The Storyteller inclined her head. "Yes. In time, the Atu who lived beyond the Wall gradually became arrogant and self-indulgent. This led to a neglect of correct planting of the seeds and an ignorance of the correct formulas and to improper use of other resources as well. The kongs became wild beasts, not servants. The Tagu fell into decadence and fought amongst themselves whenever their comforts were disturbed."

Vincent shook his head. "How could such an advanced people make so many mistakes? Couldn't they see what they were doing?"

The Storyteller's smile was knowing. "You consider yourself an 'educated' man, Vincent, do you not? But would you not agree that the most important learning is not in the head but in the heart?"

Before Vincent could respond, the Storyteller raised her hand, silencing him. "My story is not finished.

"The Tagatu had become a great tree whose branches spread high and wide above the ground. High up in those branches the Atu culture flowered. The multitude of their achievements blocked the view beneath them, and their pride deceived them into thinking their flower needed no support from the tree below. When they banished the Tagu, they were cutting into the trunk of that tree. The Atu refused to acknowledge that their survival depended on combining their abilities with the Tagu. In turning on them, the Atu destroyed much of their own strength. Before another full generation had passed, the Atu found that they were no match for the animals of the island."

The kongs had long since been set free on the far mountain and had become completely wild. They were no longer there to shield the people from the giant saurians, which did serious damage. But on occasion the giants could be controlled or killed and their carcasses used for food and other materials. A far worse problem were the death-runners. They were cunning, able to solve problems. And they favored the taste of human flesh. They could communicate, and they learned how to set traps. When the Tagatu first landed, the deathrunners decimated the populace one, ten, fifty at a time. For mysterious reasons, at certain times some of the strongest never stopped growing. Eventually one would prove smartest and strongest by killing its rivals and become leader of all. It was believed this super-deathrunner was their queen, necessary for the continuation of their species.

Gaw was the worst of these malevolent monsters. She could direct the others in attacks, and men were no match for their teeth and their claws. After many long years of battle, the Atu dwindled in numbers and power. In one final overwhelming attack, the death-runners obliterated any final pretense of civilization the Atu had. The lucky survivors who made it back to the Wall, Bar-Atu's ancestors among them, had to beg the Tagu for shelter. The Storyteller's gaze had become distant, as if she were looking into the past. She said softly, "This final humiliation was never forgotten by the Atu."

"What happened to Ishara?" Vincent asked.

"She fell into darkness," replied the Storyteller, her old eyes focused on something far away.

~⋈~

SKULL ISLAND
The Past

Ishara came back to consciousness slowly. Her body ached with a deep, burning pain. She rolled to her side and retched, dizzy and sick. A dim shaft of light, dancing with dust motes, slanted down from overhead. When at last she felt able, Ishara rose to her feet, trembling and dazed. She listened, but heard no sound from above.

Why had Kublai led Magwich and his men to the Old City? Why was Kublai letting them destroy the gifts that her ancestors had left for her and her people? Once again Ishara's resentment flared. She had to remind herself that Kublai did not have her gifts, nor did he know what the Storyteller had told her. She forced herself to be patient. Her mind raced as she considered what to do next.

She now knew where the seeds were, but that was not enough. Where were the formulas? She froze. What seemed like a far-off flutter suddenly grew louder as dust and debris fell all around her. She shielded her eyes as she ducked into a shadow just as she heard a familiar voice: "Ishara!"

Ishara winced. "Oji! Here. Not so loud!"

The creature hopped across the dusty leaf-strewn floor to Ishara. Around its neck still hung the small pouch containing the seeds and extracts the Storyteller had put there before sending him after Ishara. Ishara was so relieved she picked up her feathered friend and kissed him.

"I found a store of seeds," Ishara murmured to Oji. But, she wondered, did they hold the spark of life after so many years? If they were planted, would they grow? And then how were they to be combined? There was so much to know, and so little hope.

Taking deep breaths, Ishara peered upward. The walls were sheer, the opening through which she had fallen far above her head. There was no way to climb. With her muscles clenching in pain, she limped into the darkness, her right hand on the stone wall. Beneath her feet was a cool stone floor, dry and covered with a deep drift of soft, yielding dust. She could only hope that the passage would find its way back to the surface. At worst, she could turn around, put her other hand on the wall, and trace her way back here. Oji pranced, hopped, glided, and sometimes hitched a ride as the two proceeded on together into the darkness.

She could see nothing, no trace of light. Her steps were uncertain and slow. If she stepped into another drop, it might kill her. She counted her paces. A hundred and twenty. A hundred and eighty. She took a deep, shuddering breath and realized that she felt a breeze in her face, not much of one, but a gentle draft of air that smelled of green growing things. Somewhere the passage opened up to the outside.

Holding her teeth tight against her desire to cry out from her aches and her fears, Ishara took her slow steps in the dark. Two hundred and forty.

Now the stone floor seemed to incline upwards, and a dull hope began to grow inside her. She paused to rest and heard only her own breath, startling and loud in the darkness. How long had it been since a human had walked this passageway? What kept the creatures of the island from seeking a den in its cool, dark depths?

Questions she could not answer. She began to move again, limping because her muscles had become stiff. She was thirsty.

But the air in her face was cool and the scents helped to refresh her. She had to go on. And, if possible, she had to learn more about the seeds and the compounds—that, too, was part of her mission.

Alone of all the islanders, only the Storyteller could understand the full use of the seeds—if Ishara could bring back the knowledge. As for the golden statues the men above her were taking, let them go. Her knowledge was worth more than all the gold put together. The problem was that Magwich and his men were close, dangerously close, to where Ishara needed to go. One more explosion in the wrong place and her hopes—the hopes of all her people—would be gone forever.

CHAPTER THIRTEEN

SKULL ISLAND
The Past

Ishara lost count of her paces. She stumbled on endlessly in the darkness, her legs dead under her, her mind almost a blank. And then—

Light.

She licked her cracked lips. Her lungs heaved, but she had no tears to shed. Ahead she saw an arch of light, daylight, sunlight. She was too weary to run. She limped forward, thinking only of the Storyteller and of how she had to deliver her message.

Something cold trickled onto her shoulder. She looked up and felt water splash her face. She realized that a spring must have found its way through the stonework of the passage. It pattered to the stone floor like a heavy rain, collected, and meandered in a winding streamlet toward the far side of the tunnel. Oji hopped over and drank greedily as Ishara cupped her hands. The water was fresh and tasted clean. She drank in small sips until she felt strong enough to move ahead. Oji stood beneath the drip and took a splashy bath before following, preening along the way. Ishara could only smile.

A sloping ramp of earth and rubble led up to the low arch. Ishara climbed it, emerging into the light of late afternoon.

She stood in a vast circular ruin. The stone walls to her left bore bas-relief sculptures, carved into them ages ago, showing Atu fighting Tagu. Vines spilled down from the rim of the far side of the enclosure, and Ishara made her unsteady way toward

them. She saw now the scrapes on her legs, the ugly bruise that stained the flesh of her left arm. No matter. If she could climb to the top, she could find her way back to the village. Ishara paused, closed her eyes, and entered Oji's mind, impressing on him the need for silence. He chirped once, then fell quiet.

She reached the vines, took a bundle of them in her hands, and tested their strength. They seemed sturdy enough to take her weight. Ishara breathed deeply and began to haul herself up—

"Ishara! What are you doin' here, now, pretty lady?"

The shock of hearing the voice made Ishara release the vines as if they had been red-hot. She dropped a couple of feet and spun as soon as she landed. The tangle of vines ensnared her as she leaned back into them.

Magwich stood at the top of the far wall, a pistol in his right hand. He smiled down at her. Behind him, other people moved, sailors laden with heavy burdens and—

"Bar-Atu," Ishara said bitterly.

"Queen Ishara," the old priest said in a voice cold as hail. He turned and called, "King Kublai! See what has followed us!"

Kublai pushed past the others. For a long moment he stared down at her, his face stern and cold. He made his way around the rim, dropped his spear, and climbed down the vines. "Here," he said. "I'll help you."

"Why?" Ishara whispered.

"Come. It isn't safe here."

She took his offer of help and they climbed up together. She poised to run, but Kublai hauled himself up and seized her arm. "You're hurt!"

"I fell," she said, trying to pull away from him.

Magwich had motioned to the others to stay put, but he made his way around the circumference of the hollow, passing the disjointed skeleton of a triceratops. "Little lady, you shouldn't come here alone. The animals here will grab you up, and just like that"—he snapped his fingers— "toss you in the air, swallow you down whole."

Ishara glared at him.

Magwich's friendly smile did not change. "King Kublai, your queen seems a bit upset with me. Maybe you'd better explain things to her."

"They are going to help us," Kublai said, staring into Ishara's eyes. "They'll give us weapons, make us masters of the island—"

"No!" The word escaped Ishara's lips before she knew she was going to yell. In her own language, she whispered fast and feverishly, "Kublai, listen to me! I am sorry I did not understand earlier, but I do now. I know what you have been trying to do and the dangers you face. Husband, I support you. I am your wife, I love you. They do not! We have been together since we were children—listen to me! There is a better way, a safer way, for you to achieve your goals, *our* goals. I carry it with me! All we need is—"

"Tie her!" Bar-Atu ordered, looking over his shoulder. "Take what she is holding and bring it to me!"

Ishara took a half-step away, but Kublai quickly spun to face the two men Bar-Atu had sent. "How dare you! She is queen!"

Magwich aimed his pistol at her. "Take one more step, my boy, and she'll never take another."

Kublai's face wrenched itself into a mask of rage. He struck down Magwich's arm. "You lied! You have sided with Bar-Atu!"

"Easy, lad. I haven't sided with anybody. I only hedged my bet." Bar-Atu's men looked back at their leader, and Magwich said easily, "Let's not do anything hasty, Bar-Atu, until we see what's what. Kublai, outside this bloody island of yours there exists another world. And that world values gold. I'm only making sure that I can get along in my world, the same way you are trying to make sure you can get along in yours. You see, there's not much difference between us."

Bar-Atu growled something too softly for Ishara to hear, but his men started forward.

"Remind 'em who has the guns, lads," Magwich said, and his seamen worked the bolts on their rifles.

Everyone knew what that sound meant. Kublai, Bar-Atu, and their men froze where they stood. Drips of water echoed in the silence as they fell into the opening below. Then a spear streaked through the air, missing its target and striking sharply against stone. Magwich whirled, his gun spoke thunder, and the Atu warrior who had launched the spear screamed, reeling backward. He fell back across the frill of a ceratopsian skull, then crumpled to earth, dead.

In the island's language, Magwich spoke loudly, calmly, firmly: "Nobody else needs to die. Give us our gold and we'll be on our way. Kublai, get your boys to pick up the loot. Bar-Atu, keep yours back. We can kill 'em all as easy as I did that one."

The sun was low in the west. Bar-Atu carried his staff in one hand and in the other an apparently dead torch. But he blew on it and it began to send up a thin blue smoke. One of the sailors pointed a rifle at the priest, but Magwich said, "No, leave him be. He's planted the boat we need to get off this blasted island just where I need it. If he wants to go down in this hole and follow the tunnels, let him."

Bar-Atu kept his eyes on Magwich as he breathed on the torch. The smoke billowed thicker, but the torch did not burst into flame.

In English, Kublai said to Magwich, "You promised us weapons—what did you promise him?"

Magwich shook his head, a smile of mock apology still on his lips. "Lad, I like you, and that's a fact. But it's also a fact that we got a long, long way to sail before we can reach a port to spend some o' that gold. Now, that ship of ours for some reason took too much time to repair—lots of unusual mishaps, if I recall. I found out that there was a reason for them all, and that reason was you."

Ishara put her hand on her husband's shoulder to keep him from lunging at the man.

Kublai said, "I never did anything to your ship! If anyone did, it was him, Bar-Atu!"

"Well, somebody did it. Anyway, I had to cover my bets, lad, so I sided with both of you. I couldn't take the chance of me or my men bein' sacrificed to that god-awful

Gaw, now could I? Now, what if I'd been your friend, and then somethin' happened to you, and old Bar-Atu here decided he'd be better off without me? Get my meaning? See, all I ever wanted was to get my ship seaworthy, collect a little loot for my troubles, and set sail. I'm not your enemy, lad, though I might not be exactly your friend."

Bar-Atu waved the smoldering torch. "You gave your word, Magwich! Do what you promised!"

Ishara felt a rising despair, but she said nothing. Magwich grinned at Bar-Atu, but when he spoke again, it was to Kublai: "My other little bargain. You'd help me if I'd give you guns and powder, but the priest offered to help me, too, if I'd give him something."

"What?" asked Kublai.

"You, lad. You."

Kublai glared.

"Sorry, son. But look at it this way: I'm a man of my word, after a fashion. I promised the powder and shot to you, so the witch-doctor here doesn't get it. I promised you to him, but between us, I think you could take the old man in a fair fight. 'Course you'd have to find some way of makin' it fair."

"Ishara, you were right," Kublai said between his teeth. "I was a fool to trust him!"

"Hold on, son," Magwich said. "I like you, and I never liked this here baboon. We're precious short o' powder ourselves, but I'll leave you some. We'll come back to this island in a year, two years, an' I'll bring all you need then—and I'll give it to whichever side has won out. What you and Bar-Atu work out, well, that's none o' my business. That's up to you. But just between us, I hope you win."

Fury rose in Bar-Atu's eyes. He opened a pouch slung at his belt and took from it a fine gray powder, which he sprinkled over himself. "Kublai," Ishara said in a warning voice, "Stop him!"

"Heathen superstition," Magwich said with a shrug. He squinted as he focused on the men from every side, who were already shifting in their places. The sinking sun shone in his eyes and in those of his men, a position Bar-Atu had stealthily orchestrated with every slow movement he and his men had made. Eyes darted nervously as hands shifted on guns, knives, and spears. The ones with the guns held the others at bay.

"Stand by for squalls, son," Magwich said softly. "All hell's likely to break loose in a minute. Stand by me, and I'll stand by you, and that's a promise."

Ishara felt her skin tingling. Oji had flown up into the treetops. Something was building, but it had nothing to do with the Atu warriors. She realized that Magwich was focused just on Bar-Atu, but something else was coming, something *other*—

From every side, as quick as lightning, deathrunners bolted out of the brush with ear-rending screeches. Razor-sharp sickle claws on snake-quick feet struck, and men fell: Kublai's, Bar-Atu's, Magwich's.

Magwich snatched his rifle to his shoulder and fired once, twice. Other guns thundered. Screams burst from everywhere. From the trees, Oji fluttered to Ishara's shoulder. She grabbed the pouches around his neck, opened one, and flung the dust it contained first over Kublai, then over herself.

Charlie lurched to his feet, still dazed, and Kublai leaped past him, lowering his spear as a deathrunner charged. Instantly Oji made a screeching swoop into the creature's eyes. The deathrunner flailed to remove the nuisance. Kublai lunged, thrusting his spear through its heart. As it hit the ground others of its kind began to devour it. "This way!" Ishara cried, pulling Kublai into an opening where ancient worked stone had fallen in a jumble. The space was hardly big enough for two, but somehow she, her husband, and Charlie jammed into it.

Without warning a terrifying guttural roar froze even the deathrunners. Before Ishara realized what had happened, the remaining marauders were gone and in their place a shadow loomed, rocking ever so slightly as though to camouflage itself as a gentle breeze.

The survivors looked up in mute horror as Gaw's massive form blocked out the low-lying sun. Ishara had never seen the monster this close, this clearly. Gaw's sinister eyes, set deeply in an oversized cranium, gleamed with intelligence. Without warning, her head flung back and roared as she sprang forward. Her great tail balanced the heavy body, sweeping as Gaw charged.

Magwich froze, too awestruck to pull the trigger. Men sought to run but found the deathrunners had circled, forming a living and deadly barrier. For some reason the creatures did not attack, but only prevented them from leaving.

Magwich shouted to his men to reload.

Kublai cried, "Where is Bar-Atu?" Ishara had seen the greater part of the priest's men cut down, but not Bar-Atu. He had faded from view, and now the remnant of his men and Kublai's had rallied around the Europeans, facing the saurian enemy.

The great flesh-eater Gaw charged, ignoring spears and bullets. Men scattered in every direction. Deathrunners fell from shots fired at point-blank range. Kublai, Ishara, and Charlie stared at the slaughter.

Magwich thundered, "Run, mates! Get to the far side of this pit!" The Europeans obeyed, and Charlie fled after them.

"Come on!" Kublai ordered, pulling Ishara from their hiding place. They ran, too, away from the carnage. The deathrunners were feeding on the fallen, pursuing the last of the islanders.

Magwich had dropped his empty rifle but held a pistol. He glowered at Ishara. "What did that old devil dust himself with? This stuff?" He wiped a finger against Kublai's arm, leaving a trail. "What's this do, eh? Keep him safe from the blasted monsters?"

Ishara heard something, a low sound, like thunder far off. Someone shouted from across the pit. Some of the men leaped into the pit, seeking escape, but two deathrunners followed them and savaged them.

Magwich glanced aside at the screams, but did not lower his pistol. Kublai struck, lightning quick, but Magwich dodged back. "I'll shoot her!" he threatened.

Kublai roared in anger and dived forward. Magwich jerked the pistol toward him and fired, but Kublai had smashed into him and the shot went wild. Someone shrieked, and Ishara saw a huge form had burst from the forest from the other direction. It was a gigantic longneck, a horde of deathrunners driving it. Magwich snapped off an ineffective shot.

Rifles and pistols fired uselessly. The longneck lashed its tail, catching three of the Europeans and tumbling them into the pit. They landed heavily and did not stir.

Kublai again lunged at Magwich and dragged him to the ground, rolling to the very rim of the pit. Magwich, his face scarlet with effort, hung onto his pistol but could not break free of Kublai's grip. Ishara shouted a warning. The longneck had rounded the pit,

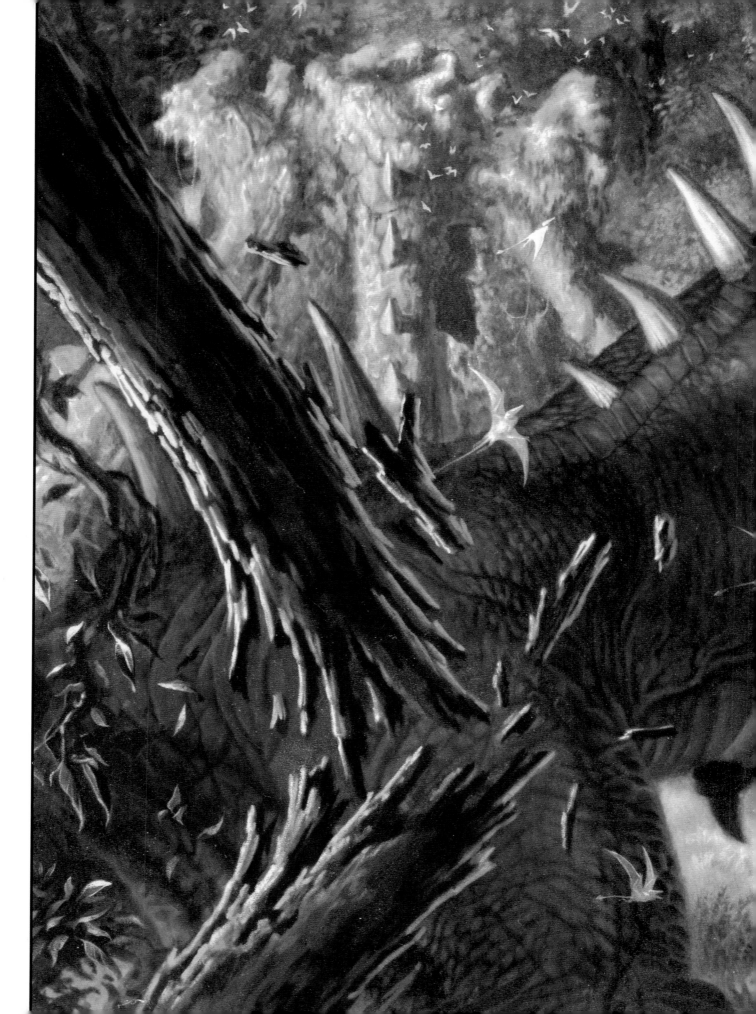

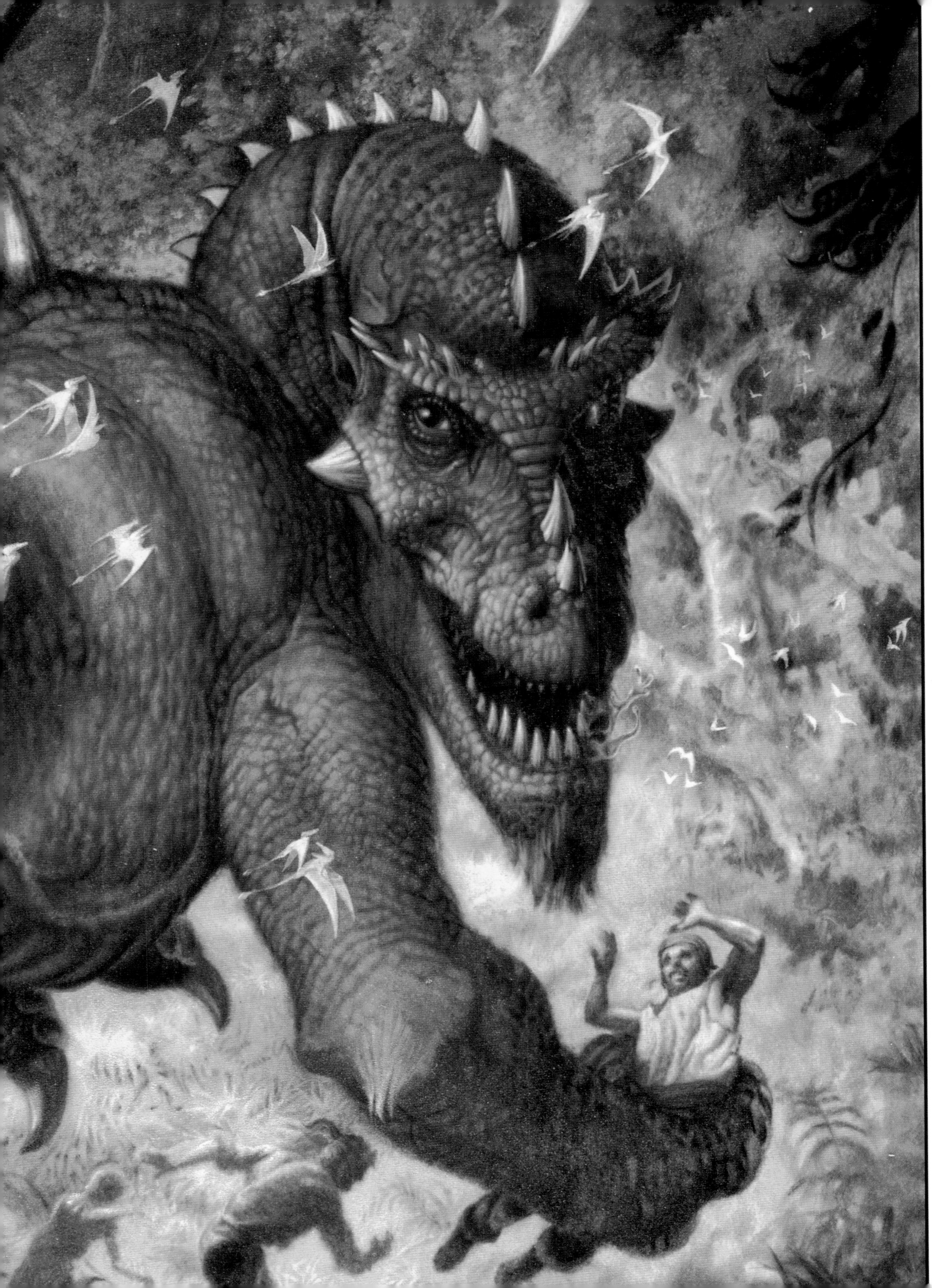

killing two more men. A moving mountain, cunningly provoked by the deathrunners, it raged toward them. Kublai and Magwich separated, forced back toward Gaw.

The longneck's great weight loosened stone and earth. The dank smell of old jungle mixed with the ammonia reek of the creature itself. The edge of the pit caved beneath the creature's weight, and it fell screeching, crashing to the floor of the amphitheater. That gave way, dropping the monster even deeper, snapping its neck. Dust and debris erupted like a volcano.

The commotion sent even the deathrunners into the forest, but not Gaw. She stalked forward, her head lowered, her jaws gaping. Kublai and Magwich stood shoulder to shoulder, facing the deadly creature.

Ishara drew a deep breath and was aware of silence—a curious silence. Then a hundred flying creatures screamed and scattered into the air from the forest. A challenging roar, shattering, deep, and the splintering of wood jerked Gaw's massive skull around as she focused on the sounds.

"Kong!" Ishara gasped, staring with wide eyes. The last of the kongs advanced like an avalanche towards Gaw. No longer a juvenile, he was a muscular, ferocious giant, twenty-five feet tall. The two deathrunners from the pit scrambled up and charged, but Kong flung them aside like rag dolls not even worthy of his attention. Gaw braced as Kong hurtled into her at tremendous speed, fists and teeth doing damage. Ishara felt the earth itself tremble, and the saurian staggered under Kong's blows. She lashed her tail, hammering her foe hard, but Kong seized the brute and struggled with her, reeling on the edge of the drop.

"Kong is winning!" Kublai said.

The smashing blows crunched bone. Gaw, stunned, lowered her head, snapped. Kong was too quick. He seized a length of bone, a rib from the long-dead triceratops, and used it as a club, as a spear. With bones broken and a half-dozen wounds spurting blood, Gaw reeled, fell, and instantly the Kong was beside her and was about to strike at the juncture of spine and skull when the last four deathrunners attacked Kong's head and neck all at once. Kong rolled off Gaw, flailing at the writhing mass which obscured his vision and ripped into his flesh. He roared in fury, snatching and smashing the creatures one after the other to the earth. The last one collapsed in death, and Kong beat his chest, whirling to meet Gaw again.

The gigantic ape snarled, lips drawn back, eyes darting, his weapon in hand. Ishara wanted to tear her gaze away, but she could not. Gaw, wounded but still formidable, wasted no time in roaring, but sped toward Kong, bent low and glaring at him with malevolent intelligence.

Kong met the charge head-on, but the impetus toppled him backward. As he tumbled, he flung up the weapon he carried reflexively, thrusting it inside Gaw's snapping jaws, keeping them from closing on his neck. For seconds they moved slowly, locked in a contest of strength. Gaw grabbed at the base of a tree with one hind claw and gripped the ground to gain traction with the other, trying to throw her opponent to the ground. Kong gave way, falling back, pressed to earth, but his muscles rippled as he gathered strength to attack again.

Ishara could not look away. The hatred in the eyes of both huge combatants was ancient, powerful, unyielding. Kong's fierce, expressive eyes offered stark contrast to the steel-cold glare of Gaw's reptilian face. Ishara felt Gaw's drive, her visceral need to kill Kong.

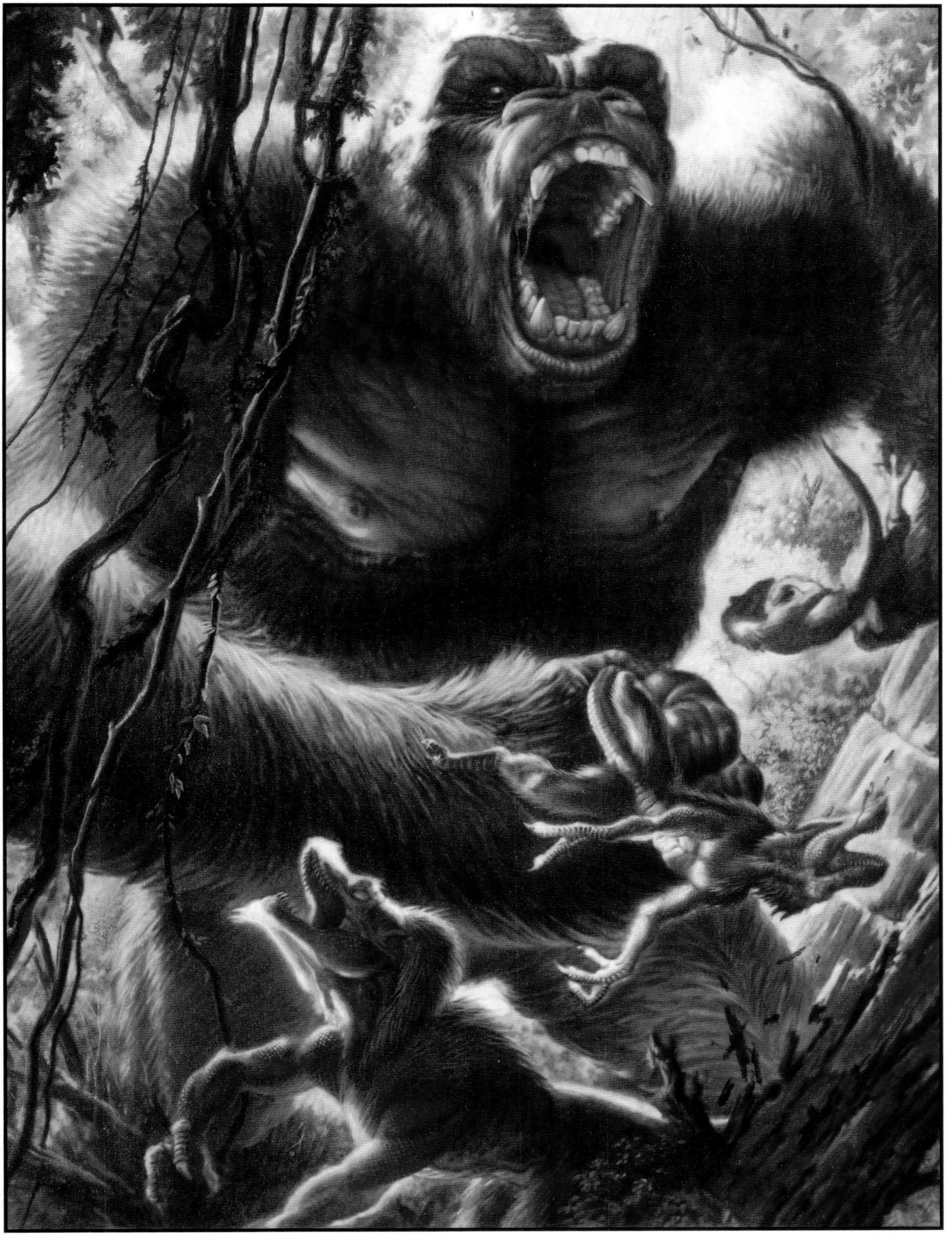

And Ishara also sensed Kong's deep-seated fear of this thing that had killed his parents. But beyond that, overpowering his fear, was a red rage. Kong, gathering a deep surge of energy, threw Gaw bodily back. Kublai had his spear at the ready, Magwich his pistol, but Ishara pulled both of them back. "No. There is hope."

Gaw had smashed into what seemed a tree, but it shattered, revealing one of the buildings wrought by the Tagatu in time unknown. The monster charged from the debris, and Kong splintered the bone he held against Gaw's skull, making the saurian reel back, shrieking in pain.

Ishara began to circle, toward the ancient structure.

"What are you doing?" whispered Kublai fiercely, grabbing her arm.

"I have to see what Magwich's men left behind," Ishara returned.

Kublai followed her. The battle between Gaw and Kong was working its way around to the right. They inched to the left. As far as Ishara could see, not one of the Europeans was still alive. Lifeless deathrunners strewed the earth. What had attracted her attention was a handcart loaded with earthenware jars. It had tipped over, but the jars had not broken. Ishara snatched some sacks from the ground, emptied them of jewels, and began to stuff the jars into them.

"What's that?" Kublai asked.

"Maybe the only things that can save the island," Ishara replied fiercely. "Come, Kublai, carry as many as you can" she said.

The two behemoths were closer than ever, breathing hard, both of them bloodied, weaving from side to side as each sought an opening, an advantage.

Kublai and Ishara stopped in their tracks, not wanting to draw attention to themselves. Ishara knew that the end was near. She felt the building tension, the last gathering of waning strength of ape and saurian. "It is finished," she whispered.

At that instant Kong let out a deafening roar and rushed forward with astonishing speed. Gaw, caught off guard, fell, knocked sideways and flattened to the ground. Directly beside her was the huge skull of the triceratops. Its studded frill and horns were mostly intact. Kong made for it, as if in the grip of a sudden inspiration. Before Gaw could recover, Kong had seized the skull. Gaw's powerful head jerked up, jaws snapping, but Kong was already upon her, using the skull as a shield. Gaw's maw was hopelessly stuck in one of the two huge fenestrations of the skull's frill. Kong used his great strength to force himself forward, keeping the monster's jaws engaged.

Gaw's arms flailed. She tried to push away the frill, but her strength was not equal to Kong's. Kong lifted his adversary completely off the ground, then smashed her to the earth. Gaw's neck bent sharply, nearly breaking. The force of the impact shattered the frill, the two great horns breaking loose. Kong yanked one of them free. Gaw, on her back, raised her arms, attempting to fend off Kong's downward thrust—but too late. Kong stabbed into Gaw's neck, and the great creature's mouth bubbled blood as an inhuman gurgling hiss burst from her.

Impossibly, Gaw clawed at the horn, reared to her feet. She shook her head, sending slavers of blood spraying through the air as she staggered wildly. Magwich, flushed from his hiding place to avoid the monster, was crushed as the beast collapsed.

Kong struck at Gaw's chest with short, heavy blows, not retreating, not giving the wily creature a chance to recover. Kong snatched up another bone from the same skeleton, a heavy leg bone, and used it as a club, beating Gaw without mercy.

Ishara saw that Kong was hurt, that open wounds on his chest and shoulders spilled his own blood and wondered how he could relentlessly fight on. But then she understood that the memory of his parents' death explained his deadly determination. It was, she realized, Kong's great advantage: Like a human, he felt emotion, not just the deep, reptilian cunning of Gaw. Perhaps they were equals in intelligence, but their minds were of different orders. Gaw lacked the ultimate strength and determination born of spirit.

Gaw's arm swung up to rake his chest. Kong intercepted it and Ishara could hear the crunching of bone as Kong's enormous canine teeth bit into it. A horrifying, hissing scream escaped Gaw's muzzled jaws. Gaw struggled to attack again, but her body was no longer able to respond as Kong pounded down with both enormous fists. The monster's bloodshot eyes strained to focus, then slowly, shakily, rolled up into her skull. A moment later, Gaw was dead.

There was a sudden, dead silence. Kong stepped back, not fully able to grasp that it was over. Suddenly, he viciously pounded the lifeless body. When nothing moved, he nudged and shook the misshapen head of Gaw to make sure no spark remained.

Kong threw his head back and let out a sustained, deafening roar as he savagely pounded his chest. The sound made the very air vibrate. It came from all over, everywhere, and seemed to go on forever.

Kublai said in tones of wonder: "The kong has killed Bar-Atu's god."

Ishara understood exactly what that meant. Their world would never be the same. Every living thing on that island had now better bow before . . . "King Kong," she said in a reverent whisper. Beside her, she felt Kublai tremble.

CHAPTER FOURTEEN

SKULL ISLAND
June ?, 1957

Jack Driscoll's luck ran out as the sun sank toward the west. He had left the labyrinth of underground passages hours earlier. More than once he had heard the stealthy skitter of two-toed feet not so very far behind him. In the confined darkness of the tunnels, the flesh eaters had too much of an advantage. Driscoll had come back to the surface and now was betting his life on a last dash to reach the Wall.

He had two choices of pathway: the rocky top of a sinuous ridge, where he would be exposed, or the depths of the jungle, free of undergrowth but difficult to navigate with no glimpse of the sky.

The ridge won. He needed to see if the creatures were following him. He could see more than that, for at one point, he even glimpsed a dark line far ahead that might, just might, be the Wall. The trouble was that the ridge wound and twisted at a slanting angle toward it. The direct route led through impassible brush and tangles of low scrub trees.

And from the brush came occasional crackles, as if the creatures were pacing him, a few hundred feet off to his left. Driscoll cradled his rifle and made the best time he could along the ridge's rocky spine.

Then he took a wrong step. The ridge gave way, sloped downward, buried itself in grasses taller than his head. Driscoll frowned. Ahead he could see that the ridge climbed up again, but it emerged a hundred yards away. In the thick grass, he wouldn't be able to see anything that might be following him.

"Double-quick," he told himself, and dived into the grasses. The turf underfoot was treacherous, springy and yielding. Driscoll realized he probably wasn't even walking on real soil, but on thousands of years of compressed and decaying grass. Insects zinged and whined, and he forced his way through the grasses, step by step. "Worse than the subway in New York," he grunted.

Then he heard the chittering. The man-sized hunters were close. Moving a millimeter at a time, Driscoll brought his rifle up. He could see nothing in the grass. He edged toward the place where the rocks rose again, step by careful step, his ears sharp for the rustle of a charging enemy.

Another sound, a rhythmic *tok-tok-tok*. Not a woodpecker, but with that insistent quality, from somewhere not too far away. Rock underfoot. Driscoll took a step up. Another, carefully. Another, and his head was above the surface.

A green-gray blur, coming fast! Driscoll fired, and the creature fell or feinted, vanishing in the grass. He turned to keep its line of passage in sight—

And a heavy weight crashed into him from behind, sending him sprawling. He was trapped beneath a massive body, and he steeled himself for the slash of teeth.

It never came. Something warm ran over his arm—blood, not his own. Driscoll grunted and heaved. The dead body of one of the dinosaurs rolled off him, and he saw that a spear shaft protruded from one of its eyes.

A hand closed on his arm.

Hours later, Driscoll said, "You fellows could take off the blindfold. It's night now, anyway."

The two men escorting him gave no sign that they understood. They hustled him along, guiding him, catching him when he stumbled. He had never been so tired.

"So are you guys from around here?" he asked. "How about those dinosaurs, huh? I'll bet they taste like chicken."

No response. "Tough crowd," Driscoll muttered. He hoped they weren't in the mood to see what *he* tasted like.

His legs were dead under him, numb with effort. At last his guides paused. Driscoll heard a strange creaking, then a hand placed on his head firmly pressed down, making him duck as he was guided forward. A slam and a sense of being inside.

And then at last one of the natives pulled the cloth from Driscoll's eyes. He blinked. He was in a cave, or perhaps the largest longhouse on the island. Torches flared, washing everything in a ruddy light. The two tall islanders looked at him impassively. One carried his pack and rifle, the other a formidable spear. "Got a deck of cards?" Driscoll asked. "A pair of dice? No sense in wasting the evening."

The spear bearer gestured, and Driscoll preceded him. From somewhere ahead he heard voices, two of them. One sounded like a woman. The other—

"Vincent?" Driscoll called.

The spear prodded him in the ribs.

"Okay," Driscoll said in a lower voice. "I get the point."

The islanders shoved him into a room and pulled a heavy door closed. Driscoll heard a bar drop into place. He looked around. A kind of cot, leather stretched over a wooden frame, stood against one wall, and on a triangular table rested an earthenware pitcher of water and some fruit.

Driscoll drank deeply from the pitcher, then sat on the cot. He was almost sure he had heard Vincent's voice. That was the best news he'd had in days.

Well—if you didn't count not being ripped apart by a dinosaur, it was.

Driscoll settled in to wait.

SKULL ISLAND
The Past

Kong seemed maddened beyond all control. Again and again as he vanished into the forest, the air reverberated to the great beast's roars. Gaw's lifeless form lay before Ishara and Kublai, the crushed figure of Magwich barely visible beneath the chin.

Behind Kublai someone cowered in the darkness. "Who's there?" Kublai demanded. "Just me."

Kong retreated, his roars of triumph fading. Ishara went to the huddled figure of Charlie. "Are you hurt?"

"I don't think so. What happened to the Captain?"

"Dead," Kublai said shortly, raising his spear. "I should kill you—"

"No," Ishara said. "He's not like the others, and we need every hand. Quickly—help me gather the jars. They are our only hope!"

"We'd better grab some of these, too." Charlie sounded frightened, peering in all directions as he gathered three strewn rifles. "Something tells me we'll need 'em."

It took them hours, but by torchlight, they found the jars. Or what was left of them. Ishara fell to her knees in disbelief. Many lay beneath the body of Gaw, the rest were shattered and their contents scattered. They dragged the broken body of Magwich from beneath Gaw's head. Kublai stared into the dead man's face. "Even now he looks like he's scheming."

"His schemes died with him," Ishara said.

"Can we bury him?" Charlie asked. "Don't seem right to leave him—"

Kublai lifted the limp body and rolled it into the pit. "His grave is a huge one," he said.

They salvaged what they could of the seeds and the few unbroken jars. It was tedious work, doubly hard in the flickering light of the torch. Ishara was silent for a long time as they searched the trampled earth where the battle had raged, hearing the shrieks of animals from time to time, the far-off roars of Kong. Pterosaurs circled high over head, but it seemed Kong's ferocity had frightened off the land creatures. Ishara could neither see nor hear any sign of them.

At last, when half the night was gone, Kublai said, "Let's rest. Ishara, what troubles you? There must be more of those jars left. We can come back in daylight and seek them."

"There are no others," Ishara said with a deep certainty. How she knew she could not say, but something told her that even in death Gaw had struck at them, crushing the jars, spilling their precious contents. What they had scavenged might be useless—especially without the ancient knowledge of the formulas required to combine the plants. Ishara felt only a deep sense of failure.

Kublai touched her gently. "You can't give up now."

"You don't understand. I had hoped so much—and now we have nothing."

"We have each other," Kublai said simply. "I love you, and you love me. We will survive. Our people will survive. I promise you."

He went back into the open and was gone for a long time. When he returned, he bore a bloody burden wrapped in the shirt of one of the Europeans. "Proof that Gaw is dead," he told Ishara. "I don't know if Bar-Atu is alive, but with this, we can break Bar-Atu's cult. His god is dead. There is nothing left to sacrifice our people to. The old priest has failed, and now my people, and yours alike, will rally around me. Even now they are waiting for my return and will have overthrown the last of Bar-Atu's henchmen. You will see."

They were exhausted. A foggy dawn broke well before they were within sight of the Wall, and they found another entrance to the maze of tunnels. They spent much of the morning resting in the mouth of one of these, taking turns watching. Unknown creatures passed close by but did not disturb them, though once Ishara, standing staring into the fog, was almost sure she heard human voices not too far away. Ishara hissed a warning for the others to be quiet. She could see nothing, though, except vague shadows. But she was very weary. Could it be her imagination?

Kublai slowly cocked his rifle, and the echo reverberated in the tunnel. A hushed silence. "Nothing," he whispered at last.

They set out again at noon, exploring the tunnel for miles before it opened again to the sky. Kublai looked around. "I know where we are. This is the clearing past the place of sacrifice." Ishara sensed his unspoken hope: That the sacrifices had ended for good now, that the place of sacrifice would fall into disuse. "Come, follow me," he said.

He found a hunter's path, and the three of them hurried along it. They burst out of a final thicket into the opening before the great gate. Kublai put his hand beside his mouth and called out, "The King has returned. Open the gate!"

Heads peered over the edge of the Wall, and a jabber of voices rose. Kublai unwrapped his bloody package. "Look! Gaw is dead! I have his teeth and claws!"

More excitement. At last the gate tentatively opened, and Ishara, Charlie, and Kublai made their way inside. A circle of villagers, all armed, stood staring at them, spears at the ready. Several aimed rifles directly at Kublai. Immediately five men rushed forward and disarmed Kublai and grabbed Charlie, who struggled vainly to get away. Something was very wrong. None of his men were present, and none of the villagers looked friendly. Kublai flushed. "Let him alone! I tell you, Gaw is dead!" he yelled, brandishing in each hand a tooth nearly a foot long. "I show you the proof! No other creature on the island has teeth such as Gaw's!"

"We know that," one of the warriors said. "Bar-Atu killed Gaw."

"Bar-Atu!" Ishara exclaimed in surprise. "No! King Kong killed Gaw!"

"King Kong! That is good, a true and proper name! Bar-Atu used his magic to call forth this new King," the man said. "He granted him the strength to overcome the old god. Now Kong is our King!"

Another pointed accusingly at Kublai. "You captured the kong and promised to tame it, to control it. You were not strong enough! Now Kong is god!"

"And I am his high priest," said a stern voice. Bar-Atu, wearing his priestly regalia, stepped forward, madness in his eyes. "When he could not help, I helped. It was I who had the outsider Magwich and his men killed as they were about to steal the treasure of our people with their rifles!" Bar-Atu's men stepped forward, holding aloft the few last rifles that remained. "The stranger's treachery was made possible by this liar who wanted to be your king! Gaw failed us by letting outsiders enter our island. Their ship had stood ready to take them back to their world so they could return with the others. I prevented them! This boy, this so-called king, cares nothing for you!"

"You lie!" Kublai shouted.

"Who helped the outsiders find materials and food for their ship and to take our women for their beds?" taunted Bar-Atu. "It was Kublai! But I have killed the outsiders and all those who sided with them. They will never threaten us again!"

Ishara felt horrified. She knew many of the island women who had married the strangers, who had borne them children . . .

Kublai shouted in anger: "You wanted to enslave the people with fear. I want to set them free!"

"Kill him," Bar-Atu snarled.

Ishara stood by Kublai's side. She realized that, behind them, a short sprint away, the Gate was still ajar. "To the jungle—run!" she said in a tone so soft only Kublai could hear, and they both sprang back at the same instant.

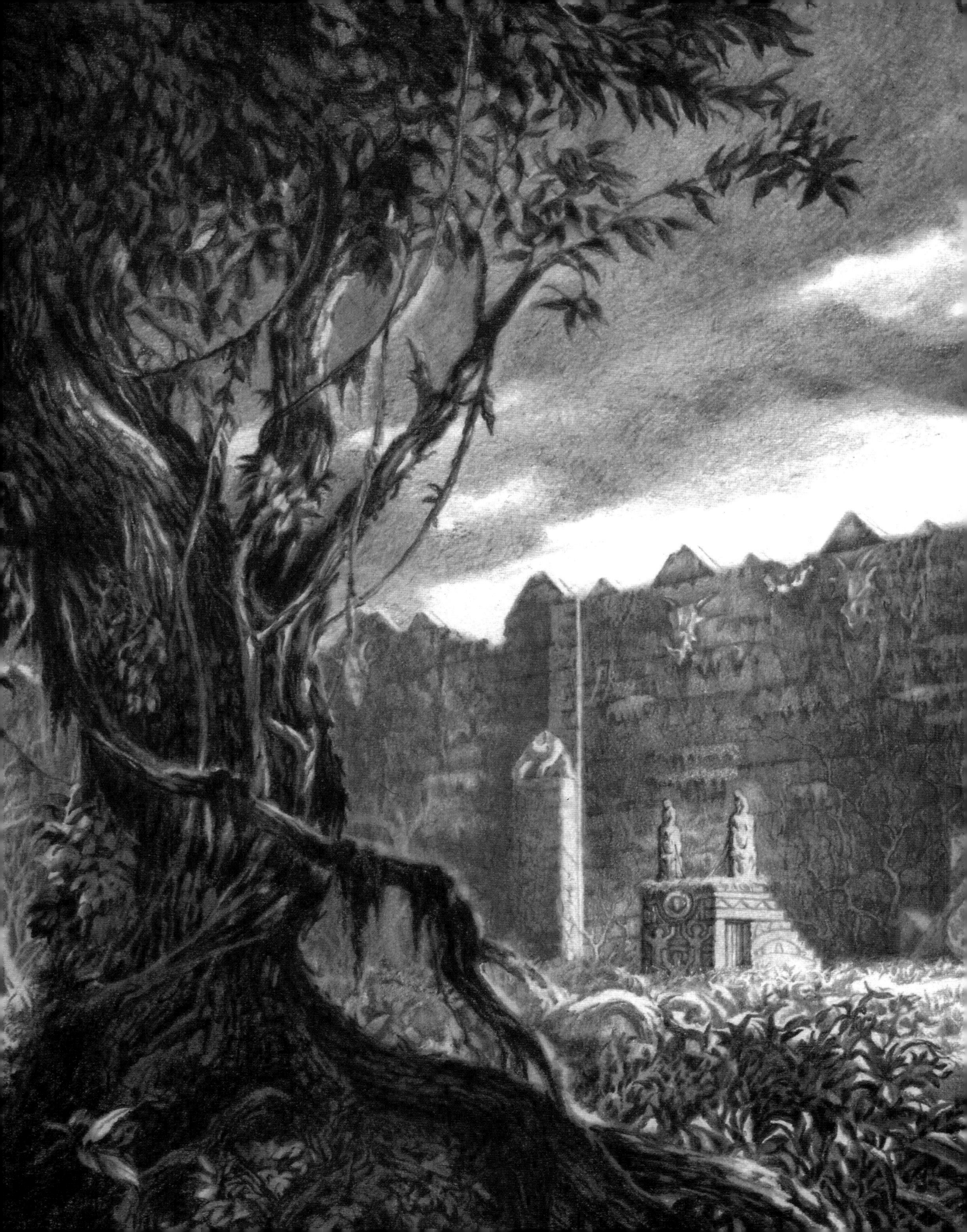

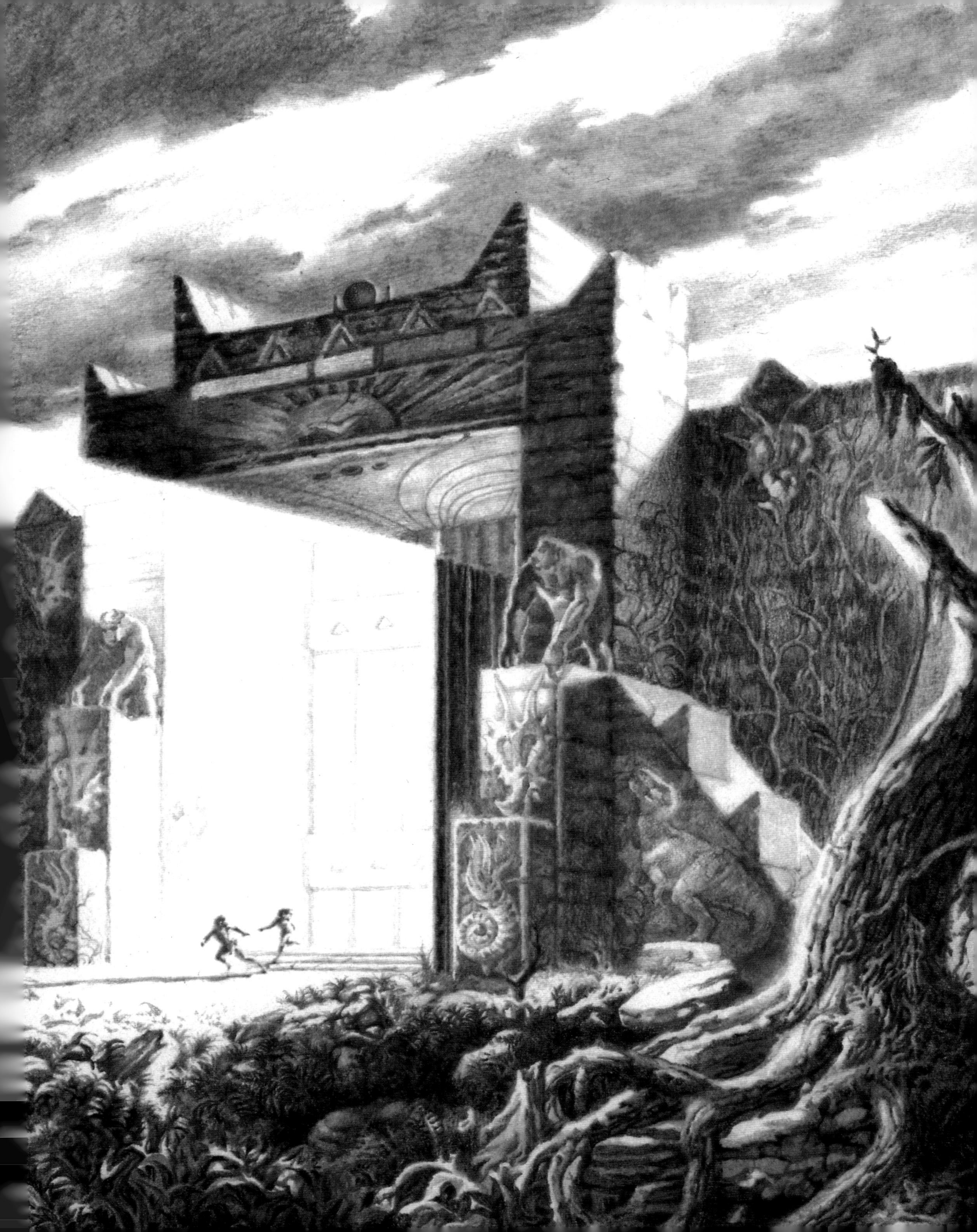

Late sun streamed through the open Gate. Kublai was the faster as they dashed from the great portal and turned to reach for Ishara's hand. She reached forward—

A rifle cracked, and an invisible hand struck Kublai in the chest, knocking him back as blood spilled from a great wound. He fell, many steps beyond the Gate. Ishara flung herself over him, trying to protect him, too late, too late. "No!" she screamed, her hands cradling Kublai's head.

Kublai's breath rasped and rattled. "Run, Ishara! Find a way!"

"No!" she screamed, dropping to her knees, lifting Kublai's head.

Kublai gasped, his words a whisper, "Don't give up, Ishara, find a way. . ." He could say no more, but Ishara could see the love in his eyes—and then the life left them.

"Kublai!" all hope left with him, and her faith deserted her. In an instant, her world was shattered. Ishara sprang up, consumed with hatred for Bar-Atu, wanting to tear him apart with her hands. But his followers had spilled through the Gate, and were already upon her. They overpowered her, dragging her back inside the Wall. She heard the boom of the great Gate closing and knew despair. Bar-Atu stood with legs apart, his gaze self-righteous and full of contempt. And behind him, forcibly bowed, was the Storyteller, looking weak and faded.

Through hot tears of anger, Ishara spat in Bar-Atu's face and cried, "Murderer! Are you not satisfied that you have won? Do you have to leave my husband's body out there to be ripped apart by scavengers?"

Bar-Atu wiped the spittle from his face, but his smirk remained. He stepped forward and slapped Ishara hard, buckling her knees, then lifted his staff. "Silence, before the same thing happens to you! Your husband mocked the protection of the Wall, so let him lie beyond it, free as he wanted to be—free to be refuse, food for the saurians and scavengers that the Wall protects us from!"

The Storyteller took a step forward, and Bar-Atu struck her with his fist, bringing a cry of pain from the old woman.

Panting, Ishara said, "Is this how a leader proves worthy? By striking a defenseless elder? Coward! Let her go back to her hut. She cannot harm you!"

"Hear me!" Bar-Atu thundered over the crowd that had gathered before him. "See what happens when one takes protection for granted! This Kublai said that he could conquer the god! That old hag, the Storyteller, says not to rely on the Wall, but on the strength within yourselves. Fools! Where is their arrogance now? What protection do they offer you now? They cannot even protect themselves!"

Ishara struggled against the men who held her. "Don't provoke him," the Storyteller said sharply. "This is Bar-Atu's time." Unspoken, but clear in Ishara's mind, was the thought, *Your time is yet to come.*

The people were murmuring. Bar-Atu's sharp eyes darted, slyly. Respect for elders was a deeply held belief of the islanders, Tagu and Atu alike. In a measured voice, he said, "This useless creature is harmless. Let her go back to her perch, then. Her power has ended."

The warriors dragged her forward, to the small doorway that led to the stairs climbing to the top of the Wall. She went silently, with bent head, as the men ridiculed her, even spat on her.

Ishara fought against her captors again, and one of them struck her hard on the side of her head, causing a blinding explosion of yellow light and then darkness.

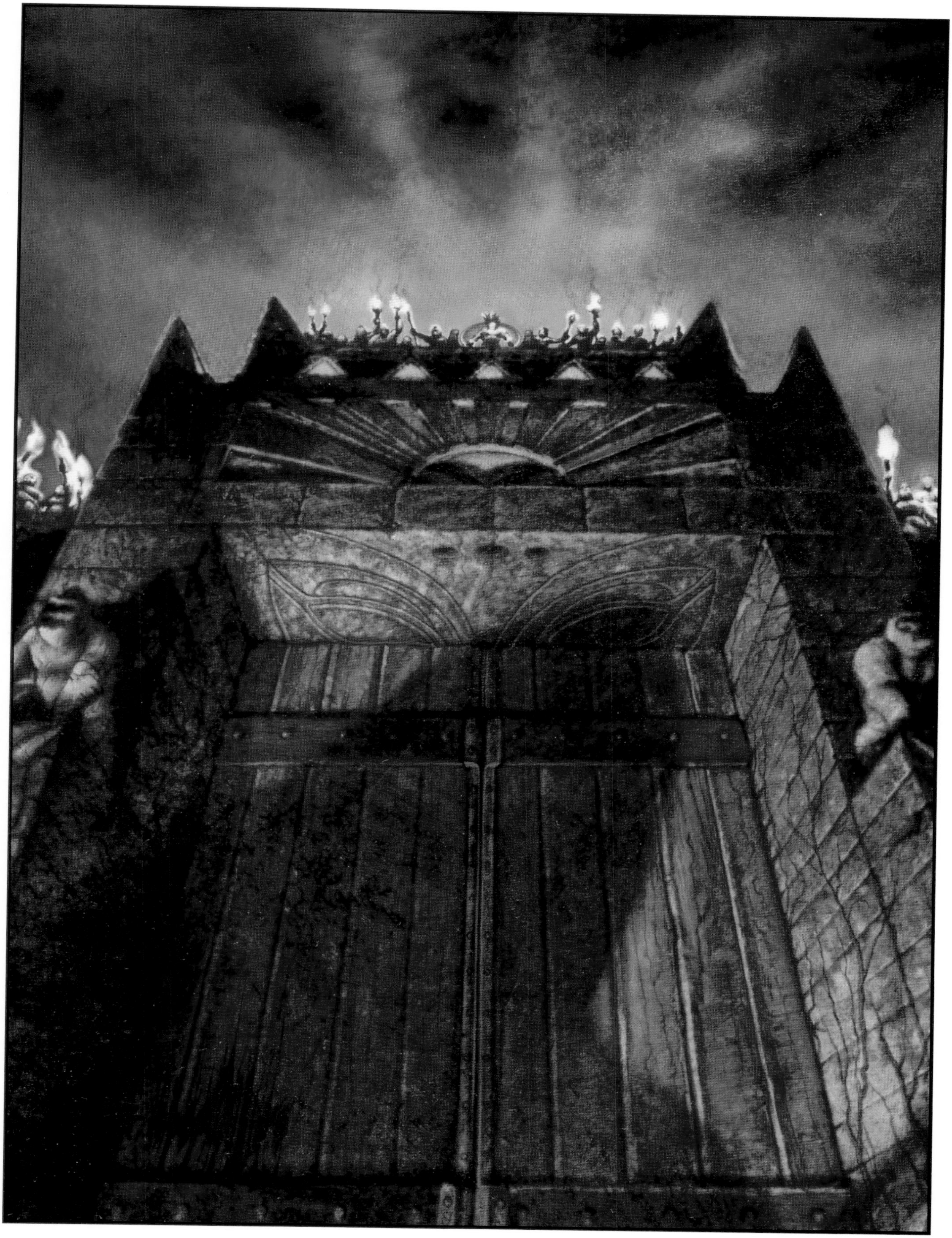

She came to consciousness some time later, feeling air on her face, sensing someone bending over her. Ishara tried to sit up, but gentle hands held her down. "Don't yell out," Charlie whispered. "They don't know we're loose."

"Where are we?" Ishara asked, groaning, trying to sit up.

"That little corner where we used to meet. I slipped away when they went after you and Kublai, and I hid. They think they've locked you in a hut, but I got you out of there. We're safe here for a little while, I think. Listen to 'em."

Then Ishara realized that the drumming she had been aware of was coming not from her aching head but from the village. Bar-Atu was leading the people in some kind of frenzied ceremony.

"The Storyteller—" Ishara said.

"She's up in her hut. When you feel strong enough, we'll go see her."

Ishara and Charlie made the climb in the dark of night. The old woman seemed more concerned with Ishara's loss and with her hurts than with herself. Ishara took comfort in the old woman's consolation, and there in the hut she mourned the loss of her Kublai. That night they rested, and the next morning they watched from the top of the Wall as two warriors bound a struggling woman in preparation for the first sacrifice to Kong.

The Storyteller sighed. "Bar-Atu has made a misstep. This time he has chosen the wrong god. This one is not like Gaw. This is a kong, a descendant of the ancient warriors of the Tagu. This creature is still less than human, but more than animal. Gaw fed on the sacrifices without caring anything for the reason why they were given to him. Gaw saw us only as food. On some level Kong will *know* he is being given dominion and will react to that."

"I don't believe Kong means to hurt us," said Ishara.

"Not after we hurt him so badly?" the Storyteller asked. "And remember the horrible things he has experienced. Even more, he is no longer a child. He is grown into adulthood—with all its passions."

"I failed," Ishara confessed. "We brought back only fragments from outside. If I had done as you asked—"

"You did your best," the Storyteller said. "And you have a part to play yet. I will not be with you long now. But I think you are ready."

"I cannot fight against Bar-Atu now that he has become king of the island."

The Storyteller's smile was grim. "He only thinks he is king. Because he is merciless, he believes Kong is merciless—merciless and mindless. But Bar-Atu will find soon enough that Kong must be appeased. Bar-Atu is not a king, but a slave— the slave of a god he made. In willingly sacrificing others for his own selfish desires, he has unwittingly finally sacrificed himself!"

In the distance, Kong roared.

The Storyteller said softly, "Kong is King of the island now." She was silent for a long moment, and then, surprising Ishara, the old woman added, "How I pity him."

CHAPTER FIFTEEN

SKULL ISLAND
Date Unknown

Vincent Denham thought that he had been awakened by bad dreams. His mind played tricks on him, he knew. Sometimes he saw moving shapes that were not there; sometimes he heard stealthy movements that existed only in his mind.

But one of these voices—

"Jack?" Vincent asked, and his voice came out as a harsh croak. He rolled out of bed, rose staggering to his feet. One small torch burned a long way off, giving him coppery dimness instead of light. He felt as if he were back aboard the Darrow. The stone floor beneath his bare feet seemed to tilt and roll like the deck of a ship.

But the voices were louder. Vincent reeled toward them, stumbling over his own feet. His shoulder hit the rough wall, and half supporting himself against it, he edged forward. A doorway, low. He ducked and stepped through and saw an open door to his left, with yellow light spilling from it.

"Killing's in your blood," Jack's voice said. "This bit of the island is like Australia was in the beginning—where the killers and thieves were sent. That's why you're going to kill me. Come on, say something!"

Silence, and then Jack roared, "You ever wonder what you losers are doing locked behind this wall? I know why you're here, do you? You should have picked Australia, it's a bigger island. Guess all the good real estate was taken."

Vincent grabbed the edge of the door, hauled himself through the opening, and swayed, his eyes wide.

An earthenware lamp flickered on a triangular table. Jack Driscoll stood in a corner, his back against the wall. And before him, holding a short spear—

"Kara!" Vincent shouted.

She spun on him, her eyes gleaming in the light. Jack took a step forward, but Kara danced back, threatening him with the spear. His teeth grinned fiercely. To Vincent she looked like a woman ready to kill.

"Get out of here, kid," Driscoll ordered. He did not look at Vincent but kept his eyes locked on Kara's in an effort to stare her down. "The little lady has some beef with me. I want to find out what it is," he said with a steely look. Vincent saw no fear in Kara's stance, though—she was the one in control, not Driscoll.

"He dies, too!" Kara said, pointing at Vincent.

Driscoll's eyes widened. "English! Kid, you know this woman? Looks like she's been treating you rough!"

Kara, balancing on toe-tips, yelled and thrust toward Vincent. He tried to duck away as Driscoll lunged forward. Driscoll was too slow, Vincent too unsteady on his feet. The spear blade missed him by an inch, but he fell to his hands and knees.

Kara laughed at him. "Too weak!" she taunted. "Fool! The medicines I have been giving you have poisoned you. And not even the Storyteller knew! Now your friends come to take the little we have left. You will die, both of you!"

Vincent pulled himself up, one hand on the door sill, one against the wall, steadying himself. A figure darkened the doorway. For a fleeting instant, Vincent thought it might be the Storyteller—but it was a man, armed as Kara was with a short spear, menacing Driscoll.

Driscoll made another lunge, but the newcomer was on him. This time Driscoll did not miss the opportunity. He deflected the spear with a forearm, grabbed the shaft with his free hand, and turned the man's momentum against him. He stumbled, and Driscoll swept his legs from under him, wresting the spear free. Before the man could rise, Driscoll was behind him, the spear shaft held horizontally against his throat. "That's more like it," he said softly. "Behave, now."

Kara yelled something in her own language, and Driscoll's captive grunted a reply.

Driscoll's grip tightened. "Let Vincent alone, or I swear I'll break his neck." Kara's sharp eyes nearly glowed as she kept Vincent pinned against the floor in the adjoining room.

Vincent felt a strange sensation, a sensation almost of peace. Weak though his body was, his mind seemed suddenly clear. He released his hold on the spear and spread his arms wide. "I'm getting up, Kara. I'm not as afraid to die as you are to live."

"Don't do it!" Driscoll yelled. "These people are killers. It's in their blood. I've seen their history. The people on this side of the Wall are the descendants of murderers."

Kara screamed, "Liar! You and your kind are the killers! You took everything we had and left us to die—" Her rage increased, and she fell into her native tongue. Behind her, Driscoll increased the pressure on the man's windpipe until his eyes rolled up in unconsciousness.

Vincent stretched out his neck as she drew back for a deadly spear thrust and asked calmly, "Are you Atu? Or Tagu?"

Kara froze. Vincent was no Storyteller, had no insight into the minds of others, but he saw doubt in her eyes, and he knew that she felt his strange certainty.

"An Atu shames himself by killing those who don't resist," Vincent said. "A Tagu never takes life without reason. Which are you? Or are you nothing more than a killer, as my friend said?"

Kara drew back her spear, but Driscoll let his unconscious captive fall and sprang forward to grasp it. He was stronger than she, and with a wrench and a thrust, he tossed her onto the cot, leaving him holding both spears. He held Kara's on her.

Vincent rose, took a step toward him, and pressed the spear down. "Don't," he said.

"It's a temptation," Driscoll admitted.

"Kill me!" Kara snarled. "If you don't, I promise I will kill you. Both of you!"

Vincent sank beside her, sitting on the cot. "Listen to me," he said simply. "I know why you feel the way you do. It's the same reason my friend feels the way he does. In your place, I might have done the same. But this must stop. I promise this, Kara: I will do whatever I can so that no more of my people will come to this island, not without your knowledge and your permission. Your people have known too many years of death and suffering. Nothing is worth knowing I helped to contribute to that. Not even my dreams of bringing knowledge of the island's creatures to the world. Not even—" he fought to say the words— "not even my hope of finding my father and clearing his name. The killing has to end. I am willing to take the first step."

The guard groaned, pulled himself to his feet, and stared at them. Driscoll braced for action but a moment later the guard obediently stepped to the side as an old woman stepped out of the shadows behind him.

"Be at peace, Jack Driscoll," she said plainly. "Lower your weapon. No one will harm either you or Vincent."

Driscoll glanced at Vincent, who gave him a short nod. But the spear was already down. "Who's this?"

Kara's eyes narrowed, and she spat something that sounded like a curse.

"Silence!" The Storyteller spoke with finality, and it was as if Kara were struck dumb. The Storyteller calmly turned to Driscoll. "You are as wrong in what you think of us, Mr. Driscoll, as Kara is in what she thinks of you. Where there is mystery, there is often misunderstanding. I think Vincent Denham now understands."

The Storyteller turned to look at Kara. "Vincent has passed your test, Kara. And mine. What remains to be seen is whether you will pass my test—and your own."

To Vincent, she explained, "It has never been the choice of the Storyteller, or anyone else, who the future Storyteller will be. How the gift appears is a mystery. There is no doubt Kara has been chosen to be the next Storyteller, the bearer of the wisdom of this island. In Kara's hands will lie the future of our people. Will she lead by the way of the Tagu or by the tyranny of the Atu? Has she learned enough to choose wisely? She demanded that she be allowed to test you, to learn whether you could be trusted with the knowledge of this island and our people. But she overstepped her bounds. I have known she was mixing poisons with your medicines, not enough to kill, but enough to keep you weak. Not only in body, but more deceitfully, in mind."

"I thought I was a long time healing," Vincent said ruefully.

The Storyteller nodded. "And yet, you have turned aside her attacks and shown that you are capable of sacrificing personal desire for a greater good. Your own will has overcome the weakness of your body and your inclinations and made a choice—a *human* choice. You have given the proof to the Tagu teaching that we are free to be the masters of our passions. It is the Atu belief that the people are ultimately helpless against their inclinations." A faint smile played on her wrinkled lips. "Kara, you did not realize that when you asked to test Vincent, you placed yourself under the same test? Tell me, how do you judge your own behavior in comparison to that of this outsider? Do you choose to control your passions and cast aside your anger, as Vincent has, or do you choose to be controlled by them and follow the way of the Atu, to continue the killing?

Kara's face twisted in an agony of frustration and regret. "Why?" she demanded. "Why do you ask this? To humiliate me? I'd rather die!"

"Not to humiliate you, Kara, to help you to choose wisely." The Storyteller said softly, as if to herself, "It is an awesome responsibility to receive the gifts of the Storytellers. I remember well, when I was a young woman like you, Kara, the confusion in dealing with the rush of emotions. They nearly ripped me apart."

She then spoke directly to Kara: "But with all gifts comes the strength to use them properly—if you have courage. It is your challenge to harness your gifts, and keep them within proper boundaries so that they serve you. If you do not succeed, they will rule you. At first you find joy in the release, but before long you will realize that they are cruel taskmasters!"

Kara glared at her, but could not meet her gaze. She lowered her head.

The Storyteller put an old hand on her cheek. "In the ancient, long line of Storytellers, there has never been one like you. The blood of both the Tagu and the Atu flows in your veins. This inflames your already heightened sensitivities. You are faced with a greater challenge than any Storyteller has ever faced. Because of this, your actions are understandable and forgivable. But you must come to realize that you can master your conflicting emotions. If you choose to. Vincent has taken the right path, Kara. So can you."

Vincent said simply, "Are we so different, you and I? Like Ishara, we have both had our childhoods stolen by events that were not of our making. And for the same stupid reasons: fear, ignorance, greed—it seems the whole world suffers from the same malady. I guess some just suffer more than others," he said, unconsciously relaxing as though a great, invisible weight had finally been lifted from him. He felt drained and sank onto the edge of the cot. "I guess we both want the same thing Ishara wanted: to be at peace inside." He looked at the Storyteller and said, "Because of *her* story, I may have finally learned how to feel that way."

"Rest," the Storyteller said. "This has taken much of your strength."

Vincent couldn't argue that point. He lay back, but speaking dreamily, as though to himself, he said, "Ishara thought everything was lost. But maybe not—if we can find our way through together, perhaps she will have succeeded after all. We can be the proof that Bar-Atu was a liar."

"You okay, kid?" Driscoll asked.

Vincent nodded. He felt so worn that he hardly cared that the two of them had been in mortal danger just minutes before.

Driscoll leaned against the wall. His expression was one of utter confusion, mixed with an almost fatherly admiration. "I don't know what Vincent is talking about, but I'll grant you that I might be wrong. I can tell things aren't what I thought—Vincent looks like death warmed over, but he seems clear-headed enough, so I guess you did take care of him."

"They did well enough," Vincent said with a crooked grin.

"Guess so. You're weak as a half-drowned cat, but somehow you seem happier than I've ever seen you. You know, your old man would have been proud of you, Vincent. I wish Ann could be here now. Maybe her nightmares about this island could end, too."

The Storyteller said, "Friend of Denham, I welcome you. Come with me."

"You're sure he'll be okay—"

"He is safe now. Come."

Vincent heard those words from far away. Then he was asleep, asleep and at peace . . .

Vincent had no idea how long he had slept when he awoke to find the Storyteller sitting on his cot with Kara and Jack standing across from them. "What did you dream about, Vincent Denham?" asked the Storyteller. "You smiled often in your dreams. I almost did not recognize you."

Vincent's words were almost random at first, confusing even to him. But he quickly, eagerly, began to talk of rediscovered memories. Words spilled from him, words about his mother, his childhood recollections of his father. He smiled and said, "One thing my father always insisted on was that I paid attention at Mass. Funny. Somehow I thought I had outgrown my religion, but I suppose the things that are real sink right into the bones. Ishara knew that, didn't she? Like you of the island, we believe in God, and our beliefs are the roots that nourish our lives and give meaning to existence. On this island, the Storytellers were like stars showing the way."

"You sound like a Storyteller yourself," Kara said, her tone half-doubtful, half-derisive.

Vincent shook his head. "No, I'm no Storyteller, I just can't help seeing the irony of it all. If not for this island, I might not have lost my parents—yet because of this island and the story of Ishara, I'm beginning to find myself. I may not be there yet, but I am seeing things in a new way."

The Storyteller said softly, "You are surrendering much in making your promise to leave the island to our people, Vincent Denham. I do not know if Kara wholly understands what you are surrendering. I tell her now, it is one stronger even than blood, as deep as the soul. Your pride in your work and in yourself is at stake, and you have offered that as your sacrifice."

The Storyteller took Vincent's arm. "The Tagu humbled themselves before the Infinite, as Vincent humbled himself before you, Kara. True humility is the ultimate strength, because to have it one must have the strength to master himself first. I think the teachings of the Tagu are alive in him, because they are a reflection of his own belief."

Kara stared at the floor and then slowly slipped into the dark, her footsteps softly echoing behind her. And ahead of her. The Storyteller patted Vincent's arm. "Vincent Denham, my apprentice has learned from you, I think. Now you must regain your strength."

Vincent sat up, leaning on one elbow. "But I want to know—"

Driscoll shook his head. "Rest up, kid. We can all talk later. Take it from me, things are going to work out all right."

The Storyteller turned to Driscoll and said, "For two days, Vincent must rest and recover from the poisons he has taken. And then I will guide you all to a place where questions may be answered. That will give Kara time to think. She has much to consider— far more than any of you know, especially for someone so young. Let us hope and pray that she, too, makes the right choice."

CHAPTER SIXTEEN

SKULL ISLAND
July 3, 1957

Vincent Denham sat blindfolded, leaning against a tree. He was conscious of others near him—the Storyteller, Kara, and two guards. Sunlight felt good, warming him to the bone. He heard a grumbling voice approaching: "Don't know why you have to blindfold me every time we go anywhere."

Then his blindfold was taken off, and he found himself looking up at Jack Driscoll, similarly blinking in the sunshine. "Well?" Vincent asked.

"Yeah, I've been in touch with the crew," Driscoll said. "They jerry-rigged the repairs—" he looked around. "For the love of Mike, we're outside the Wall!"

"Nothing will harm us here," the Storyteller said.

"I'd feel better with my rifle, anyway," grumbled Jack.

But the Storyteller shook her head.

"They've repaired the ship?" prompted Vincent.

Driscoll blinked at him. "Oh, yeah. Enough to get us to a civilized port, anyway. We can go aboard any time."

"Okay," Vincent said.

"Come now," the Storyteller urged. "It is a long way. Follow me."

She led them to what looked at first like a low hill. It turned out to be a man-made dome of stone, with one low opening. They crept into it, and then Vincent found he could stand upright. "It's a tunnel!" he exclaimed.

"I have a little acquaintance with it," Driscoll said dryly. "Or with its family, anyway."

"This is the way Bar-Atu took when he surprised Kublai and Ishara the day Kong became King. It is also the path that took him back to the Wall before anyone else. Kublai never had a chance," said the Storyteller.

"You mean Bar-Atu knew about the Old City all the time?" asked Vincent incredulously.

"Yes. And the seeds as well—that is how he was able to summon Gaw for the sacrifices. That is why he would disappear for days at a time. But it was far too dangerous to chance alone too often. He could never let on that the city existed lest others find some glimmer of hope. He had chanced upon the seeds and was running out. That is why he allowed Kublai and Magwich to form their expedition without interfering. He could not lose: on the one hand, Magwich had promised to deliver Kublai, and on the other, the journey provided Bar-Atu the perfect opportunity to discover more seeds under the protection of so many armed men. However, he did not know what the Storyteller knew. The ancient Atu knew certain ways to use the seeds of wild plants, but never how to cultivate them properly. Bar-Atu discovered some of the secrets of his ancestors and used them to make it seem as though his prayers could summon Gaw."

For Vincent the pieces began to fall into place. They explained a great deal. Driscoll nudged him. "I suppose you can fill me in on this?"

Vincent shrugged and chuckled. It's a strange story, Jack. So strange a story that you may not believe it. But I do."

"I've heard words like that before. Seems dramatic turns of phrase run in your family."

They passed the murals, which Driscoll described to Vincent, but the Storyteller allowed no dawdling, much to Vincent's frustration. They kept a quick-march pace, and though Vincent soon tired, he tried not to show how exhausted he was feeling. Especially since Kara strode grimly beside him, not looking at him and showing no signs of weariness herself.

They paused twice; and three times they passed through chambers at least as wide as the one Vincent had recovered in. He wondered if the network of tunnels continued under the village. Was this the kind of place where he had lain helpless for so long?

After a whole day of marching, they made camp for the night, with the Storyteller lighting torches and staking them around their campsite. The torches burned with a faint green flame, sending out an oddly soothing aroma. When they woke the next morning, the torches were still flickering green. The Storyteller put them out and carefully handed them to one of the guards. They had a quick meal and then resumed their journey.

Now and then sunlight shafted down through openings in the stone ceiling, or the tunnel itself emerged onto the surface. At these times, the guards went ahead and called when they were sure no predators were lurking in ambush. "We will be there soon," the Storyteller announced. "When Ishara sought the Citadel, she did not know the short ways, through the tunnels. The pathway there is more direct, and less dangerous. What took her many days has taken us only a day and a half."

And finally, with the sun already at zenith, they emerged in a range of low, green hills. The Storyteller did not hesitate, but led them to a mound as tall as a two-story house. A figure sat on a stone near it, and he rose as they approached. Vincent heard Driscoll catch his breath. "My God, it's him!"

Vincent felt frozen in place. Before him, his face gaunt, his hair gray, was a familiar figure. He had seen that face in films, in photographs, often enough. He remembered it from childhood.

Bitterness roiled in him. Carl Denham had deserted his wife and child. He had brought ruin on them all. And here the man stood—

Vincent closed his eyes. He fought down his resentment, fought down his anger. At the bottom of everything lay another feeling, the feeling of a son for a father, and in the end that was stronger. He found he was weeping. When he opened his eyes, the old man was still in the same place, his expression warm. No, Vincent saw, not just warm. Hopeful. After all these years, Carl Denham still had hope.

And one look in his father's eyes told Vincent that the old man still loved him. Now he could see that his father had also suffered, that the distant image he had created in his mind was not the real Carl Denham. His father was a man, just like him. Whatever decisions he had made, whatever mistakes he had committed, had not been done out of heartlessness.

"Dad," Vincent said, nearly choking. Then somehow his father was embracing him, and Vincent could not speak at all.

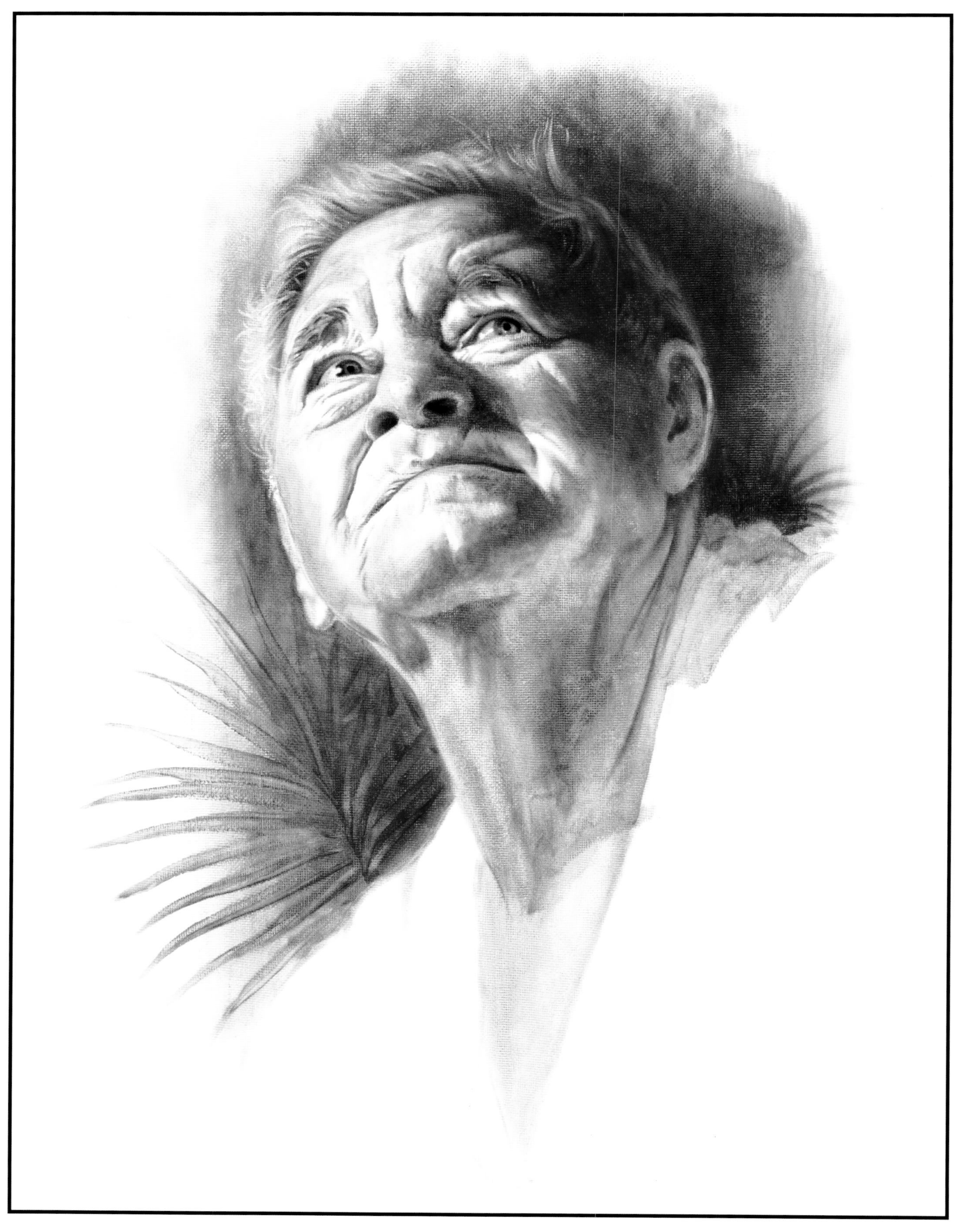

"Twenty years," Carl Denham said. "Englehorn was a good man and a brave one, but the ship cracked up and the monsters in the lagoon took the crew, one by one. So there I was, the only survivor. I can't tell you what it was like, bringing supplies and equipment ashore, never knowing whether one of those sea-serpents was gonna snap me up."

Driscoll asked, "What exactly happened to the captain—did you try to save him?"

"Yes, Jack, I tried," Denham said solemnly. "Englehorn got a bad bite, and it became infected. I got him to shore, but he didn't last long. The Storyteller will back me up— she did her best for him even though every other person on the island wanted to throw both of us back. Englehorn's buried beyond the Wall."

Driscoll sighed, but his expression was respectful. "I guess if anyone could make it, it would have been you. I know how tough an old buzzard you are. My sympathies are with the critters."

"Not so tough," Denham said. "I'm not going to live so very long, the Storyteller says. And she knows. She knows. But Vincent, you're right about one thing. The world can't learn the truth about this island, not yet."

"Secret's safe with me, Dad," Vincent said.

Driscoll chuckled. "Me, too. I don't have a single seaman aboard who could navigate, and nobody's seen the charts except Vincent and me. I don't ever plan to come back here myself."

Denham nodded. "The islanders deserve to be left alone. I did a terrible thing to them when I came and took Kong. I've spent a quarter of a century trying to make up for it. Come with me." His eyes twinkled. "I might just show you the *ninth* wonder of the world."

Laboriously, he stood and, leaning heavily on his cane, he led Vincent to what seemed another tunnel opening. It led into the green hill, into a domed room equipped with a bed, a simple fireplace, a chair, a table, and stacks of notebooks. Carl Denham gestured at it. "My diary, son. What I've learned about the island. Sketches of its animals. Translations of writing that even the Storyteller had forgotten." He coughed. "See, I had a pretty fair education once upon a time. Learned six, seven languages during my travels. And you know how I always loved to draw—Lord knows I had the time to develop my skills. I hope you feel my work meets with your approval. You know, if my life had been different, I could have made a pretty fair scientist. I guess we're not so different after all," he said with a grin. He sat at the table and waved his hand at the storehouse of paper. "It's yours, son. Use it. Use the knowledge in it. But keep the island secret, at least for now. You'll understand more when you've read some of it. Start with these."

Carl Denham reached to the table and retrieved a thick sheaf of paper. "Letters to you," he said. "And to your mother, God rest her soul. I hoped some day someone would find them and get them to you. I never expected to hand them to you myself. Son, I've done a lot to be ashamed of and a lot that I regret. I can't ask you to forgive me, but maybe you can sort of understand."

"I can do more than that," Vincent said, taking the letters. "And I can forgive you, Dad."

"You're a better man than I was at your age," Carl said, sounding as if he meant it.

"I hope to be as good as you when I'm your age," Vincent returned, and he meant it, too.

Carl smiled and patted his son on the back. This was the way Vincent always imagined it should have been growing up. They walked together, Carl's arm around his son's shoulder, out of both pride and the need for physical support. For a man on the mend himself, Vincent never felt better. He was amazed at how easy it was to release what he had suppressed for so long, now that he was talking to his dad. And saddened that he knew their time together was going to be too short. He told his father about his mother and the hardships that they both endured. Vincent could feel his father's old body react as though struck by a blow. Several times he had to stop and allow the old man to recover his composure.

After a long silence Carl wiped the tears from his eyes and muttered, "It was the hardest decision I ever made, son. There were a lot of important people involved in that voyage and a great deal of damage done by Kong. So many people were killed, and if I didn't leave so that they could lay it all on my back, a lot of other people would have been hurt. Wrong as my decision may have been regarding your mother and you, what I envisioned happening if I stayed was far worse. Fortunes and reputations were on the line, and they needed a scapegoat. I would have stayed on my own account, but I had to protect your mom and yourself. Lawsuits, physical threats—I couldn't let you be exposed to that."

Vincent said, "I think I understand."

Carl Denham drew a deep, unsteady breath. "And then there was Kong. I was so blinded by fame and money that I never considered what the costs would be. When we left this island, Kong wasn't the only one we took. The Storyteller and the last of her helpers came with us. I didn't know why or how at the time, but I couldn't tell her no."

Vincent had never heard that. He said, "So that's how she learned English."

Carl said, "Well, how she learned more of it, let's say. She and I have had lots of time to practice talking each other's language since then. You know, during the whole return voyage back from the island with Kong, she sat down in the hold of the *Wanderer*. She wouldn't leave him. She constantly burned these mixtures. By the time we arrived in New York, I had heard quite a bit of the story you heard, and I was beginning to wonder about what I had done."

Vincent had never supposed that the Storyteller had been outside the island, let alone in New York. He wondered what the city had meant to her, what knowledge she had brought back.

Carl went on, "Well, son, under the bright lights, all that self-recrimination went out the window. It was all so much bigger than life, if you get my drift. I was deep in debt, and I thought a week of exhibiting Kong would clear me. What happened next was worse than what happened on the island. So many people died and were injured."

"I've read about it."

Carl sighed, leaning heavily on his son. "The Storyteller had predicted what would happen before we left the island if we took Kong. As I sat alone in the dark hours of the morning after Kong's rampage, it all came flooding back. She was the only one in the room with me. To this day, I don't know how she got there. She was so sad, but hopeful that some good could come out of it all. It was with her urging that I finally left to—as she put it—make things right with myself and with the ones I loved. There was time a I might have come for your mom and you, but even so, how could I have asked the two of you to take such a risk as coming to this island? At any rate, what's done is done."

A pterodactyl cruised over, banking on the thermals. Carl shaded his eyes and watched the graceful, soaring creature. "They're so beautiful when they aren't trying to kill you," he murmured. "So beautiful."

Vincent could only stare in awe. "I've always dreamed about dinosaurs," he said. "To see them alive—"

Carl still seemed lost in the past. He said, "You know, I couldn't decide which wanted my carcass more, the creatures on this island or the bigwigs in New York. They still talk about me back home, Vincent?"

Vincent shrugged. "Your early movies are still shown now and then. But as for Kong, there was a complete cover-up. You must have had some powerful people wiping out your tracks. I never could learn much of anything past what the newspapers said."

Carl leaned on Vincent's arm. "Ah, well, we were in a Depression, son. People were desperate and nobody wanted to be responsible for making things worse than they already were. People were paid off from top to bottom to get Kong into New York. When he went berserk, heads were ready to roll. There was blood in the water and the sharks were ready. Believe me, I had no real choice but to leave with Kong's body."

"Lucky you had a friend with a ship. But how did you supply it?"

Carl coughed. "I, uh, well, sold a map to the island." He looked sheepish. "It was a pretty good map, too. Only thing was, it wouldn't lead anybody to within a thousand miles of this place. Of course, I made a photographic copy of the real one, and then I hid the original behind the only family picture I had near me when I left. I guessed you'd find it if you were meant to. The Storyteller seemed to always think that was possible. I never believed her. But after—what is it, twenty-five years?—with her on this island, I'm not so much of a pragmatist any more. She's a strange old woman, and a very dear fried. Anyway, the Storyteller had me add several bits of information to make things a bit easier if you made it back, marking the jungle trails and so on. I translated her language as best I could, a sort of pidgin-Tagatu I've used often in my notes. You'll figure it out—give you something to do on your long voyage home."

"I remember Jack saying the map was the real one, but that it was different. He said the tunnel information saved his life."

"I'm glad of that. Driscoll's a good man." Carl shifted uneasily, and in a softer voice, he added, "Be careful when you get back, Vincent. Others may still be wondering how to find that map."

"I don't like the sound of that word—*others*. But don't worry, Dad. Jack and I will make sure no one else gets his hands on it."

They talked endlessly. Vincent filled his dad in on what had been going on in the world —World War II, the atomic bomb, jet engines, the Cold War, television. The rush of history that turned Kong into a myth, a legend, a dimly remembered story that might be a hoax.

Carl heard it all, shaking his head. "Another Great War and an atom bomb," he said. "Sounds like stuff out of the pulp magazines. Maybe I had it better on this island than I knew. What about you, son? I hope you sleep better now that you know something about what really happened."

"I'd sleep better if I knew what you've been doing here for twenty-five years. What have you found? And what happened to Kong's body? What happened to Ishara after Bar-Atu gained power? She seems like someone I know now. Wish I could've met her."

Carl leaned on his cane. "Another day, son. Besides, those aren't my stories to tell. Maybe you'll hear them in time. There's always tomorrow."

SKULL ISLAND
July 14, 1957

That morning Carl Denham simply did not wake up.

Vincent knew his father was dead the moment he saw his still face, although the expression might have been that of a serenely sleeping man. Vincent couldn't help staring at him. His thin, withered body was a shadow of the dynamo who was willing to take on the world. But his face still reflected the indomitable spirit that once dwelled there. Vincent thanked God for the opportunity to see his father one last time. Grief welled up in him, but it was grief tempered with a sense of peace.

They buried him on the green hill, covering his grave with a cairn of stone. Driscoll read the burial service, then said with emotion, "I had my share of disagreements with Carl Denham, but I'll say this: he was a man who held onto life with both hands. Vincent, your father was a good man, better than most. I'm glad you had the chance to get to know him these last few days."

The Storyteller and Kara watched Vincent closely. He nodded and then said a short prayer for his father's soul. The Storyteller slowly approached and stood beside him. "I asked your father about this cross that you sign over yourself many times. Its meaning speaks to me. May its sign bring you peace, Vincent."

When he looked up, his eyes were clear. "It does. In my heart, my father had been dead for so long. Now—well, I've never felt so much that he's alive as I do at this moment. My prayers were answered. But what about your people? My father told me many amazing things, and one was that you traveled with him to our country. You're more than a Storyteller—you're a Storyweaver. My father wouldn't tell me what happened to Ishara, or much about what happened to him here." Vincent thought deeply for a second. "Tell me, did my father's return help your people? Have they found peace? Now that I know what I missed, it would make all those years without him easier to take if I knew he did some good."

The Storyteller looked over at Kara and thought for a moment before answering. "There is an old saying among your people, which has its equivalent with ours: 'God works in mysterious ways.' I will give you time to yourself. We will talk later." The Storyteller and Kara turned to leave, but as they did, Kara hesitated and glanced back at Vincent. But her thoughts did not leave her lips.

That evening, as he tried to bring some order to the mass of papers his father had left, Vincent looked up and was startled to see Kara standing silently nearby, watching him. She said impulsively, "You did not ask if *I* have found peace."

"I thought you would tell me when you were ready," Vincent replied.

She took a deep breath. "I am, as you say . . . 'working on it.' I understand now, at least, that your father wanted to help us. That he has helped us. Your father was a great mystery to us and very few were allowed to get close to him. Because of that there were many things said about him. The Storyteller said that was best for our sake, and for his. Only she really knew his mind. She always told me that as the next Storyteller, I must remember what is good for all of the people of the island, not just for myself. Tell me, did you mean what you said? Will you go away from the island and never return?"

"You'll see me leave," Vincent told her. "Soon. I will take nothing with me that would give away the location of the island and I will destroy whatever I already had. You have my promise."

"Perhaps that is asking too much," Kara said. "I'm no longer sure what is right. But I thank you for your promise. I know it cost you much."

"Not so much," Vincent said with a crooked grin. "Just my future as a scientist and my father's reputation. But I can live with it now, I think. The important questions are the ones I asked myself, not the ones the world asked me."

Kara's expression was one Vincent could not read, although he sensed it held nothing of hatred. Suddenly she asked, "May I help you with your father's things?"

As she turned and gestured toward the voluminous papers and artifacts, Vincent stood frozen. He could never have imagined a more beautiful woman. He could not understand how he had never noticed her that way before. Her perfectly proportioned limbs, the slender curve of her body, flowed with a sureness of purpose and a natural grace that were extraordinary. If she were aware of his gaze, she said nothing. A casual flash of her eyes unnerved him and he self-consciously sprang into action shuffling papers. "Thank you," he said, his voice a dry croak. Under his direction, Kara began to stack and organize. After long hours, Vincent saw some order to the mass of materials, but as he turned to thank Kara, he found she was gone.

The next morning The Storyteller, Kara, and Driscoll woke Vincent from a sound sleep. Several men shouldered Carl's effects. Under the open sky, Kara asked, "Where are we going today?"

The Storyteller looked at her and said with a smile, "Perhaps a place you least expect. There are many things that can only be learned when one is ready to accept them. Knowledge must be earned, or its real lessons are wasted." The Storyteller turned to Vincent and said, "Your father was right when he said that I had more to tell. But a story must be told in its correct order to have its full effect. This is a living story, and the end is not yet written. Come my children." As though reading his mind, the Storyteller added with a smile, "Yes, you too, Mr. Driscoll—I am old enough to be your mother as well!"

Driscoll grinned. He seemed to be developing a genuine like of this mysterious old woman. As Jack had told Vincent, it had taken him some time to place her from their having been together on the *Wanderer* during the trip back from Skull Island a quarter century ago. Then he had seen her face only once or twice and had never heard her utter a word. Carl was mysteriously silent concerning her and always pensive when questioned about why she was allowed on the ship.

This time, though, the Storyteller led them to one of the underground vaults and lifted a torch high. "You should see this," she said. "See what Carl Denham brought back to the island."

The skeleton was gigantic. It was a completely unknown species, clearly related to apes but certainly not a gorilla. The bones were laid out in proper order, though not articulated. At first, Vincent could only stare. And then the thoughts came flooding back: as a boy, he was confronting the very source of his nightmares. The very thing that took his father, took his mother, and ruined his family's name. For the first time, Kong's existence, his reality, struck Vincent with all the force of a physical blow. Somehow seeing Kong's bones caused the knot of emotions that had bound him for so long to finally unravel completely. He could no longer hate and fear the creature that had stalked him in his dreams. Kong had paid a price, too—the ultimate price. Vincent felt a curious sympathy, a strange sense of peace. It was as though an enduring weight had been lifted. It seemed Kong's bones were the hub around which all of his questions and their answers converged. He felt exhilarated! His mind was free to wonder as never before.

And as a paleontologist, he felt at a loss. In a flash, the skeleton triggered Vincent's recurring vision, the one he last had during his convalescence on the island: Kong mounted in the Museum of Natural History astride the famous skeleton of the tyrant lizard king in the Great Hall of Dinosaurs, returned to New York once again as "The Eighth Wonder of the World."

Vincent was only vaguely aware that both the Storyteller and Kara were intently watching him.

"It's tempting, Dad," he whispered. "But no. You brought him back here to rest. You gave up your family and yourself. Let him stay here. This is where he belongs."

Kara was weeping. "I have never seen this," she said. "Now I understand. They are so like the bones of a man. I can feel his loneliness. He was not too far from what we are—"

"He wasn't quite human," Vincent told her. "But he was more than an animal. King Kong. Yes, I think he was well named."

Driscoll sighed. "We didn't treat him very well," he said, as he surveyed the remains. Fractures and breaks were everywhere. Vincent could tell that some, acquired earlier in his life, had healed. Most were not. Many showed unhealed breaks and shattered places where bullets had entered the great body. It was evident that this creature had suffered greatly in life and in death. Driscoll shook his head. "Vincent, this may sound strange, but I think Carl had more respect for Kong than for most people. Kong never backed down an inch. In hindsight, Denham respected that and felt bad for getting Kong killed. They had a lot in common. We should have left him here."

"With every evil comes good," the Storyteller said. "Had Carl Denham not traveled to our island, he would have not returned, and much knowledge would have been lost forever. Although it was wrong to take Kong, it was equally wrong to worship him as a god. We were created for a higher purpose, Mr. Driscoll—as I know you now believe. We are not mindless savages and murderers."

Driscoll looked away, flushing. "Yeah. I made a bad mistake," he said.

Yet Vincent thought the Storyteller's words were not meant as a reprimand so much as a kindness in acknowledgment of Jack's acceptance of her and her people.

The Storyteller touched Jack's arm. "Please help an old woman walk. The day has been long and I need a strong arm to lean on. The night is not so far off, and we must hurry." Jack offered his arm with a rough, yet delicate gallantry, and Vincent saw from his smile that he fully understood the forgiveness and acceptance in the Storyteller's gesture.

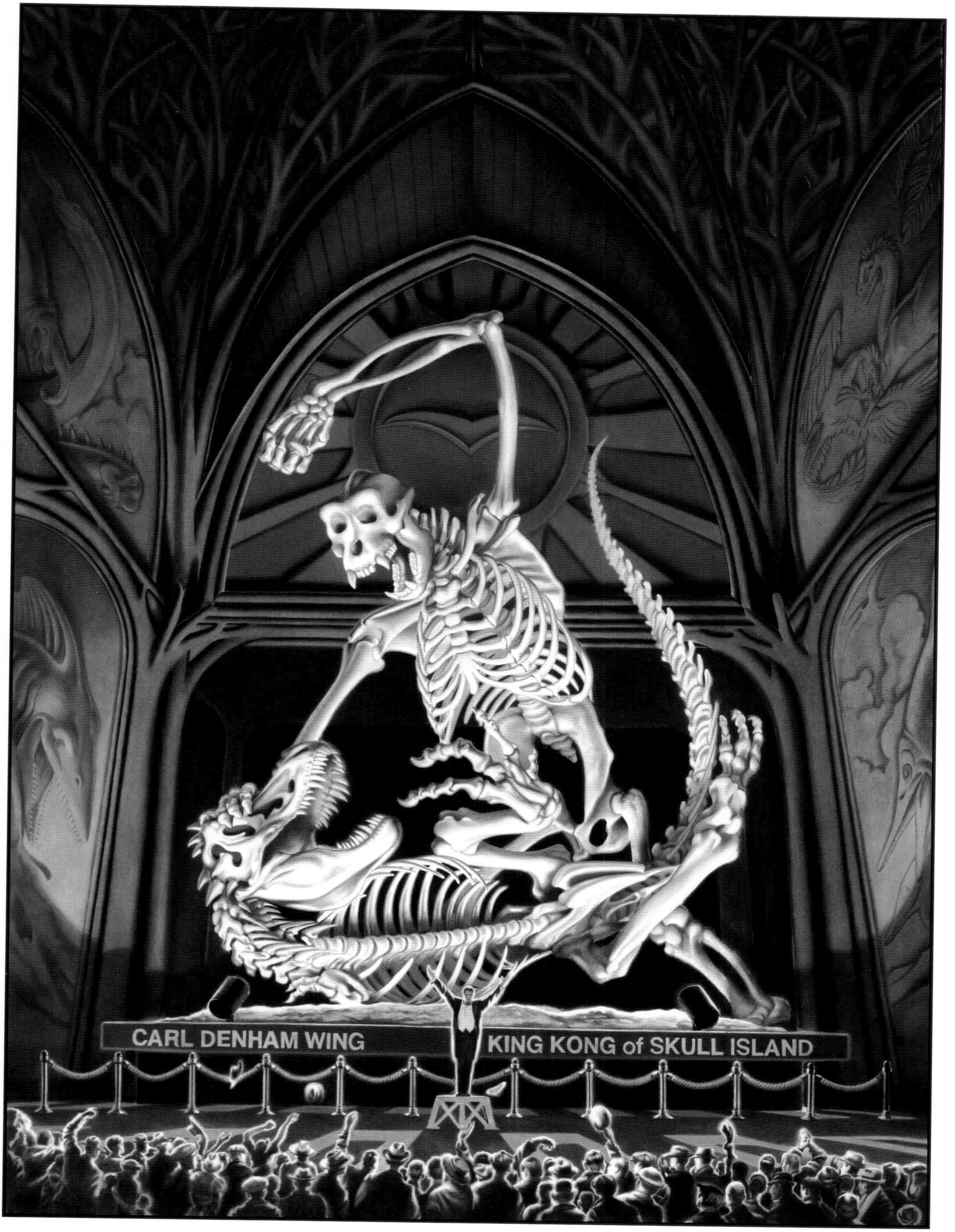
CARL DENHAM WING
KING KONG of SKULL ISLAND

CHAPTER SEVENTEEN

SKULL ISLAND
July 22, 1957

"**D**on't want to miss the tide. I'd better shove off. You gonna be okay, kid?" Driscoll stood with one foot on the thwart of the launch, the other unseen beneath the creaming waves rolling into the beach below the village.

Vincent grinned and offered his hand. "Don't be away too long."

"Figure four weeks, tops," Driscoll replied, shaking Vincent's hand. "Don't worry about the chart. I'll keep it under lock and key, and like I say, there's not a man aboard the *Darrow* who could find his way back to the island without me to lay in the course. You take care, now. I can see you need some time alone here. I found out all I need, but I get the feeling you have more work to do." Driscoll winked, leaving Vincent feeling genuinely confused.

Driscoll hitched up his gunbelt. "We'll provision the *Darrow*, make sure all the repairs are good, and be back by the last week in August. I mean what I say about being careful. Don't try to climb inside any caves that happen to have teeth."

"I'll be okay. Take care. And, Jack . . . thanks for your promise." Vincent held out his hand.

Jack grinned and shook hands. "My promise not to let anybody know about the island? Vincent, my wife means a lot to me. I think Ann would up and leave if I let anybody know about Skull Island. I'm not about to let that happen. Besides, I owe your old man."

Vincent helped Driscoll shove off, then stood and watched the older man fire up the outboard engine and thread his way out toward the waiting ship. The Storyteller had assured Vincent that the monsters of the bay rarely showed up here, in the shallower waters. But all the same, Vincent watched until his friend had scrambled aboard the *Darrow* and the winches had lifted the dripping launch onto the deck. Then Vincent turned and made his way up a worn path toward the village, thinking of the million and one things he hoped to accomplish in four short weeks. So much to see, so much to catalogue, so much to learn.

And there was Kara.

Although greatly diminished, the distrust that occasionally still showed in her eyes stung Vincent. He knew now that she had her reasons, that her past, the island's past, and—face it, he told himself—his father's past all joined in a jagged pattern of pain. For someone as young as she to have grown up with the stories she had heard. How could he expect her to change so quickly? But at least, he thought, she tolerated him now. It also occurred to him that even though she lived here and was to be the next Storyteller, she had not seen many things. They were kept from her for a reason. He was soon to find out why.

SKULL ISLAND
August 12, 1957

A steaming, hazy Monday morning, and for hours Vincent, the Storyteller, and Kara wound their way along underground passages, now and again emerging into the jungle. The Storyteller carried a staff, whose head was a torch, burning with a slow flame, brilliant in the tunnels, pale in the sunlight. Nearly colorless vapors roiled from the flame. Every half-hour or so, they paused to discard the burned-down head of the torch and replace it with a new one, laced with an incense that smelled of spice and a calming aroma, not quite floral, not quite musky. Twice Vincent saw creatures start toward them—a carnivore ten feet tall, and later a pteranodon that swooped into a clearing. In both cases, the creatures hesitated before they sheared away.

The virtue of the essences held them off, the Storyteller explained. The vapors of the torch were enough to calm the beasts, to turn them aside from prey. The trail grew rougher; climbing over saddleback passes over the tops of ridges, descending into cooler valleys, but always rising toward the rounded form of the mountain that wore a skull as a face.

And at last they climbed a tortuous, winding path up the shoulders of that mountain. As they entered the gaping cavity of the mouth, Vincent saw unusual indications. Then, as they climbed higher, he realized something that had never occurred to him: The skull face was not wholly natural—there was evidence that human hands had worked it! Clinging to the bare stone here and there lay patches of masonry.

The Storyteller paused to rest at a turn not far below the nasal cavity. "Ages ago," she said in a low voice, "After the Atu had taken over the Old City, in an act of final defiance of Tagu beliefs, they attempted to fashion the mountain's natural caverns into a human face here, to look out over the island to stare defiantly into the heavens, as though they could make even the stars bow down before them. It was never finished. Earthquake and weather have worn away most of what was done. All that is left is the eroding skull. It stares over us to remind us of past follies, a reminder of the true face of pride." Vincent could not help but marvel at their ingenuity. He understood the temptation. He pitied them, and offered a silent prayer of thanks for turning away from it before it was too late.

They toiled up a steep passage, no doubt the one Kong had once blocked with stones, and a quarter of an hour later, they stepped into the main cavern itself, from bright afternoon sunshine into gloom. Again he realized that he was in the presence of something any other scientist in the world would give anything for. Dinosaur bones—not fossilized rock, but *real* bones! The graveyard of Gaw! Vincent gasped in astonishment. Each time he thought he had seen the ultimate, something more incredible loomed before him. This time he could not believe his eyes. Proof of the Storyteller's tale took his speech away. Lying in front of them, atop a mass of skulls and other bone debris, lay the skull of Gaw. Unmistakable in its physiognomy, the huge cranial case indicative of higher intelligence. It dwarfed the famous *Tyrannosaurus rex* skull in the Museum of Natural History in New York City. Vincent could only imagine the size of this creature in life. Even in death it intimidated and awed. Vincent bent over it, noting the gaps where years before a triumphant Kublai had wrenched fangs from the jaws. "How did it come to be here?" Vincent asked.

"Kong brought it. It was a symbol of his victory. As were the others."

Strewn beneath the remains of Gaw were similar skulls in miniature: the dreaded deathrunners! Their craniums rivaled in size those of any primate. These finds could turn paleontology on its ear forever. Vincent turned to speak, but the Storyteller stood mesmerized by a human skeleton mixed in with the debris. She seemed on the verge of tears as some event unfolded before her eyes that only she could see.

Kara stood riveted in place as they beheld the remains of the "god" that had terrorized her people in life and legend. Even in death Gaw's jaws looked ready to kill.

Vincent could do nothing but wonder at the sight before him. With no intent to go back on his word, he could not help feeling that the world needed to know of such treasures. The temptation that the science was simply too great to ignore gnawed at him. He kept his feelings to himself and struggled mightily to suppress them.

The Storyteller turned and led them as they climbed higher, toward the other eye, the one Driscoll and Ann had never entered. Light began to flood from everywhere as they neared the huge expanse of its orbit. As they rounded a corner of stone Vincent and Kara both gasped. A kong loomed before them!

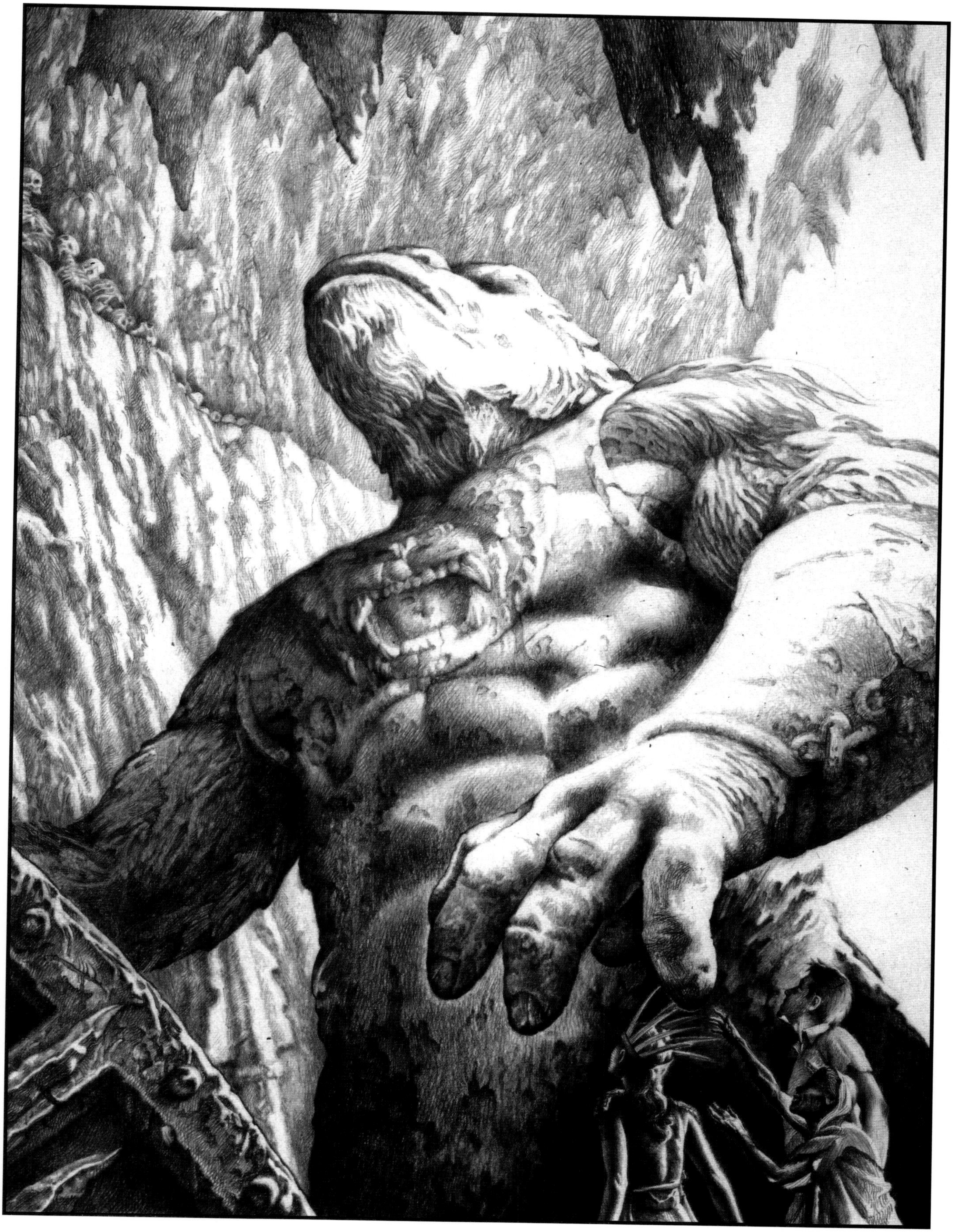

No. Not a real creature, he saw, but a life-sized statue of a kong, somewhat stylized. It stood, arrayed in some sort of strange garb amongst other cast or sculpted artifacts of a gargantuan scale. An icon of veneration, or a portrait of fact? "Your people made this?" he asked the Storyteller.

"But we did not bring it here," she said. "He did. The last kong. The most lonely one."

"There are more," Kara said, pointing to a lower level. Arranged there were smaller statues of kongs, some so lifelike that Vincent could almost convince himself they moved and breathed in the half light, others cruder but made with evident mastery.

"Do you know what this place is?" asked the Storyteller.

Kara bowed her head. "The last home of the kongs," she replied softly. "Legends speak of it. After the fall of the Old City, the last living kongs came here for refuge. Our people forgot their ties to them and sometimes hunted them."

"They survived in the open for a time," the Storyteller acknowledged. "But fierce as they were, they were not what King Kong was. He was a giant among giants. Without their keepers to maintain their armor and weapons, the kongs were more than evenly matched by some of the great saurians of the island. The final blow was the arrival of an ancestor of Gaw, before the fall of the Old City. This was a foe none of the kongs could match. Intelligent, vicious, and with a keen sense of survival, it organized the highly intelligent but relatively solitary deathrunners and attacked the kongs without mercy. Their numbers were always few, and over the course of years, they dwindled even further. They came here, to watch and to wait because it was more easily defended and they had used it in the past. And when at last only one small band of kongs survived they left for the shelter of the high mountain in the distance. Their saurian enemies could not reach them there. They passed out of our knowledge and into legend. But for long, long years that small group of them survived there, until they had at last all died, all except one."

Vincent realized that Jack Driscoll had told him about this place. On the other side was where King Kong had brought Ann Darrow, and where Driscoll, then a young man, had followed. Driscoll had called it a place of death, but Vincent, seeing it now, thought of it more as a place of a great yearning loneliness.

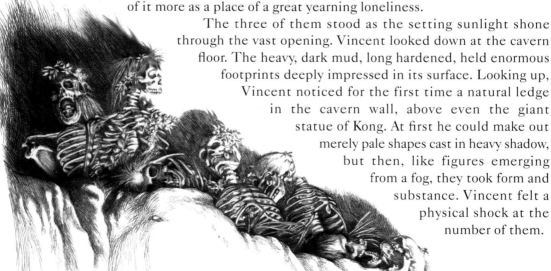

The three of them stood as the setting sunlight shone through the vast opening. Vincent looked down at the cavern floor. The heavy, dark mud, long hardened, held enormous footprints deeply impressed in its surface. Looking up, Vincent noticed for the first time a natural ledge in the cavern wall, above even the giant statue of Kong. At first he could make out merely pale shapes cast in heavy shadow, but then, like figures emerging from a fog, they took form and substance. Vincent felt a physical shock at the number of them.

Human skeletons. They had been carefully placed against a mud wall, pressed into it so they retained their human semblance and their attitudes. They looked like a shelf of dolls.

"The sacrifices," Kara said. "All the sacrifices that Bar-Atu made to Kong. He killed them."

"No," the Storyteller said simply, "not intentionally. But they died of fear. And he kept them."

Vincent's head was spinning. Why had the great Kong arranged these remains in this way? An extended row of figures atop a ledge, possibly an artificial ledge at that. And then, with a gesture and two words, the Storyteller made it clear: "The Wall."

The puzzle came together instantly. But a more baffling question remained. Why? Vincent imagined the rows of humans standing atop the Wall, worshiping Kong, urging him to take his sacrifice. Everyone assumed the bloodthirsty beast ripped them to shreds and devoured them. It seems they were only half-right: the beast was hungry, but not for human blood. Could it be that what he really needed was some sort of interaction? Kong was, after all, a type of ape, a mammal, the only one living on an island populated by reptilians. What else was there, who else was there, that he could look to? Was that the only time the gigantic beast felt he belonged? The implications rocketed through his mind.

Although the giant saurians could not have scaled the Wall, the same was not true for Kong. Going on Jack's descriptions, Vincent surmised that Kong could have climbed it at any time. Did he not do that because he remembered what had happened to Gaw when he approached too closely? Or for other reasons?

"You were the only creatures on the island that even resembled Kong," Vincent said softly. "He felt kinship. He allowed you to live because without you he would be completely alone. These aren't trophies, but his family. They're a way to stave off the loneliness that only an intelligent creature could feel."

The Storyteller nodded gravely. "We were all he had, the only ones who moved, were somewhat shaped like him, made sounds that were not saurian."

Against all his training and against reason, Vincent felt a painful lump rising in his throat. Kong had not been a great ape, exactly, but a member of an unknown species. Perhaps he had been more than that. Had he stood on the threshold? Something had attracted him to Ann Darrow. "Beauty and the Beast," his father had said. Was he evolved enough to have felt the impossible gulf that separated him from the tiny, glowing creature he gave his life for? Vincent realized that he would never know for certain.

For three days they stayed there, exploring the caverns, finding piles of scattered artifacts. Bones of a dozen species of dinosaur.

A paleontological treasure he could open for the world, but it would remain locked away by his promise. As a scientist he scoffed at such a promise in the interest of knowledge. The temptation pulled at him. As a man of his word, he turned his back on all of it and followed the Storyteller and Kara.

CHAPTER EIGHTEEN

SKULL ISLAND
August 16, 1957

They passed the night in the cavern, and in the morning they got an early start. To Vincent's surprise, the Storyteller led them into yet another maze of underground passageways, this one in better repair than the ones that had brought them from the Wall. He asked her several times where they were going, and she did not respond at first. Finally, she turned on him, glaring. "Young man, do you want me to stop this trip right now?" she demanded.

Her tone catapulted Vincent back to a time when he was six and his father was at the wheel of the family Packard. He almost gulped, "Nossir," but stopped himself and merely shook his head. He marveled at her vitality. Perhaps, due to hardships, she was younger than she looked.

They passed dark chambers, stonewalled and stone-floored, but the Storyteller refused to pause. "Time to explore them later."

After hours underground, the old woman told Kara and Vincent to rest. She left two torches with them and took a third with her, vanishing down a broad, dark corridor that seemed to tilt ever so slightly upward. Vincent sat with his back against the cool stone wall, Kara near him. "She can be grumpy, can't she?" he asked.

Kara sniffed. "You should try being her apprentice."

Something screeched far off. Without realizing he had moved, Vincent found that he had an arm around Kara's warm shoulder. "That was probably just a bird or something," he said.

She pressed softly against him. "Probably."

Vincent's mouth was dry. "It's probably nothing to worry about."

Her breath came warm against his cheek. "Probably."

It was hard to swallow. "I think—"

But whatever he thought, he couldn't talk about it. Not with Kara's lips so close.

It might have been only a few minutes later that the screech, now much closer, repeated itself. Both Kara and Vincent sprang to their feet. A pale light appeared in the distance, and then a raucous voice echoed in the corridor: "For the luvva Mike!"

"Oji!" both Kara and Vincent exclaimed at once. And sure enough, the Storyteller came into view, the archaeopteryx perched on her shoulder, bobbing its head at every step.

The Storyteller was grumbling as she approached: "The torch keeps all the big creatures away, but I think this one likes the scent. Come, come! I told you two to rest. Your faces are so hot you must have been running! Follow me now."

Vincent's face did feel hot. They fell into step behind the Storyteller, and before long, Vincent could tell the passage was indeed climbing upward. A patch of sunlight showed ahead at last, and the three of them scrambled up a slope and into the open at last.

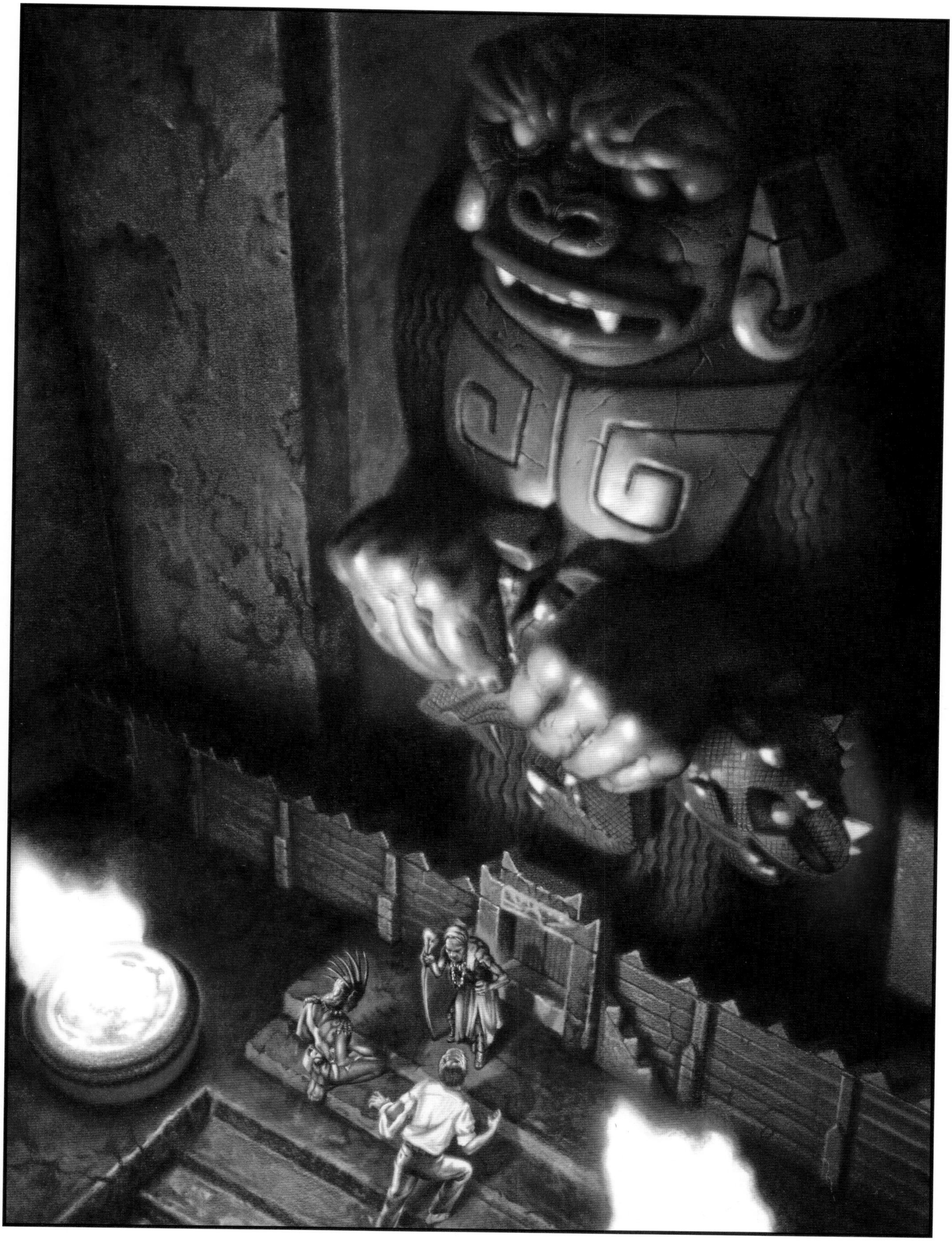

Vincent's first impression was that they had emerged atop a vast rounded green hill studded with ancient, mossy tree trunks and rock pinnacles. Then he blinked in the sunlight, seeing that what looked like a natural opening in one of these pinnacles was of the right size and shape to be a doorway. Beyond the rocky outcrop was a tall, leaning stake, topped with a metal basket in which pale fire roiled a greenish, thin vapor.

"The Old City!" Kara exclaimed. "I've asked you to bring me here time after time!"

"But you never asked me when the time was right," returned the Storyteller tartly. "Now it is."

Vincent was turning. Now he saw a half-dozen tall, slender statues, all of them holding metal baskets filled with the same strange fire that burned in the Storyteller's torch. He understood. "The statues are guardians. They keep the dinosaurs away."

"Very good," the Storyteller agreed with a wrinkled smile. "Yes. The burning spices and compounds control the great beasts, take from them their savagery. Yes." Oji fluttered and launched himself from her shoulder, spiraling upward to perch, finally, on the top of what had to be a thirty-foot tower, pierced here and there with rounded windows.

Vincent could not take in the full extent of the city. Its outlines were deceptive, even in the strong light of afternoon. The buildings hardly seemed the work of hands—everything had an organic, living feel to it, as if the island itself had grown the city from its soil. But in the center, even though overgrown to a great extent after so many years, the truth of the Storyteller's tale was born out: there was major devastation. As they slowly traced its outline by carefully walking its camouflaged edge, the remnants of a gigantic crater were clearly evident. "This is where the collapse took place. The great dinosaur fell into the opening, and its fall took away our hopes of learning how to use the seeds of the island."

Kara said, "How can this be? In your story Ishara was driven out by Bar-Atu, and it seemed that all hope was gone. Yet there burn the herbs all around us! I had thought the old ways lost forever."

"They had been lost for many ages," the Storyteller said softly. "It has been the calling of the Storytellers since the beginning to keep the flame of hope burning in the hearts of our people. It was the message of Ishara's Storyteller to her: never lose hope. All will be made right in the end."

The Storyteller turned toward Kara and looked directly into her eyes before saying, "And this is the teaching I pass on to you. The lessons we learn firsthand are the lessons we learn best, and that is why you needed to face your own self-doubts and prejudices in order to gain the strength to overcome them. This is where your inner character is forged, it is where you gain the authority to lead your people."

Vincent said, "I don't understand. Bar-Atu won, Kublai was killed. All hope was lost—or was it? What happened to Bar-Atu's cult and to Ishara? Did she survive—did her *dream* survive?"

The Storyteller sat on a stone and stared over the old City with brooding eyes. "Ishara's soul fell into a blackness that seemed to have no bottom. But Ishara, though terribly wounded, persevered. Even she could never have predicted what would happen in the years to come. Only her hopes kept her alive. And her dream. Do you understand now, Kara?"

Kara bowed her head. "I understand that I was wrong to be angry because you told an outsider stories of Ishara that I had never heard. And I begin to see that things may not always be what they seem, so I must be strong to see them through to the end, no matter how hard it is."

"Yes, you speak well. Because the blood of both the Atu and the Tagu flows in your veins, you walk a path no Storyteller has ever taken. You will speak with authority on the problems of each. And it is those problems which you must acknowledge and overcome yourself, before you can teach with true understanding and once and for all heal the age-old rift that has afflicted our people."

"I do not fully understand why I have been put to the same test as Vincent has been," said Kara.

"Your gifts are extraordinary, Kara. But they are not enough. The key is choosing to use them properly, and that requires wisdom. How can I be sure that I pass on my authority safely? By putting you to such a test as to burn away anything that could fog your vision. But that is enough for now. After all this time my story is almost finished. Do you want to find out the ending?"

Both Kara and Vincent nodded yes.

"As I left off, and as you can see, the most vital part of the Old City was destroyed, and the seeds, their formulas, and so much other ancient knowledge was destroyed along with it. It was also true that Bar-Atu gained power in our village. He murdered Kublai and shortly thereafter the old Storyteller died as well, under very mysterious circumstances. But before she passed, she conferred her authority on Ishara with one last word: 'Believe.'

"Not long after that, Charlie left the island, sailing in one of the small boats that Magwich's ship had brought. He had small hope of surviving, but he carried with him a supply of food and drink and a rough chart he had made. Somehow, he did survive—for many years later, others followed that chart to the island.

"As for Ishara, she held onto the Storyteller's final word. For a long time that was all Ishara had to go on. But something unusual began to happen to her. Others were naturally attracted to what made them feel good and they joined her in secret. Ishara taught them the old ways that were passed down to her.

"Something unexpected lived on after the destruction of the Old City in spite of the fact that she knew the herbs were gone forever: In a very short time Bar-Atu had run out of his supply as well and he was no longer able to safely move secretly about outside the Wall. The people quickly began to grow restless when there was no longer the abundance gained from the previous hunts. Their allegiance to Bar-Atu was based on bribes, and when he could not deliver, they began to turn on him.

"In the past he had held them in check with the threat of Gaw, whom he was able to summon with the herbs. But not so with Kong. It was no longer only the people, but Bar-Atu as well, who lived in fear. Kong was absolute ruler. Once Bar-Atu's hunters disturbed Kong when he was feeding, and he turned on them in great fury, destroying them all. Bar-Atu could not explain why his god had turned against the people who were doing good for the village, who were seeking food for the feast."

The Storyteller said that in time, support for the new Storyteller grew because it was not bought with bribes and fear. It was genuine. Ishara, bolstered by this support, became bolder until she dared walk and talk freely among the people. There were not enough to resist Bar-Atu at first, but his trouble with his own followers prevented him from disbanding

Ishara's followers as he might have. Eventually Bar-Atu was forced to act and plotted to murder them all. But then something completely unforeseen happened. . .

"But it grows late," the Storyteller finished. "I am weary, and tomorrow is time enough for the story."

Both Vincent and Kara sounded like two children as they sprang up in unison saying, "But you can't stop now!"

To their frustration, it was too late. The Storyteller had already dozed off and was resting comfortably, with a ghost of a smile on her face.

The next morning everyone awoke early. But instead of continuing their journey, Vincent and Kara refused to depart until they heard the end of the Storyteller's tale.

She looked at their eager faces and murmured, "Where was I?"

"Something happened—something unexpected," Kara said.

"Oh, yes. It was at this time, when Ishara was on the verge of becoming a threat to Bar-Atu, that he made plans to kill her after the impending sacrifice to Kong. She had no real hope of survival. It was at that time that, as I said, something completely unexpected happened.

"During the ceremony to prepare the sacrifice, strangers were discovered. It had been over half a century since outsiders had arrived on our island. It was your father, Vincent."

"You mean because of my father, Ishara was not killed?" asked Vincent, stunned.

"Far more than that, Vincent Denham. Far more than that."

Kara sat, pensive. "I understand. If Vincent's father had not come to the island to take away Kong, Bar-Atu would have won in the end. He would have killed the Storyteller, and the line of Storytellers would have come to an end."

The Storyteller nodded. "Yes, exactly. Carl Denham destroyed Bar-Atu's plan. He brought with him the one named Ann Darrow. She was the one whom Kong could not resist. When Jack Driscoll stole her back from him, Kong lost all control and came off of his impenetrable mountaintop to a place where he could be captured. But before he was, several things happened. During his rampage, he killed most of Bar-Atu's followers, who for years had been the only ones allowed to bear weapons. Bar-Atu's mind had been damaged by the herbs he had used for too many years to put himself into his trances. He ranted like a madman, ordering the rampaging Kong to obey him. Kong crushed him like an ant and then bit him in half. The cult died with him, one reign of terror ended by another. But in all the destruction wrought by Kong, one more thing happened that no one ever expected. But this is a part of the story which is better experienced than heard. I will stop now and ask you both to be patient. Follow me."

She led the way through what had to be an ancient street. Now Vincent realized that the landscape wasn't as unfamiliar as he had thought. He had seen this before, but from a different perspective, and at the time he had not realized what he was seeing.

They camped in the Old City that night and the next morning Vincent saw what an immense task of exploration and learning lay ahead. They left the hilltop before noon, plunged back into the underground network, and by twilight they emerged close to the Wall. The Storyteller led them through a small door, then up a long stair, zig-zagging in switchbacks to the very summit of the Wall. Her house waited there. Oji fluttered to its roof and in the last light of day began to preen himself.

The Storyteller sent Kara into the village, and she and Vincent stepped into the open doorway of the hut. To Vincent's right the vast jungle rolled away into the darkness. To his left he could see the cooking fires and the torches of the village. The Storyteller smiled and nodded toward the inside of her hut. Only then did he see an enormous chest, well made to withstand the moisture and temperatures of the island. Something his father had brought a quarter century before. And inside it—

A profusion, a wealth, of photographs. Stacks of motion-picture film canisters. A stack of yellowing pads of paper, carefully wrapped.

"Your father's," the Storyteller said quietly. "Yours."

And for all the rest of that day, Vincent looked through the stacks of pictures, even partly unrolled some of the photographic film. The pads were journals and sketchbooks. He never realized how much his father loved to draw! Many were roughly dated. And the dates began in the year 1934—the year after Kong's appearance in New York, the year that Carl Denham returned to the island. Most of the photographs came from his father's original visit, but some he had taken on his return. An entry dated 1935 noted, "Some film left, but out of developer. Guess I'm strictly a sketch artist from now on."

Vincent was amazed at his father's curiosity and his ordering of facts and images. He laughed aloud. "I never realized how much like Dad I am. He would've made a good scientist."

Sketches of animals, of people, and of a strange kind of writing, not quite hieroglyphic, not quite pictographic. Vincent realized that his father had been working out the island's forgotten written language, working at the problem patiently and for years on end. He found a battered notebook in the stack and realized it was a dictionary of sorts, or a cross between a dictionary and a journal. He read one of the latest entries, dated January 1955.

Carl Denham had written, "I am now certain. The dinosaur life of the island is gradually dying out, as it died out millions of years ago in the rest of the world. In twenty years I have seen the species of dinosaur reduced by a third. In a hundred years, how many of them will be left? Will any be left? I am glad that I never made it clear where this island was. I hope that the maps I gave them were effectively misleading. Still, I wish there were something I could do. Could more civilized people have stopped the dying— or would they have hastened it? No one will ever know. It is up to the islanders now. It is up to them to save everything."

And the photos! Carl Denham had never lacked nerve. They showed dinosaurs in intimate detail, feeding, grooming, mating—even charging toward the camera. Vincent felt his eyes brim with tears.

A tentative hand touched his arm, making him flinch in surprise. Kara looked at the photograph he held, an eight-by-ten print of a valley jumbled with bones. Denham had written in the margin "Dinosaur graveyard."

"I have never seen these things," Kara said. "How could images be captured like this and stopped in time? What do they mean?"

Vincent cleared his throat. "They mean that my father wanted to save the creatures of the island. Even if he could save them only in pictures."

Kara frowned in thought. "Like . . . like Kong kept the bones."

"Yes," Vincent agreed. "Like that. For the same reasons, perhaps. To belong to a wider world. To preserve memory even beyond life."

They paused by the window opening, and watched a golden sunrise over the dark green jungle canopy.

"Vincent Denham," Kara said in a tremulous voice, "I ask you this: These things tell more of the life of my island than I know. More even than the Storyteller can speak of. Will you—I have no right to ask. Will you return one day to help me learn about the meaning of these things? Will you teach me the things your father learned?"

Vincent reached for her hand and held it. She squeezed his hand softly, a pressure both childlike and imploring. He looked into her eyes and nodded. "I will."

Kara looked in his eyes and smiled before leaving Vincent to his thoughts. From behind him Vincent could hear the Storyteller's sigh. "And the circle is complete," she murmured. "Journeys end, and the old find rest. Now at last my quest, too, has ended."

Vincent turned. "What do you mean?" he asked, feeling a tremor of uncertainty.

"I think Kara will be well now," the Storyteller murmured. "Her heart has been awakened to what I have tried to teach." She signed. "For a long time I have been afraid that she would choose the path of Bar-Atu, the path of fear and hatred. If that happened, I think my people would die in the next generation. But now I know the ancient break will finally be healed."

"Who is she?" Vincent asked.

"She does not even realize it," the Storyteller said, "but her great-grandfather was Kublai, and her great-grandmother was Ishara. Their only child was a daughter, born seven months after the death of Kublai. The child was adopted by an Atu family."

"Adopted? Why?"

"Storytellers do not raise their own children," the old woman said simply. "We regard all the people of the island as our children."

"You are Ishara," Vincent said.

The old woman nodded again. "That was my name."

At first, Vincent could not say anything. Finally, he stammered, "B-but that's impossible. You'd be over—"

"I am very old." The old woman smiled.

All Vincent could do was wonder.

The next morning Oji woke Vincent with a screeching "Ya gonna sleep all day?" so exactly in his father's tones that he lurched from sleep feeling ten years old. Kara emerged from the far rooms of the hut with a basin of water. He washed the sleep from his eyes and then Kara said, "The Storyteller wishes us to go down into the village."

They climbed back down the stair—Vincent realized that at this point, on either side of the immense doors, the Wall was very thick, and the stair actually was buried inside its body—and emerged through another small door on the village side. But instead of taking the winding pathway, Kara led Vincent off to the left. "Here," she said. She pressed a section of the Wall, and it swiveled on hidden hinges. A doorway barely large enough for them to pass through was revealed.

Vincent felt his heart pounding strangely. The door did not open to the jungle side of the Wall, but to a dark, cathedral-like room, at least twenty feet wide at the base—

"We were inside the Wall!" he said, comprehension breaking through. "This was where the Storyteller nursed me back to health!"

The Storyteller herself stepped from the shadowy darkness. "This is something else your father discovered," she said. "Look at the walls, Vincent Denham." She handed Vincent a torch.

He stepped to the wall and touched it. It was not, as it appeared, a great structure of wooden logs. Instead, to his hand it had the rough feel of concrete. Petrified wood?

"It is another of the Old Ones' creations," the Storyteller said, answering Vincent's puzzled expression, not any spoken question. "A kind of mortar that becomes harder and firmer as time wears on. The strongest construction material they knew. Here, and for many paces back, the Wall is a double thickness. This is their second Citadel; here they stored the whole of their secret knowledge after the Tagu were banished from the Old City. Upon returning to the shelter of the Wall, which was originally a simple barrier, they built a second Wall here and sealed their secrets within it. The Storytellers knew the eventual fate of the Atu, as surely as knowing a dropped stone will hit the ground. They wanted to protect the greatness of the Tagatu culture, and the beliefs upon which it was built.

"After the fall of the Old City, the surviving Atu returned to the Wall and begged forgiveness. It was granted them and they again made their home among the Tagu. You have heard the story of what happened next. The Storytellers and their beliefs were nearly wiped out and all knowledge of their culture's achievement buried. The Wall was sealed. Over centuries, the way in—and there was only one—became wholly forgotten."

"How was it rediscovered?" asked Vincent.

"When your father first arrived here and Kong rampaged through our village, there was a miracle of sorts found in the wake of the destruction. The shock of Kong's blows had loosened sections of mortar, which had been used to seal and repair the Wall for millennia. In restoring the Wall, my followers found the passage—and they told only me."

"I wondered how a wooden Wall could have lasted all these years," Vincent said.

The Storyteller smiled. "The frame is made of wood, but wood that is soaked in the mortar. Otherwise, the Wall surely would have fallen to rot. Or to the lightning. The Gate has been patched many times when it caught fire. Can you imagine what would have happened had the whole Wall ever burned?"

Vincent could not. The structure was too big, too solid. "It would have looked like the burning of Atlanta," he said. Kara looked at him quizzically.

"When I entered the Wall for the first time," the Storyteller said, "I saw that the fallen mortar inside had uncovered hidden things, ancient signs and symbols. There they stayed, meaningless and the Wall in disrepair except in those areas that were essential to keep the creatures at bay. It was your father who first studied them when we returned. He was the first to realize that maybe there was more to the Wall than we had imagined. We had few symbols that meant words, and from those few your father worked at the meanings of the others, until he had recovered the formulas of my ancestors. And from the writings we learned which seeds and spores to gather from the jungle."

Kara stepped forward. "Now the Storyteller says the time has come to reveal the knowledge. Our people must learn to follow the way of our ancestors. We must find peace or die."

She reached for Vincent's hand, and again he felt the soft pressure that seemed a hesitant request. He squeezed her hand in response.

"It seems the answers were here all the time, waiting until we were ready to accept them. The Storyteller has always taught me that life has a plan and that we will be given the things we need when we are able to make the best use of them," Kara said.

"No one knows the whole Story of Life," said the Storyteller. "We are all meant to learn from each other, and the end of the Story can only be guessed at. The story of King Kong has had the power to reach across time and act as the center around which all of our stories revolved. It is only right that we should honor his memory. Follow me."

The Storyteller led them into the Wall, down into subterranean chambers and then back up into a large vault where scented braziers illuminated a stunning sight: the tomb of Kong.

"We have labored on it for twenty-five years," the Storyteller said as Kara knelt and Vincent stood staring. "It is finished now, and soon we will move Kong's bones here to rest." The vault was vast, as quiet as a cathedral, and in its simplicity as majestic as a palace. "Here he will remain for as long as the island exists," the Storyteller said. She bowed her head. "And here my story ends."

Later that day, they sat on the crest of the smaller hill. Overhead, pterosaurs, vast and majestic as legendary dragons, wheeled and flashed in the sun. From the crest of a jungle ridge came the cry of some enormous creature, not angry. It was natural to Vincent, the sound of a creature that was simply itself, not an imagined god.

Vincent had been in silent thought for a long time when he said, "My father didn't understand what he was doing when he took Kong from the island. He caused so much suffering, all without meaning to."

Kara touched his hand. "And how many of us really know what our actions mean or what ends they lead to? I now understand that your father had a good heart and no wish to injure anyone. The Storyteller taught me that somehow suffering always raises to greater heights a spirit willing to endure. Like Ishara, your father never gave up. Like her—" Kara took a deep, cleansing breath. "Like her, he believed."

EPILOGUE

ABOARD THE *DARROW*, AT SEA
September 28, 1957

Tropical sunsets were becoming a flamboyant memory as the ship worked her way into higher latitudes. San Francisco was not so many days ahead. Vincent Denham stood at the rail and watched the white wake sketching itself back across the Pacific, toward the smoldering red twilight, toward Kong's island.

"Your old man would be proud of you," Driscoll said quietly.

"I'm proud of him," Vincent said simply.

"You're not taking much back."

"I'm taking more than you know," replied Vincent. Briefly he smiled, remembering how he had once imagined the skeleton of Kong poised in the Museum of Natural History. A brass plaque would have given the name of the specimen—a Latin tag in which *carldenhami* would have figured. And crowds of people would stare and wonder.

But in the end, what was he taking back? A very few bones and a wealth of memories. And plans for the future.

Driscoll sighed. "Well, I've seen the island twice now, and that's enough for me. You know, all these years I thought those islanders were the most primitive of savages, but from what you say, they may be the greatest ancient civilization the world has ever known. I'm sorry you can't let the world know—but I'm glad, too, in a way. Let your old man and Kong rest in peace there."

Vincent turned and leaned on the rail. Night was climbing in the eastern sky, and already a few stars studded the growing darkness overhead. "I'm going back to a different world from the one I left," Vincent said. "Different because I see myself differently. You took a big risk in helping me. In hindsight, it was kind of selfish to ask you to put yourself on the line like that."

Jack flicked his cigarette into the ocean. "Don't kid yourself, Vincent. It wasn't only for you that I went back. I had a few things I had to straighten out myself. Besides, if it weren't for your old man, I never would have met Ann."

"Thanks, Jack. That reminds me. I'll be going back myself. I think they need someone to finish the work Dad started. Besides, Kara asked me to."

Driscoll smiled but did not reply. They simply stood companionably on the deck while the night came on and the wake stretched ever more to the west.

NEW YORK
November 3, 1957

As the airliner tilted back and fought for altitude, Vincent Denham stared out the window at the pinnacles and canyons of New York City. Night was fast coming on here.

Looking down, Vincent saw the glare of streetlights and advertising signs. Somehow they reminded him of the village on Skull Island, viewed from atop the great Wall.

And out there, on the island, halfway around the world, daybreak would be coming on just now. The light of a new dawn would wash across the sea, touch the ichthyosaurs leaping in the lagoon, set the tilting wings of the pterosaurs ablaze with ruddy light, reveal the rounded surface of Skull Mountain, bring life to a village of hopeful people.

And the light of day would break like a rising tide on the Wall, the great and enduring Wall, no longer an imaginary barrier of the past, but a gateway to the future—a future that awaited his return.

Vincent eased back in his seat, closed his eyes, and dreamed.

END

Pages from the sketchbook of
CARL DENHAM

These creatures called 'moposaurs' are beloved by everyone + are something of a cross between a koala + a parrot. They're a favorite pet, their feathers are used for everything. They 'talk' + hang out everywhere

The moposaur above is still growing its feathers after being plucked. The smaller one shows one full feathered. They have pink heads mostly

It has been raining for several days. There is nothing to do but draw. I wonder if it is raining all over the world.

The blow-pipe + harness on the right were retrieved from inside the Wall. It is held in high esteem by the storyteller — I believe it might have been Kittah's. The 'plant' is called a 'Gort' (？) It seem a cross between a pineapple + an artichoke — I was shocked to see that this thing moves on its own! It uses its roots to slowly slither. It is an essential ingredient in some of the most valuable herb mixes.

The leaf on the left has poison sacs + needles used in blow gun — on the right is a tasty melon type fruit

I have been working for years in the lost
city & am getting a glimpse into just how
advanced the Atu scientists had become.
If my translations are accurate. This
giant bridge-like structure was bio-eng-
ineered. It was half built & half 'grown!'
Astoundingly, the huge triangular extensions
were originally covered with a thick moss-
like covering. They plates were used to gather light for photosynthesis. The energy
was somehow transmitted through the
thick vines entwined around the main
structure, down through the struts and
into the ground. From here it seems
the energy was distributed through a
preplanned root system. There are
indications that one function of this
was to activate the membranes
stretched over the fenestrations
of many of the structures. These
membranes had their own bio covering that then began to glow & provide
ambient light. There were other uses
as well, it seems. The mind reels!

This combi-
nation natural
+ grown arch
is hundreds
of feet long
- over 200'
high

The shock of Kong's fist have shaken
loose sections of mortar. I could clearly see
writing underneath! None seemed to
notice this - they we too concerned with
survival. But this extraordinary occur-
ance has led to the deciphering of the isl-
and's ancient language & secrets. Slowly, the
storyteller & I have labored to uncover more.

Upon arriving back on the island the
effects of Kong's rampage were everywhere - and still are. The great doors
remain unusable for the most part. I
doubt they can ever be restored as they
once were, but they still provide some
protection.
   I cannot help but feel remorse.
Yet I have found the proverbial 'silver
lining' in the exposed ruins mentioned
above. The secrets they contain
have slowly begun to transform life
for the people here.

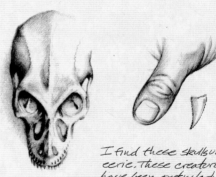

I find these skulls unusually eerie. These creatures must have been particularly horrific. Is it possible they still exist?

I did not believe the storyteller when she first told me of creatures called 'Death-runners'! But I cannot deny my own eyes. The brain of this creature was at least the size of a chimp. I have used its razor sharp teeth to shave. The legends say they were almost as smart as humans, & possibly could even talk. That they were deadly is without question as this extraordinary find shows. From what age was this unfortunate warrior: Greek, Roman? It seems others have been here before. This island contains mystery upon mystery & unimagined dangers. The spider-like creature below which is covered partly with fur & feeds its young with milk, was caught today after killing several villagers. It has two huge eyes, legs with fleshy muscles on the outside & hands, to go with its massive fangs. Is it insect or mammal? I must endeavor to do further research. If only I had a camera...

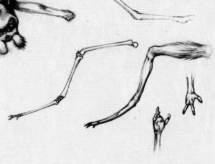

This creature can turn its head & is supposedly fast enough to run down a man with ease. It grabs with its 'hands' & injects massive amounts of venom causing painful death. So far as I know, it spins no web & rarely travels beyond deep ravines

DeVito ArtWorks, LLC

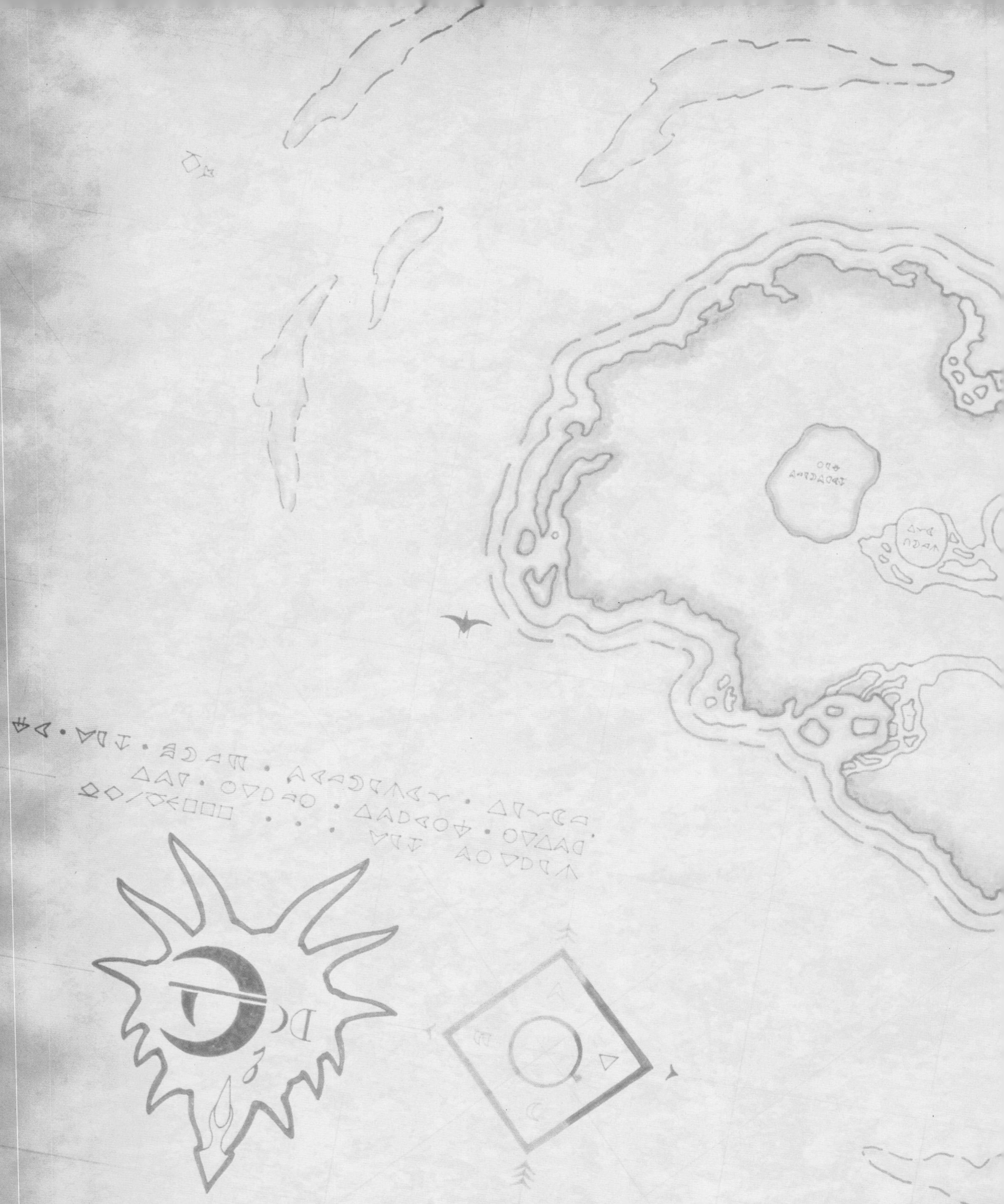